Digging In
Literature for
Developing Writers

Digging In
Literature for
Developing Writers

Albert Garcia
Sacramento City College

Upper Saddle River, New Jersey 07458

Library of Congress Cataloging-in-Publication Data
Digging in: literature for developing writers /
   [compiled by] Albert Garcia.
        p. cm.
   Includes index.
   ISBN 0-13-049388-0
   1. College readers. 2. English language—Rhetoric—Problems, exercises, etc.
   3. Report writing—Problems, exercises, etc.   I. Garcia, Albert J., 1963-
PE1417.D54 2004
808'.0427—dc21   2003051154

Senior Acquisitions Editor:
   Craig Campanella
Editor-in-Chief: Leah Jewell
Editorial Assistant: Joan Polk
Sr. Marketing Manager:
   Rachel Falk
Marketing Assistant:
   Adam Laitman
Production Liaison: Fran Russello
Production Editor:
   Marty Sopher/Lithokraft
Manufacturing Buyer:
   Brian Mackey

Art Director: Jayne Conte
Cover Design: Suzanne Behnke
Permissions Coordinator:
   Mary Dalton-Hoffman
**Composition/Full-Service
   Project Management:**
   Lithokraft/Marty Sopher
Printer/Binder: Courier
   Companies, Inc.
Cover Printer: Phoenix Color Corp.

Credits and acknowledgments borrowed from other sources and reproduced,
with permission, in this textbook appear on page 293.

Pearson Education LTD., London
Pearson Education Singapore, Pte.
   Ltd
Pearson Education, Canada, Ltd
Pearson Education-Japan
Pearson Education Australia PTY,
   Limited

Pearson Education North Asia Ltd
Pearson Educación de Mexico, S.A.
   de C.V.
Pearson Education Malaysia, Pte.
   Ltd
Pearson Education, Upper Saddle
   River, New Jersey

10 9 8 7 6 5 4 3 2 1
ISBN: 0-13-049388-0

Contents

4 Learning and Teaching   98

5 The Emotional Side   142

Ideas for Writing   182

6 Work and Dreams   183

Ideas for Writing   229

7 Issues/Positions   230

To the Instructor

If you are holding this book in your hands, you are at least considering the notion of teaching your developmental composition class with literary selections. I applaud you for this. For years I've been asking myself why we don't assign literature to our students who are just beginning to develop their writing skills. So much accessible and enjoyable fiction, poetry, and nonfiction could be offered to our students, yet traditionally we have taught our classes with the same kinds of readings they have been exposed to over and over again—articles about current issues. I don't intend to criticize that approach; one can certainly teach reading and writing skills successfully with that kind of text. However, I hope you agree that teaching developmental composition with literature offers exciting possibilities for both students and instructors.

What You Will Find in this Book

This book starts with an introduction to the three genres of literature I've included: poetry, short stories, and essays. (Certainly, drama is another important literary genre, but for space considerations, I have not included any plays.) This chapter gives students a brief introduction to reading literature with a focus on some essential questions they can ask of each genre. I offer the basic vocabulary for discussing literature but keep it deliberately simple and not focused on memorizing terms or concepts.

More than anything, this chapter is aimed at helping students feel comfortable with literature.

The main feature of this book is the literature itself. I've included poems, short stories, and essays. You will find that most of the selections are accessible for students who are still developing their reading skills. A range exists, of course. Pieces like Tim O'Brien's "Beginning" might challenge students a bit, but I have taken care to choose selections that are generally comprehensible on a first read. Most of the readings are contemporary, by well-known and lesser-known writers, and the topics cover a broad extent of human experience. The chapters—Family History, Growing Up/Growing Old, Learning and Teaching, The Emotional Side, Work and Dreams, and Issues/Positions—offer instructors an opportunity to teach within a theme, although you will find that an individual selection in one chapter might easily have been placed in another.

Each chapter starts with a brief introduction to its theme and a preview of the literary selections. Students can read this to get a general sense of what they can look forward to in the chapter. Each selection of literature is preceded by a short biography of the author as well as a *Before Reading* prompt. This prompt will start students thinking about the topic of the piece before they encounter the author's treatment of that topic, engaging them more thoroughly in the work. Following each poem, story, or essay, students will find *To Understand* and *To Write* questions. Some of the *To Understand* questions test a student's basic understanding of what has happened in the piece. Others require more critical thinking and ask students to ponder particular parts or aspects of the work. The *To Write* questions ask for personal responses to the literature. These can be used in several ways. You can assign them as take-home journal assignments, or you might use them as quick-write prompts at the beginning of class. Either way, students will be more prepared for class discussion if they have done some writing in response to the literature. These prompts might also be used for formal writing assignments, depending on the goals you have for those assignments. In general, the language in both the *To Understand* and *To Write* questions is not the language of literary analysis nor of literary criticism. Students should be able to read the work and answer the questions without being intimidated by terminology or theory.

At the end of each chapter, you will find a list of *Ideas for Writing*. These writing prompts address the general theme of the chapter (though not one particular work) and are meant to offer opportunities for formal paper writing. You might have students choose one assignment (or you might choose one for them) after they have read all or some of the literary selections for that chapter. I've phrased these prompts so you can use them for paragraph or essay assignments, depending on the direction of your class.

A glossary following the last chapter is a final feature of this book. Although the literature in this text is quite accessible, you may find it helpful to direct your students to the glossary for words that are not familiar to them.

Overall, I hope this book provides both students and instructors an enjoyable classroom experience.

—Albert Garcia

Supplements

Online Instructor's Manual   Written by the author, the Instructor's Manual for DIGGING IN contains a paragraph or two on each literary selection, describing suggestions for how to present the piece to a class, pointing instructors toward some of the study questions, and other helpful hints. In addition, the author discusses the advantages of teaching literature in the developmental classroom.

The IM will be posted online, by unit, for instructors to download at *www.prenhall.com/english*. Contact your local prentice hall representative for a password to access the Instructor's Manual or for information on how to obtain a printed copy.

Acknowledgements

I could not have completed this book without the help and support of many people. To start, I want to thank Craig Campanella from Prentice Hall for his belief in this book's approach and his willingness to try a literature-based developmental composition text. I am also grateful to Joan Polk, Mary Dalton-Hoffman, Marty Sopher, and Jennifer Murtoff, each of whom helped to guide me through the process of pulling the final manuscript together. Further, I'd like to mention the reviewers whose constructive comments helped me revise the early draft of this book: Jennifer Blackman (San Jose State University), Janice Hunter (Valencia Community College), Shirley Hart Berry (Cape Fear Community College) and Susan Ahern (University of Houston).

Thanks also to my many colleagues at Sacramento City College who have supported this project—in particular to the fine people in the Language and Literature Division who suggested many great authors and titles to include here. (I'm sorry I couldn't use them all.) Thanks to Jeff Knorr for his help on the introduction. And a special thanks goes to Terry, Anna, Michael, and Ben for their encouragement, understanding, and frequent help.

—*Albert Garcia*

Digging In
Literature for
Developing Writers

1

Reading Literature:
A Brief Introduction

Getting Started/Digging In

If you are like many students, the very idea of reading
literature may be intimidating. There are several reasons for this. In past classes, you may have had to read
works that were written in a style of English that was
difficult to understand. You may have worried that your
interpretation of a certain piece was not the same as your
instructor's interpretation. No one wants to be wrong
about anything, yet that is what many beginning students of literature fear the most: being wrong.

Let's set things straight. You will not be wrong about a
piece of literature unless you respond to it in a way that
suggests you didn't read it. A response that is thought
through clearly and can be supported by what is in the
text is a valid response. When you read a poem or short
story, you bring your entire lifetime of experience to that
piece. The author has supplied the words on the page, but
you help to create the meaning by taking the author's

words, images, and story and filtering them through your imagination. No two people, then, will read that piece of literature in exactly the same way. Therefore, if you read and respond conscientiously, you won't be wrong.

That is not to say that all responses to a piece of literature are equal. Good readers will recognize their own understanding of a piece but will also be able to make reasonable guesses about how other readers will respond. In other words, a reader's reactions should be more than personal opinion.

Let's think about an example. In Chapter 2 you will encounter a short story by Tobias Wolff called "Powder." In this story, a father takes his son on a snow skiing trip. He is supposed to return the son to the boy's mother for Christmas Eve dinner. However, the father, already in bad favor with the mother, delays in bringing the son home. He and the boy go on several last ski runs and end up being stranded in the mountains as a result of a storm.

There is more to the story, of course, and if you have read carefully, you should, as a start, be able to state what has happened in this story. This does not involve interpretation or explaining meaning. It does involve paying careful attention to the story's events and to what the characters are saying. This task may sound simple enough, but for some pieces of literature it is difficult simply to say what has happened. Nevertheless, it is a good starting point in determining how well you have read a piece.

All readers will have some kind of personal response to "Powder." If you have experienced a divided family, that will influence your reading. If you have been involved in winter sports—skiing or snowboarding—that will affect the way you read the story. Perhaps you are not from a divided family, nor are you experienced in winter sports. Still, you will have a personal response because you are a son, a father, or a mother; because you have an interest in parenting; because you're interested in driving cars in the snow (one aspect of the story); or because you're fascinated by people who reject authority (another aspect of the story). In some way, you will be able to make a personal connection to the story.

However, good readers will go beyond their personal responses. Whether or not you have anything in common with the characters and situations in "Powder," you should be able to sense how the author wants you and other readers to respond both emotionally and intellectually to the story. You should anticipate, for example, that some readers (probably more than *some*) will judge that the father is irresponsible. Also, if, in your background, you have little experience with Christmas, you should nevertheless realize that most readers will recognize the significance of Christmas Eve dinner. The key is to acknowledge your personal reactions while looking for ways that the author wants all readers to respond.

Here are a few tips for reading any kind of literature:

- Read carefully and read at least twice.
- Circle any words that are unfamiliar to you, and then look them up. Do not pass by them and assume that they are unimportant. (This book has a glossary, and chances are good that the word you circle will be listed in it with a clear definition.)
- On your second reading, jot personal responses in the margins and underline passages that seem important.
- Answer the *To Understand* questions as thoroughly as you can. These questions will help you understand not only the basics of what happens in a poem or story but also focus on key ideas and passages in it. If you are reading literature outside of this book, a good strategy is to write or ask your own questions. You might be surprised at how good you are at this because of your intuitive ability to sense what is important in a piece.

- After reading the piece once or twice, leave it alone for a little while, at least overnight if possible. Then read it again. You will be amazed at the new ways you see the poem or story. Good literature will reward many readings. You will get something new out of it each time you return to it.
- Talk with your classmates about the piece that you're reading. This will help you see the work from other perspectives. It's also enjoyable.

Reading Short Stories

People have been telling each other stories for as long as they have used language to communicate with each other. Long before we created modern alphabets to record our words, and long before we had printing presses to mass distribute them, people sat around a fire or beside a path and shared stories. Some of these were true stories about their lives; others were made up fictions meant to entertain or teach. We still do this, of course. Most of us truly admire the skills of a person who can tell a good story. But in recent times (the last 200 years or so), we have had an opportunity to enjoy a certain kind of written story called the short story. These pieces of fiction are notable for their brevity (much shorter than a novel) and power. Writers of short fiction know that, since they are working in a limited space, every word must count, must contribute in some way to the story's impact. As readers, we have to take this into account. We can assume that the author has not included a paragraph here or there just to fill space. Therefore, we must read carefully, enjoying the tale but also thinking critically about how it is put together and how the writer wants us to respond.

In general, there are a few areas in all short stories that are worthy of looking into in order to ensure that you have read them well. The **characters**, **setting**, **conflict**, and **point of view** are good starting points for studying short fiction.

Characters

- Who is the main character?
- Which character do you care most about?
- How do we come to know the characters?
- What motivates the main character? What makes this person act in certain ways?
- What forces is the main character battling?
- Which characters play a less significant role in the story? What purpose do they serve in the story?

Answering these questions about the **characters** in the story will take you a long way in understanding the work. Remember that the characters have been constructed by the author. Some of them have been made for us to love and some to hate, some to admire and some to scorn. Try to get a sense of how the author wants you to respond to a character by asking the above questions. While it's true that readers may have various reactions to a given character, the author has crafted the character to create a response that is generally common from one reader to another.

Setting

- Where does this story take place?
- Is this a rural, urban, or suburban setting?
- In what country or state does the story take place?
- What year is it? What season?
- What time of day?
- Is this taking place indoors (what room?) or outdoors?
- Is a character acting a certain way or doing something because of the setting?

Most of these questions are fairly easy to answer, yet they are of great importance in reading a short story. A story's **setting** can be thought of as the place, time, and overall situation in which the events occur. Consider how important setting or place is in your life. Where you are at a given time will considerably affect the way you act and feel. Consider how you feel when you are in a class-room, a secluded forest, your grandparents' house, a church, your own living room, or on a crowded street. You probably feel and act differently in each place—because of the place. A story's setting, likewise, will affect both how the characters act and how you will respond emotionally. Therefore, read carefully, noticing every little detail that makes the overall setting. Assume that every detail is important because the author has put it there.

Conflict

- What is the main character struggling through or against?
- What person, idea, or problem has the main character encountered?
- How is the character trying to overcome or solve the conflict?

Writers of short stories know that conflict is at the heart of a story. Without conflict, there is no story, at least not one that will hold a reader's attention. It may be pleasant to encounter a character that is absolutely content—but not for long. We read stories because we are intrigued by the struggles fictional characters encounter. **Conflict** occurs when a person or force keeps the main character from reaching his or her goal. Some conflict is obvious. If a character is in a fistfight, there is immediate conflict. Many stories, however, involve more subtle conflict. Often a character faces an inner struggle (with religious belief, for instance, or values within a family), and this conflict can be even more compelling than a car chase or a police shootout. Regardless, you should be able to discern what the conflict is, what the character is up against, and how that person goes about trying to solve the dilemma. In the end, we look for any way the character might have changed as a result of the conflict.

Point of View

- Who is telling the story?
- Does the story have a first-person "I" narrator?
- Does it have a second-person narrator, addressing a "you"?
- Is it a third-person narrator, mentioning "he," "she," and "they"?
- If third-person, what capabilities does this narrator have? Is this storyteller able to enter the minds of all the characters or just one character? Can the narrator tell about the past and/or the future?

In fiction, the term **point of view** refers to who is narrating (or telling) the story and what powers of narration that voice has. Most short stories are written in either first or third-person. In a **first-person** story, the narrator will be the "I" character. This person telling the story will be a participant in some way. Since any information we readers get about events comes from this one person, we must decide how reliable this narrator is and understand that, if the story were told by one of the other characters, it could be completely different. For instance, Frank O'Connor's "My Oedipus Complex" is told by a young boy, Larry, who, very attached to his mother, is upset when his father returns from the war. When you read this story, you will discover how O'Connor's choice of first-person narrator allows readers a very humorous look through this special character's mind. If, on the other hand, the story had been told by the mother or father, it likely would have lost its charm.

A **third-person** narrator, in contrast, is not one of the characters. It is an outside voice who is not a participant in the story. You should note, however, that this narrator is not the author. The author creates this storytelling voice just as he creates a first-person narrator. In some stories, a third-person narrator is able to describe the thoughts and feelings of only one character. You can call this **third-person limited**. In other stories, the narrator can report the thoughts and feelings of any character. Call this **third-person omniscient**. There are many other types of third-person narrators based on the capabilities their authors decide to give them. Your job is to pay attention to what kind of narrator the author has created and to ask how the writer's decision impacts the way the story's events are told.

Reading Poems

For many students, poetry is the most intimidating kind of literature. Why is this? Isn't it curious that a form of writing that is comforting and enjoyable to us as children (nursery rhymes) becomes a source of fear when we are older? Also, have you ever wondered why almost everyone loves some kind of music, another lyrical art form, yet relatively few people read its cousin in the arts, poetry? It's too bad that many students shy away from poetry. Perhaps it is the condensed and experimental use of language in poetry that makes it seem especially difficult for some readers. Whatever the reason, a poem is nothing to fear, and reading a good poem can be very rewarding. Yet you have to get comfortable with this kind of writing, and familiarizing yourself with a few poetic concepts— **image**, **voice**, **type of poem**, and **theme**—will help.

Image

- What mental pictures—or images—do you see when reading the poem?
- If the poem were a photograph, what details could you see? What details do you provide out of your own imagination?
- What senses are evoked in the images: sight, hearing, smell, touch, taste?
- Does the writer use figurative language (imagery and/or metaphor) to extend the images?

- Do the images in the poem, in total, create an overall effect? Do they create a mood or feeling?

Imagery is a main tool of the poet. While an artist creates pictures with paint, stone, or clay, a poet creates **images** with words. As readers, we should pay careful attention to any image a poet offers us. If we see grooves cut into an old maple table top, duck feathers ruffling across a lawn, or a person's hand closing on a doorknob, we should assume the poet included the image for a reason. That detail may seem a small thing to notice, but when images are combined with other images, they create an impression that helps a reader to understand and enjoy the poem. A poet will sometimes use **metaphor**, a direct comparison between two dissimilar things, to further the scope of the poem's imagery. Thus, if the poet writes, "His hands were small fragile leaves," we have metaphor. If the poet writes, "His hands were *like* small fragile leaves," we have a **simile**, a comparison using *like*, *as*, or *than*. Some poems rely heavily on imagery; others use it in a minor way. Whichever the case, pay careful attention, and ask yourself why the poet wants you to see a given picture.

Voice/Speaker

- Who is speaking the poem?
- What voice do you hear: angry, thankful, loving, rambunctious?
- What mood or feeling does this voice create?

Every poem has a **speaker**, the voice that says the words to you. Sometimes the speaker is easy to identify; in other poems it is difficult to tell who is speaking. Often, we are tempted to assume the voice in the poem is that of the poet. While it is true that poems can be autobiographical or even loosely based on the poet's experiences, we readers, without being personally familiar with the poet, have no certain way of knowing whether the events recorded in the poem are from real life or imagined. For that reason, when discussing a poem, we say, "The *speaker* mentions a pot of tulips," not "The *poet* mentions a pot of tulips."

More important, perhaps, is for a reader to understand what kind of **voice** (inflection) the poem has. A poem is much different from a newspaper article. An article's purpose is to inform you. You may not discern a substantial difference in style or voice from one article to another. In poetry, however, you will be able to hear a different attitude in every piece you read. Some poems will seem to shout at you; some will whisper. While one speaker will have a voice of confused longing, another will boast with confidence. To discover the speaker's voice in a poem, you may find it helpful to read the work out loud. Ask yourself how the poet wants you to read this voice. How is it supposed to sound?

Type of Poem

- Does the poem tell a story?
- If there is no story, what force holds together the images and ideas?
- What shape does the poem have? Are the lines long or short or varied? Is the poem arranged with a certain number of lines in every stanza, or do the stanza lengths vary? How do these factors influence the way you read the poem?
- Does the poem incorporate rhyme, meter, or other sound devices?

In its long and varied history, poetry has taken many forms. The two most useful for you to be aware of are narrative and lyric. A **narrative poem** contains a story of some kind; the speaker of the poem *narrates* this story. Sometimes these will be long poems, perhaps even book-length, but the poem's size does not in itself make it narrative. Instead, look for some of the elements you'll find in short stories, characters and setting, for example. **Lyric poetry** has its roots in music. The word lyric is derived from a Greek word, *lyra*, meaning "musical instrument." You know from any kind of popular music that lines written to be accompanied by music are called lyrics. They come printed in the CD case of your favorite singer. However, in poetry, lyrics eventually came to be written for readers and not to be performed by musicians. Many readers of poetry today will refer to almost any short poem as a lyric. Key qualities of lyric poetry you can look for are an intensity of expression and personal feeling along with an attention, on the part of the poet, to create sounds with the words, phrases, lines, and sentences that compliment the subject. You know these sounds are sometimes created with rhyming and rhythmical devices, but the methods of manipulating or creating pleasing sound in poetry go far beyond that. Whole books have been written about it. The key for you is to notice the sound and ask yourself how that element contributes to the entire experience of reading the poem.

In truth, much of the poetry we read today contains elements of both the narrative and the lyric. Poets writing narratives will frequently pay special attention to the sound of their lines. Poets writing lyrics commonly include elements of story in their work. You shouldn't be too concerned about labeling a poem narrative or lyric; rather, look for the ways the elements of these broad types influence your experience of the poem.

Theme

- Does the poem suggest a message to you? Does it seem to hint at a certain viewpoint of its subject?
- What impression do you get from the poem? How would you explain this impression to another person?

The most common question a teacher of poetry gets is "What does it mean?" This is what students most frequently want to know. They want the answer—as if the poem were a mathematical equation to solve. Most good poetry, however, cannot be limited to one meaning. Indeed, most poets do not intend only one message, nor do they come out and state exactly what they think about their subject. Your job as a reader is to consider possible themes that come from a poem. The **theme** is what the poet is saying about the topic of the poem. Often, the poet does not state a theme directly but, rather, suggests one through imagery and tone. Therefore, if a poet's topic is an elderly man's behavior, ask yourself what the poet is saying about this topic and, perhaps, about the behavior of elderly men in general. Remember, you do not have to have the only correct answer or interpretation. Sometimes a poem will not seem to reveal a theme at all. If that is the case, pay attention to the impression the poem gives you. How does it make you feel? Dive back into the sounds and images in the poem to discover what they offer you. Don't be fearful if at first you don't discover a theme. Remember that poetry is an art form that goes beyond merely presenting a message. If a poet wanted only to make a point, he or she could do so in an essay or a memo. A poem is meant to be an experience for the reader. Yes, you may be able to find a theme, but don't make that your only goal in reading a poem.

Reading Essays

The term **essay** refers to many types of prose writing that have one thing in common: they are not fiction. Essays can have a variety of purposes. In an autobiographical essay, the writer tells a story about his or her life. These essays may seem much like short stories. The difference is that the characters, setting, and events are drawn from the author's life. In a short story, on the other hand, the author invents these from his or her imagination. Writers use essays for other purposes as well: to explore a subject, to describe a place, to argue a position on a controversial issue, to explain a concept, or to propose a solution to a problem—among others. You, too, will have many opportunities to write such expository or argumentative essays in your classes. Most of the essays in this book are autobiographical; therefore, the reading tips below focus on that kind of creative nonfiction.

Subject/Theme

- What is the author's subject? What topic lies underneath the remembered events of the story?
- What is the author's point about the story? Can we readers discern a message?

An autobiographical essay will have an **obvious subject**, the event recorded by the author: the recollection of a family funeral, a trip to Paris, or a time spent in jail. However, a reader should be prepared for a more **general subject** as well. Is the author writing about a family funeral also writing about how people respond to stress in the face of a loved one's death, how the world seems oddly changed when we lose someone, or how important it is to have one's affairs in order before death? The point is to look beyond the events of the essay to see the larger topic being explored by the writer. Then ask yourself if the writer is making a point—developing a **theme**—about the larger subject. Don't oversimplify here. If you conclude the theme is that funerals are sad, you need to look again to see what the writer is saying beyond that. After all, a reader could get that message from nearly any essay about a funeral. Ask what theme is particular to the essay you're reading.

Author's Presence

- What part does the writer play in the essay?
- Is the writer a character or the voice in the story—or both?
- What do we readers learn about the author?
- What does the author learn?

Since writers of autobiographical essays write about experiences in their own lives, the writers themselves are a very important part of the essay. As readers, we can understand the essay better if we ponder carefully the writer's motivation and reasoning. Frequently, the writer will be a character in the essay, but this is different than a fictional character. We should ask ourselves why the writer has chosen to show readers this part of his or her life. It may surprise you to discover that writers of auto-biographical essays often write in order to *discover* what they think about their subjects. (This is the case for other kinds of writing—poems and short stories—as well.) Is it true then that they don't know what they think about their subject until they write it? Yes, sometimes. The essayist writing about a funeral may know that there is something significant and powerful about that event but not completely understand at first what it is. We read the essay to discover what we can but also to experience what the author has learned. In that regard, reading an autobiographical essay is a unique opportunity to look into how another person has experienced the world.

Final Comments on Reading Literature

In the introduction to his book, *The Triggering Town*, the poet Richard Hugo says, "I think literature should be studied for the most serious of all reasons: it is fun." Hugo was on to something. While reading literature can require careful analysis, we should initially approach a poem, story, or essay as a work of art to enjoy. The author wants it that way. Writers don't set out with the idea of making life difficult for us readers. Therefore, read the selections in this book carefully, read them over and over again, look up words you aren't familiar with, analyze their many features, answer the *To Understand* questions, and explore the pieces in your own writing—do all this, but first, enjoy!

2

Family History

━━━━━✦━━━━━

Family History

For most of us, our family is the one group with whom we have built our identity. Beyond school, church, clubs, friends, and coworkers, the family—for better or for worse—is the group we come home to, the people we are bound to by blood and by history. While many other groups and people play important roles in our lives, the family is where many of our most important dramas are played out. From birth to marriage to death, the grand stories of our lives take place within a group of people we call family.

It should not be surprising, then, that writers frequently find inspiration for their work in the people that are closest to them: the family. Even in fictional writings, authors understand that the family unit, however it might be composed, provides limitless dramatic situations for short stories and novels. We look to this literature—about grandparents, parents, brothers, and sisters—for two main reasons: 1) to be entertained, to get caught up in the intriguing lives and histories of other families, and 2) to gain a better understanding of ourselves and our own families.

Among the works in this chapter, you will encounter

- a poem in which a granddaughter imagines what life was like for her grandmother, a picture bride, who promised marriage to a man in a distant land before ever meeting him;
- a short story about a son who goes on a skiing trip with his father, who has separated from the boy's mother;
- an essay by a daughter who was warned by her mother not to rely on her looks.

As you read the stories, poems, and essays in this chapter, you will think of ideas for your own writing, things you want to say about your own family or families in general. The *To Write* questions following each piece of literature will offer opportunities to write on subjects related to the story or poem you've just read. In addition, at the end of the chapter, the *Ideas for Writing* section will provide you with a number of topics to use for longer assignments about family.

Robert Wrigley

A Photo of Immigrants, 1903

*Robert Wrigley is an award-winning poet who lives in the
canyon of the Clearwater River in Idaho. He has published five books of poetry including, most recently,* In the
Bank of Beautiful Sins *and* Reign of Snakes. *In this poem
he describes the lives of an immigrant family as he sees
them in a photograph.*

Before Reading: Imagine the many countries from which newcomers
to the U.S. have emigrated. In general, what do immigrants bring with
them? What do they leave behind?

You could cry at their faces.
Father forces a smile
and Mother looks into the lens
as she must have looked for weeks
into the distances of the Atlantic.
The infant dangles her feet
against sack cloth, and the boy,
four maybe, looks up at his hand
in his father's, as though surprised
to find it there. Or perhaps
the look on his face is pain, his father
holding on too hard. The ship in back
loads for the return to Danzig:
crates of pencils, pistons, bolts of linen.
By its first moorage, these four will be on their way
to Cleveland or Chicago. They will have seen
the Statue of Liberty and looked past it
for the world. They will have sweltered
on the train all through Ohio
and August.
And in five years
they will write to their friends in Cracow,

enclose a few dollars, a new and cheerful photograph.
Father will tell in his most earnest prose
the ordeal of the Atlantic passage
and the ecstasy of arrival.
He will have himself removing his hat
and blowing kisses to the city, laughing
and clapping with his fellows. And that night
he will mail his letter, walking slowly
to the post office with his daughter.
He will hear two men there speak again
of the great lake to the north of the city
and vow to visit it when there is time.
He will stop and tell his daughter of his plans.
She will nod and walk on, walking oddly
on the sides of her feet, hoping
he will soon let go of her hand,
speak English, or loosen
at least his fierce and powerful grip.

To Understand

1. Why do you think Wrigley starts this poem with "You could cry at their faces"? What emotions does the speaker express throughout the poem?

2. Where are these immigrants from? What details inform you of this?

3. Why does the father mail a letter? To whom does he mail it?

4. Notice the manner in which the father grips his four-year-old son's hand in the first stanza and also the "fierce and powerful grip" he has on the daughter at the end of the poem. How does the man's interaction with his children relate to his immigration to the U.S.? What impact does this man have on his children?

To Write

1. When and how did your family immigrate to the United States? Explain how your ancestors (or you) came to this

country. You may find it helpful to talk with parents or other family members. Imagine how the immigrants in your family felt to leave one country and find themselves in a new land.

Cathy Song

Picture Bride

Cathy Song was born in Honolulu, Hawaii. After earning degrees from Wellesley College and Boston University, she returned to Honolulu to write and to raise her family. She won the Yale Younger Poets Award for her first book, Picture Bride, and has published three subsequent volumes of poetry. A product of Chinese and Korean ancestry, Song writes frequently about the experiences of immigrants to Hawaii. In the following poem, she describes what was a common marriage arrangement for immigrants to Hawaii from 1907–1924. Chinese, Japanese, Korean, and Filipino men working sugar cane plantations, with few prospects for marriage in the islands, would arrange through photographs and letters for women (mainly from Japan and Korea) to come to Hawaii to marry them.

Before Reading: Imagine what it would take for a woman to leave her country and her family to marry a stranger in an unfamiliar land.

She was a year younger
than I,
twenty-three when she left Korea.
Did she simply close
the door of her father's house
and walk away. And
was it a long way
through the tailor shops of Pusan
to the wharf where the boat
waited to take her to an island
whose name she had
only recently learned,
on whose shore
a man waited,
turning her photograph

to the light when the lanterns
in the camp outside
Waialua Sugar Mill were lit
and the inside of his room
grew luminous
from the wings of moths
migrating out of the cane stalks?
What things did my grandmother
take with her? And when
she arrived to look
into the face of the stranger
who was her husband,
thirteen years older than she,
did she politely untie
the silk bow of her jacket,
her tent-shaped dress
filling with the dry wind
that blew from the surrounding fields
where the men were burning the cane?

To Understand

1. Why did the speaker's grandmother leave Korea to marry a stranger 14 years older than herself?

2. Notice that many of the sentences in this poem are phrased as questions. Why do you think Song has composed her poem in this way?

3. Examine the images in the last six lines of the poem. What impressions does Song create here? How are we readers supposed to feel about the grandmother's move to Hawaii and her life with her new husband?

To Write

1. Explain what you believe are the advantages and disadvantages of a picture-bride arrangement.

Tobias Wolff

Powder

The author of several short story collections including In the Garden of the North American Martyrs, Back in the World, *and* The Night in Question, *as well as a book-length memoir,* This Boy's Life, *that was made into a feature-length film, Tobias Wolff writes in this story about a father/son relationship that takes on extra tension because the father (presumably not living with the rest of the family) competes with the boy's mother for time with the son.*

Before Reading: Consider what special strains occur around children whose parents no longer live together.

Just before Christmas my father took me skiing at Mount Baker. He'd had to fight for the privilege of my company, because my mother was still angry with him for sneaking me into a night-club during our last visit, to see Thelonious Monk.

He wouldn't give up. He promised, hand on heart, to take good care of me and have me home for dinner on Christmas Eve, and she relented. But as we were checking out of the lodge that morning it began to snow, and in this snow he observed some quality that made it necessary for us to get in one last run. We got in several last runs. He was indifferent to my fretting. Snow whirled around us in bitter, blinding squalls, hissing like sand, and still we skied. As the lift bore us to the peak yet again, my father looked at his watch and said, "Criminey. This'll have to be a fast one."

By now I couldn't see the trail. There was no point in trying. I stuck to him like white on rice and did what he did and somehow made it to the bottom without sailing off a cliff. We returned our skis and my father put chains on the Austin-Healy while I swayed from foot to foot, clapping my mittens and wishing I were home. I could see everything. The green tablecloth, the plates with holly pattern, the red candles waiting to be lit.

We passed a diner on our way out. "You want some soup?" my father asked. I shook my head. "Buck up," he said. "I'll get you there. Right, doctor?"

I was supposed to say, "Right, doctor," but I didn't say anything.

A state trooper waved us down outside the resort. A pair of sawhorses were blocking the road. The trooper came up to our car and bent down to my father's window. His face was bleached by the cold. Snowflakes clung to his eyebrows and to the fur trim of his jacket and cap.

"Don't tell me," my father said.

The trooper told him. The road was closed. It might get cleared, it might not. Storm took everyone by surprise. So much, so fast. Hard to get people moving. Christmas Eve. What can you do?

My father said, "Look. We're talking about four, five inches. I've taken this car through worse than that."

The trooper straightened up, boots creaking. His face was out of sight but I could hear him. "The road is closed."

My father sat with both hands on the wheel, rubbing the wood with his thumbs. He looked at the barricade for a long time. He seemed to be trying to master the idea of it. Then he thanked the trooper, and with a weird, old-maidy show of caution turned the car around. "Your mother will never forgive me for this," he said.

"We should have left before," I said. "Doctor."

He didn't speak to me again until we were both in a booth at the diner, waiting for our burgers. "She won't forgive me," he said. "Do you understand? Never."

"I guess," I said, but no guesswork was required; she wouldn't forgive him.

"I can't let that happen." He bent toward me. "I'll tell you what I want. I want us to be together again. Is that what you want?"

I wasn't sure, but I said, "Yes, sir."

He bumped my chin with his knuckles. "That's all I needed to hear."

When we finished eating he went to the pay phone in the back of the diner, then joined me in the booth again. I figured he'd called my mother, but he didn't give a report. He sipped at his coffee and stared out the window at the empty road. "Come on!" When the trooper's car went past, lights flashing, he got up and dropped some money on the check. "Okay. *Vamanos.*"

The wind had died. The snow was falling straight down, less of it now, lighter. We drove away from the resort, right up to the barricade. "Move it," my father told me. When I looked at him he said, "What are you waiting for?" I got out and dragged one of the sawhorses aside, then pushed it back after he drove through. When I got inside the car he said, "Now you're an accomplice. We go down together." He put the car in gear and looked at me. "Joke, doctor."

"Funny, doctor."

Down the first long stretch I watched the road behind us, to see if the trooper was on our tail. The barricade vanished. Then there was nothing but snow: snow on the road, snow kicking up from the chains, snow on the trees, snow in the sky; and our trail in the snow. I faced around and had a shock. The lie of the road behind us had been marked by our own tracks, but there were no tracks ahead of us. My father was breaking virgin snow between a line of tall trees. He was humming "Stars Fell on Alabama." I felt snow brush along the floorboards under my feet. To keep my hands from shaking I clamped them between my knees.

My father grunted in a thoughtful way and said, "Don't ever try this yourself."

"I won't."

"That's what you say now, but someday you'll get your license and then you'll think you can do anything. Only you won't be able to do this. You need, I don't know—a certain instinct."

"Maybe I have it."

"You don't. You have your strong points, but not . . . you know. I only mention it because I don't want you to get the idea this is something just anybody can do. I'm a great driver. That's not a virtue, okay? It's just a fact, and one you should be aware of. Of course you have to give the old heap some credit, too—there aren't many cars I'd try this with. Listen!"

I listened. I heard the slap of the chains, the stiff, jerky rasp of the wipers, the purr of the engine. It really did purr. The car was almost new. My father couldn't afford it, and kept promising to sell it, but here it was.

I said, "Where do you think that policeman went to?"

"Are you warm enough?" He reached over and cranked up the blower. Then he turned off the wipers. We didn't need them. The clouds had brightened. A few sparse, feathery flakes drifted into our slipstream and were swept away. We left the trees and entered a broad field of snow that ran level for a while and then tilted sharply downward. Orange stakes had been planted at intervals in two parallel lines and my father ran a course between them, though they were far enough apart to leave considerable doubt in my mind as to where exactly the road lay. He was humming again, doing little scat riffs around the melody.

"Okay, then. What are my strong points?"

"Don't get me started," he said. "It'd take all day."

"Oh, right. Name one."

"Easy. You always think ahead."

True. I always thought ahead. I was a boy who kept his clothes on numbered hangers to ensure proper rotation. I bothered my teachers for homework assignments far ahead of their due dates so I could make up schedules. I thought ahead, and that was why I knew that there would be some other troopers waiting for us at the end of our ride, if we got there. What I did not know was that my father would wheedle and plead his way past them—he didn't sing "O Tannenbaum" but just about—and get me home for dinner, buying a little more time before my mother decided to make the split final. I knew we'd get caught; I was resigned to it. And maybe for this reason I stopped moping and began to enjoy myself.

Why not? This was one for the books. Like being in a speedboat, only better. You can't go downhill in a boat. And it was all ours. And it kept coming, the laden trees, the unbroken surface of snow, the sudden white vistas. Here and there I saw hints of the road, ditches, fences, stakes, but not so many that I could have found my way. But then I didn't have to. My father was driving. My father in his forty-eighth year, rumpled, kind, bankrupt of honor, flushed with certainty. He was a great driver. All persuasion, no coercion. Such subtlety at the wheel, such tactful pedalwork. I actually trusted him. And the best was yet to come—switchbacks and hairpins impossible to describe. Except maybe to say this: if you haven't driven fresh powder, you haven't driven.

To Understand

1. Why does the father keep his son skiing past when he should have left to deliver the boy to his mother for Christmas Eve dinner?

2. What kind of man is the father? What specifically does he do to lead you to your impression of him?

3. What are the differences in the way the father and the son (the narrator) think and act? Are there any similarities?

4. Why does the son seem to have a positive outlook on his father's driving at the end of the story rather than the concerned viewpoint he has had throughout most of the story?

To Write

1. To better understand the mother's role in this story, write a passage in her voice as she is waiting for the father to return their son for Christmas Eve dinner.

2. Early in the story, the father "promise[s], hand on heart, to take good care of [the boy]." How successful has he been at this? Point to particular places in the story that lead you to your opinion.

Simon Ortiz

My Father's Song

Simon Ortiz is a member of the Acoma Pueblo in New Mexico. The author of many books of poetry and prose, his work is influenced by the oral traditions of the Acoma and by the landscape of the Southwest. In the following poem, a son recalls a vivid, memorable event he experienced with his father and the way his father communicated with him.

Before Reading: Think about the manner in which fathers communicate with their children. How did your father talk with you? How did he pass along wisdom or values?

Wanting to say things,
I miss my father tonight.
His voice, the slight catch,
the depth from his thin chest,
the tremble of emotion
in something he has just said
to his son, his song:

We planted corn one spring at Acu—
we planted several times
but this one particular time
I remember the soft damp sand
in my hand.

My father had stopped at one point
to show me an overturned furrow;
the plowshare had unearthed
the burrow nest of a mouse
in the soft, moist sand.

Very gently, he scooped tiny pink animals
into the palm of his hand
and told me to touch them.

We took them to the edge
of the field and put them in the shade
of a sand moist clod.

I remember the very softness
of cool and warm sand and tiny alive mice
and my father saying things.

To Understand

1. At the beginning of the poem, the speaker mentions that he
is "wanting to say things. . . ." What does he mean by this?
Use other words or expressions to explain what he wants.

2. What impression do you get from the story about the father
and son finding baby mice? How do the details of that story
make you feel?

3. In the first stanza, why does the speaker describe what his father has said as "his song"? In what ways could his "saying
things" be considered a song?

To Write

1. Some fathers eagerly offer advice to their children while others are relatively silent, teaching by example. Others, sadly,
pay little attention to their kids. Explain what, in your opinion, is the best way for a father to communicate with his children. What kinds of ideas, opinions, or stories should a father
pass down to his children?

2. Did your father have a "song" to offer you? If so, what was it
like?

Gary Soto

Father

Born and raised in Fresno, California, Gary Soto is a poet, fiction writer, and essayist who writes for adults as well as young audiences. His essay collection, Living Up the Street, *from which this piece is taken, won the Before Columbus Foundation American Book Award in 1985. In 1995 his* New and Selected Poems *was a finalist for both the* Los Angeles Times *Book Award and the National Book Award. He frequently visits schools to read his work and to speak with students, and he now serves as Young People's Ambassador for the California Rural Legal Assistance (CRLA) and for the United Farm Workers of America (UFW). "Father," a remembrance of a particularly confusing and tragic time for the author, is a good example of how Soto's writing can appeal to both adult and young audiences.*

Before Reading: Think about pacing in a piece of writing, how slowly or quickly an author reveals details and key information. In this essay, notice how Soto reveals the central shocking event.

My father was showing me how to water. Earlier in the day he and a friend had leveled the backyard with a roller, then with a two-by-four they dragged on a rope to fill in the depressed areas, after which they watered the ground and combed it slowly with a steel rake. They were preparing the ground for a new lawn. They worked shirtless in the late summer heat, and talked only so often, stopping now and then to point and say things I did not understand—how fruit trees would do better near the alley and how the vegetable garden would do well on the east side of the house.

"Put your thumb like this," he said. Standing over me, he took the hose and placed his thumb over the opening so that the water streamed out hissing and showed silver in that dusk. I tried it and the water hissed and went silver as I pointed the hose to a square patch of dirt that I soaked but was careful not to puddle.

Father returned to sit down with an iced tea. His knees were water stained and his chest was flecked with mud. Mom sat next to him, garden gloves resting on his lap. She was wearing checkered shorts and her hair was tied up in a bandana. He patted his lap, and she jumped into it girlishly, arms around his neck. They raised their heads to watch me—or look through me, as if something were on the other side of me—and talked about our new house—the neighbors, trees they would plant, the playground down the block. They were tired from the day's work but were happy. When Father pinched her legs, as if to imply they were fat, she punched him gently and played with his hair.

The water streamed, nickel-colored, as I slowly worked from one end to the next. When I raised my face to Father's to ask if I could stop, he pointed to an area that I had missed. Although it was summer I was cold from the water and my thumb hurt from pressing the hose, triggerlike, to reach the far places. But I wanted to please him, to work as hard as he had, so I watered the patch until he told me to stop. I turned off the water, coiled the hose as best I could, and sat with them as they talked about the house and stared at where I had been standing.

The next day Father was hurt at work. A neck injury. Two days later he was dead. I remember the hour—two in the afternoon. An uncle slammed open the back door at Grandma's and the three of us—cousin Isaac, Debbie, and I who were playing in the yard—grew stiff because we thought we were in trouble for doing something wrong. He looked at us, face lined with worry and shouting to hurry to the car. At the hospital I recall Mother holding her hand over her eyes as if she was looking into a light. She was leaning into someone's shoulder and was being led away from the room in which Father lay.

I remember looking up but saying nothing, though I sensed what had happened—that Father was dead. I did not feel sorrow nor did I cry, but I felt conspicuous because relatives were pressing me against their legs or holding my hand or touching my head, tenderly. I stood among them, some of whom were crying while others had their heads bowed and mouths moving. The three of us were led away down the hall to a cafeteria where an uncle bought us candies that we ate standing up and looking around, after which we left the hospital and walked into a harsh afternoon light. We got into a blue car we had never seen before.

At the funeral there was crying. I knelt with my brother and sister, hands folded and trying to be patient, though I was itchy from the tiny coat whose shoulders worked into my armpits and from the heat of a stuffy car on our long and slow drive from the church in town. Prayers were said and a eulogy was given by a man we did not know. We were asked to view the casket, with our mother and the three of us to lead the procession. An uncle helped my mother while we walked shyly to view our father for the last time. When I stood at the casket, I was surprised to see him, eyes closed and moist looking and wearing a cap the color of skin. (Years later I would realize that it hid the wound from which he had died.) I looked quickly and returned to my seat, head bowed because my relatives were watching me and I felt scared.

We buried our father. Later that day at the house, Grandma could not stop shaking from her nerves, so a doctor was called. I was in the room when he opened his bag and shiny things gleamed from inside it. Scared, I left the room and sat in the living room with my sister, who had a doughnut in her hand, with one bite gone. An aunt whose face was twisted from crying looked at me and, feeling embarrassed, I lowered my head to play with my fingers.

A week later relatives came to help build the fence Father had planned for the new house. A week after that Rick, Debra, and I were playing in an unfinished bedroom with a can of marbles Mother had given us. Behind the closed door we rolled the marbles so that they banged against the baseboard and jumped into the air. We separated, each to a corner, where we swept them viciously with our arms—the clatter of the marbles hitting the walls so loud I could not hear the things in my heart.

To Understand

1. If the central event in this essay is the tragic death of Soto's father, why does Soto devote the first four paragraphs to his family working in the yard, preparing for a new lawn?

2. Go back to the paragraphs in which Soto describes being at the hospital and, later, at the funeral. What details in these paragraphs inform you of how the young Soto was feeling? What would you say his age was? Point to the details that work as clues.

3. In the final paragraph, the kids are rolling marbles against the baseboards in an unfinished room. What does Soto want his readers to conclude from this scene? What emotion was Soto experiencing? What should we readers feel?

To Write

1. Write about a time that you experienced a death in your family. Give your readers a sense of your emotional state at the time by including, as Soto does, vivid details about what you were noticing.

2. Recall an event (other than a death, perhaps) that seemed suddenly to turn your life upside down. What was the event? Describe your life before the event and after the event to show how it changed.

Nikki Giovanni

Nikki-Rosa

Nikki Giovanni was born in Knoxville, Tennessee, and was raised in Ohio. Her collections of poems include Black Feeling; Black Talk; Black Judgment; *and* Blues for All the Changes: New Poems. *She has won the NAACP Image Award for Literature as well as the Langston Hughes Award for Distinguished Contributions to the Arts. She has been named Woman of the Year in several magazines including* Ladies Home Journal, Mademoiselle, *and* Essence.

Before Reading: Think about what it means (and feels like) to be a member of a minority group and to be poor in this country.

childhood remembrances are always a drag
if you're Black
you always remember things like living in Woodlawn
with no inside toilet
and if you become famous or something
they never talk about how happy you were to have your
     mother
all to yourself and
how good the water felt when you got your bath from one
     of those
big tubs that folk in chicago barbecue in
and somehow when you talk bout home
it never gets across how much you
understood their feelings
as the whole family attended meetings about Hollydale
and even though you remember
your biographers never understand
your father's pain as he sells his stock
and another dream goes
and though you're poor it isn't poverty that

concerns you
and though they fought a lot
it isn't your father's drinking that makes any difference
but only that everybody is together and you
and your sister have happy birthdays and very good
    christmasses
and I really hope no white person ever has cause to write
    about me
because they never understand Black love is Black wealth
    and they'll
probably talk about my hard childhood and never under-
    stand that
all the while I was quite happy.

To Understand

1. This poem's speaker offers many details about her childhood of poverty. What are some of these details?

2. Several times in the poem the speaker suggests that she was happy despite her childhood poverty. Does this surprise you? Explain why she felt this way.

3. Do you agree that white people "never understand Black love is Black wealth"? Explain your answer.

To Write

1. Do you ever feel misunderstood because of your family's wealth or lack of wealth, where you have lived, your family's education level, or other socioeconomic factors? Explain how others have perceived you and how accurate or inaccurate they have been.

Susan Straight

Not Skin Deep—Heart Deep

Susan Straight's books include the novel I Been in Sorrow's Kitchen and Licked Out All the Pots *and the short story collection,* Aquaboogie. *Her most recent novel is* Highwire Moon. *Her many awards include a Guggenheim fellowship and a Lannan Foundation grant.* "Not Skin Deep—Heart Deep" *was originally published in an anthology of letters from women writers to their mothers entitled* I've Always Meant to Tell You: Letters to Our Mothers.

Before Reading: Consider how important physical appearance is in our culture. Look around you. How important is attractiveness to the people you interact with daily? How important is it to you?

Dear Mom,

It wasn't *ugly*. I don't recall you using that word. The way I remember it, you used to say, "Well, you're plain, and you're never going to make a living on your looks. You might not even get married, and that's why you'd better learn to use your brain . . ."

Had your stepmother told you that? I know your mother died when you were ten and lived in Switzerland, and the woman your father married treated you terribly. She must have told you much worse. We're both small, sturdy, and tough.

I know I was homely, back when I was thirteen or so and you gave me this talk. Remember my blue cat-eye glasses? And the gap between my front teeth, along with the high-placed fang I had instead of the left incisor? Remember when I was the shortest, skinniest girl in every class? And my legs—they were painfully thin and slightly bowed until the car accident broke my left thighbone and the traction straightened it. Then they didn't match—I had one leg curved and one spindle straight. Of course, you were right. I wasn't going to catch any modeling jobs or men looking like I did.

I had plenty of beautiful friends, girls I watched at school. They made cheerleader, leaned against the eucalyptus tree trunks with guys, wore hip-hugger jeans with their curves swelling out and baby-doll tops with scoop necklines showing pillow-soft shadows. The football players, who were the best for status, always went for them.

But I liked watching the game of football as much as the guys, because during all those weeks of traction, I'd combined reading, studying, and watching sports on that little hospital TV, waiting for your daily visits. Remember? We'd already had the plain talk, I think. Because I decided I wanted to be a sportswriter instead of a cheerleader. With my face and legs and glasses, I'd never get a cheerleader spot anyway. Use my brain, right? I started observing the plays, keeping stats on the sidelines, and I practiced writing sports stories at home, in secret.

You thought being a female sportscaster was a great idea, because there weren't many and it was a professional-type career. You'd emigrated from Switzerland to Canada and then America, barely getting to finish high school, having to work, and then when my father left, having to work and leave babies with sitters. But you loved sports—remember, you always told me you'd learned your American English from listening to Vin Scully and Howard Cosell broadcasts?

When my pretty friends got married or had babies or partied, I went to college and became a sportswriter. I still thought I was plain; still do, even though Dwayne has been telling me for almost fifteen years that I look okay to him. And then I moved from sportswriting to stories and novels.

Now, the "ugly" story is my favorite tale to tell on you when I give a reading. You know that, because you came to the author festival in Long Beach to hold Delphine when she was four months old. You didn't hear what I said about you and the talk you'd given me, because you were outside walking with her. But after the presentation, a "plain" woman, meaning she was unadorned, unmadeup, unpermed, approached us. She said, "Is this your mother? The one who called you plain and said you'd better use your brain?"

I nodded, embarrassed. You looked at me, embarrassed, too.

She said, "My mother told me something similar. And I'm a chemist."

We were about to take this further, to tell each other why we were glad we'd been told our brains were far more important investments than our faces, but several women crowded around to say that was an awful thing to tell a daughter, something certain to have ruined her self-esteem and confidence and femininity. But that's not what the words were intended to do. The words built me up, in an unusual way.

Hey, I thought, but I couldn't tell them, I've got a job. I've still got that brain. I'm not on the street. And that's because of my mother's words, in a way.

Because so many of my lovely friends you remember from when I was in high school, the ones who traded their looks and didn't go to class and laughed at brainiacs like me, who went for guys who had good looks, too, or who were dangerous and wild and infamous, those friends are on the street. I see them almost everyday, Mom. One has no teeth. She's a prostitute. And teeth get in the way of what she has to do now for a living. Someone knocked them out for her. Remember D, whom I've known since kindergarten, who wore glasses like me, and who took them off a few years later so she could be beautiful even though she couldn't see? She lived in the barn on Jeff's land last year, Mom. I didn't tell you. She's lost her three kids because she does speed: she trades herself for drugs.

I have three kids now, too. Three girls you love. Three daughters who are so startlingly lovely that they get modeling offers every week, along with compliments and stares and comments from total strangers on their gorgeous faces and eyes and skin and hair. No one ever calls them plain. But I work on their reading and writing every day, with your help, Mom. And whenever anyone says to them, "Look at how beautiful they are!" their father and I always add, "And they're smart."

Sometimes at night, I whisper to them that looks fade away and brains never do. I let them type on this typewriter. The little blue one you bought me for high school graduation, the Smith-Corona the exact shade of blue as my cat-eye glasses, finally wore out. But I keep it nearby now, and never forget what you taught me.

With love,
Susan

To Understand

1. Do you think the advice Straight's mother gave her—". . . that's why you'd better learn to use your brain . . ."—was mean or helpful? Or would you categorize it in some other way?

2. What options did Straight see available for her life, given that she considered herself "plain"? Are the career paths she chose commonly pursued by women?

3. Why does Straight describe the lives of her good-looking friends who have turned to prostitution and drug abuse? What is her message with these examples?

To Write

1. What are the special challenges for people who are "plain"? Compare these to the challenges especially attractive people face.

2. Explain the advice you would give your child if he or she were rather plain in appearance or, conversely, quite attractive.

Neal Bowers

Driving Lessons

Neal Bowers is the author of several books of poetry, two scholarly books, and a nonfiction memoir entitled Words for the Taking; The Hunt for a Plagiarist. *He lives in Ames, Iowa, and is Professor of English and Distinguished Professor of Liberal Arts and Sciences at Iowa State University.*

Before Reading: Recall when you first learned to drive—or when you learned some other activity that was of great importance to you. Think about what you went through, but also try to remember what the experience was like for the person teaching you—one of your parents, perhaps, or some other adult.

I learned to drive in a parking lot
on Sundays, when the stores were closed—
slow maneuvers out beyond the light-poles,
no destination, just the ritual of clutch and gas,
my father clenching with the grinding gears,
finally giving up and leaving my mother
to buck and plunge with me and say,
repeatedly, "Once more. Try just once more."

She walked out on him once
when I was six or seven, my father
driving beside her, slow as a beginner,
pleading, my baby brother and I
crying out the windows, "Mama, don't go!"
It was a scene to break your heart
or make you laugh—those wailing kids,
a woman walking briskly with a suitcase,
the slow car following like a faithful dog.

I don't know why she finally got in
and let us take her back

to whatever she had made up her mind to leave;
but the old world swallowed her up
as soon as she opened that door,
and the other life she might have lived
lay down forever in its dark infancy.

Sometimes when I'm home, driving
through the old neighborhoods, stopping
in front of each little house we rented,
my stillborn other life gets in,
the boy I would have been if
my mother had kept on walking.
He wants to be just like her,
far away and gone forever, wants
me to press down on the gas;
but however fast I squeal away,
the shaggy past keeps loping behind,
sniffing every turn.

When I stop in the weedy parking lot,
the failed stores of the old mall
make a dark wall straight ahead;
and I'm alone again, until my parents get in,
unchanged after all these years,
My father, impatient, my mother
trying hard to smile, waiting for me
to steer my way across this emptiness.

To Understand

1. Why does the mother leave the father (if only momentarily) in the second stanza? Look for clues in the first and third stanzas.

2. The speaker describes his mother's leaving as "a scene to break your heart / or make you laugh." Explain how it could be both.

3. In the second stanza, the speaker describes his family's car as "a faithful dog" as it follows his mother. Later, he imagines his own life and its "shaggy past [that] keeps loping behind, / sniffing every turn." Explain why the speaker employs these dog metaphors. What do they suggest about the way he sees his life?

4. In the poem's last line, the speaker describes his life with his parents as "this emptiness." What details throughout the poem suggest emptiness in the speaker's life?

To Write

1. Do you have a "stillborn other life" you have thought about? Imagine how your life might have been had one or both of your parents made different choices.

Maxine Hong Kingston

Catfish in the Bathtub

Maxine Hong Kingston grew up in Stockton, California, where she worked long hours with her brothers and sisters in her parents' laundry. In her writing, she explores the experience of being raised by Chinese immigrants in the United States and of the clashing of cultures and generations. Her memoir, The Woman Warrior: Memoirs of a Girlhood Among Ghosts, *won the National Book Critics Circle Award, and its sequel,* China Men, *received the same award. Her other writings include the novel* Tripmaster Monkey: His Fake Book.

Before Reading: Recall the kinds of foods you were asked (or made) to eat when you were a child. What else did you have to do because it was "good for you"?

My mother has cooked for us: raccoons, skunks, hawks, city pigeons, wild ducks, wild geese, black-skinned bantams, snakes, garden snails, turtles that crawled about the pantry floor and sometimes escaped under the refrigerator or stove, catfish that swam in the bathtub. "The emperors used to eat the peaked hump of purple dromedaries," she would say. "They used chopsticks made from rhinoceros horn, and they ate ducks' tongues and monkeys' lips." She boiled the weeds we pulled up in the yard. There was a tender plant with flowers like white stars hiding under the leaves, which were like the flower petals but green. I've not been able to find it since growing up. It had no taste. When I was as tall as the washing machine, I stepped out on the back porch one night, and some heavy, ruffling, windy, clawed thing dived at me. Even after getting chanted back to sensibility, I shook when I recalled that perched everywhere there were owls with great hunched shoulders and yellow scowls. They were a surprise for my mother from my father. We children used to hide under the beds with our fingers in our ears to shut out the bird screams and the thud, thud of the turtles swimming in the boiling water, their shells hitting the sides of the pot. Once the third aunt who worked at the laundry ran out and bought us bags of candy to hold over our noses; my mother was dismembering skunk on the chopping block. I could smell the rubbery odor through the candy.

In a glass jar on a shelf my mother kept a big brown hand with pointed claws stewing in alcohol and herbs. She must have brought it from China because I do not remember a time when I did not have the hand to look at. She said it was a bear's claw, and for many years I thought bears were hairless. My mother used the tobacco, leeks, and grasses swimming about the hand to rub our sprains and bruises.

Just as I would climb up to the shelf to take one look after another at the hand, I would hear my mother's monkey story. I'd take the fingers out of my ears and let her monkey words enter my brain. I did not always listen voluntarily, though. She would begin telling the story, perhaps repeating it to a homesick villager, and I'd overhear before I had a chance to protect myself. Then the monkey words would unsettle me; a curtain flapped loose inside my brain. I have wanted to say, "Stop it. Stop it," but not once did I say, "Stop it."

"Do you know what people in China eat when they have the money?" my mother began. "They buy into a monkey feast. The eaters sit around a thick wood table with a hole in the middle. Boys bring in the monkey at the end of a pole. Its neck is in the collar at the end of the pole. Its hands are tied behind it. They clamp the monkey into the table; the whole table fits like another collar around its neck. Using a surgeon's saw, the cooks cut a clean line in a circle at the top of its head. To loosen the bone, they tap with a tiny hammer and wedge here and there with a silver pick. Then an old woman reaches out her hand to the monkey's face and up to its scalp, where she tufts some hairs and lifts off the lid of the skull. The eaters spoon out the brains."

Did she say, "You should have seen the faces the monkeys made"? Did she say, "The people laughed at the monkey screaming"? It was alive? The curtain flaps closed like merciful black wings.

"Eat! Eat!" my mother would shout at our heads bent over bowls, the blood pudding awobble in the middle of the table.

She had one rule for keeping us safe from toadstools and such: "If it tastes good, it's bad for you," she said. "If it tastes bad, it's good for you."

We'd have to face four- and five-day-old leftovers until we ate it all. The squid eye would keep appearing at breakfast and dinner until eaten. Sometimes brown masses sat on every dish. I have seen revulsion on the faces of visitors who've caught us at meals.

"Have you eaten yet?" the Chinese greet one another.

"Yes, I have," they answer whether they have or not. "And you?"

I would live on plastic.

To Understand

1. This essay contains detailed descriptions of many foods the author encountered while growing up. List four or five details that cause the greatest reaction from you.

2. Why does the mother tell her daughter the story about people in China eating monkey brains? Are there any clues to her purpose?

3. Explain the essay's final sentence. How does the speaker feel about the eating habits of her family?

To Write

1. Are there unusual food items or recipes in your family? Explain how ordinary or unusual your family's diet is. Be sure to mention specific dishes and their ingredients.

Family History: Ideas for Writing

1. Write about something that makes your family unique. Start by listing five to ten possibilities—games that you play, ways that you communicate with each other, or unusual things you do during holidays, perhaps. Try to imagine what people outside of your family would consider unusual or different about your family. Focus your main idea on only one or two items from your list.

2. Write a paper about a family member at least one generation before your own. Start by looking through a family photo album or by talking with an elderly relative. After you've chosen the person about whom you will write, decide what you want to say about him or her. What impression do you want to give your readers about this family member?

3. Most people will agree that raising a family is an enormous responsibility. It can be fraught with difficulties, filled with rewards, or both. Write a paper in which you offer advice to young people who will one day be parents.

4. We read everywhere that traditional family roles—mother keeps house while father goes to work—have changed. Mothers are clearly a vital part of the workforce although some recent studies suggest women may be starting to revisit the benefits of staying home with their children. Write a paper in which you explain the roles your parents held in your family while you were growing up.

5. Write a paper in which you focus on one particular problem or challenge families are facing in today's world. List several possibilities before narrowing your topic to what you consider the most serious problem or challenge.

6. Images of family life are presented every day in the media. Write a paper arguing how accurately or inaccurately one television show or film presents family life. Is that story's depiction of family similar to what you see in real life?

7. Write a paper comparing and contrasting family life for two different generations of your family: your grandparents' household and your parents' household. In what ways was daily life the same, in what ways different? Narrow your focus to two or three main similarities and two or three main differences.

3

Growing Up/Growing Old

Growing Up/Growing Old

If we are fortunate enough to avoid a premature end to our lives, we can be assured of one thing: that we will age, one year at a time, growing up when we are young and growing old in the later years of our lives. Regardless of our social or cultural background, this is common to all of us. The process is physical (getting taller when young and shorter when old) as well as psychological (understanding ourselves and how we fit in the world in a new way each year). It makes us who we are. Notice how we define ourselves by judging how well we are growing up or growing old. A grandmother might remark about her grandson, "He's growing up to be a fine kid," or a man might say of his elderly mother, "She's aged gracefully" or worse "She's fallen apart." It is natural for us to track our progress in how we mature.

Writers of all backgrounds and eras have known that this process of maturation is fascinating for us. When we read literature about the experiences of the young or the elderly, we have the opportunity to learn about ourselves. After all, we have been (or will be) going through the same life stages. Many people claim they read in order to escape into another world, into other lives; however, by carefully monitoring their own reactions to stories and poems, readers can also discover new things about their own lives.

The literature in this chapter includes pieces about both youth and old age. Among others you will find

- a story of a young boy who jealously fights with his father for his mother's attention;
- a poem about young boys at a birthday party—and about how their bravado makes them seem like adults;
- a personal essay about a man who visits an elderly woman in his neighborhood for her homemade doughnuts;
- a poem about an elderly man who is frightened at the reality of his failing memory.

These works will give you an opportunity to think about your own years of growing up as well as about your future. They will prompt you to think about young and elderly people around you—relatives, friends, neighbors, even whole communities—and this experience should offer you wonderful material for your own writing. Be sure to make use of both the *To Write* questions following each piece of literature as well as the *Ideas for Writing* section at the end of the chapter. With these as guides, you will be on your way to sharing in writing your own insightful ideas about growing up and growing old.

Frank O'Connor

My Oedipus Complex

In 1966 Frank O'Connor died as one of Ireland's most loved authors. He is famous for his widely anthologized short stories, both haunting and comic. In the following story, O'Connor humorously introduces readers to a young boy, Larry, who jealously fights with his father (who has just come back from the war) for his mother's attention. This kind of jealousy is a feature of what psychologists call the Oedipus complex, a term Sigmund Freud coined to describe a subconscious sexual desire felt by young boys for their mothers. (According to Greek legend, King Oedipus killed his father and married his mother without knowing their true identities.)

Before Reading: Consider how young children, before the age of five perhaps, interact with their parents. Do boys have a special connection to their mothers? Do girls experience a similar connection to their fathers?

Father was in the army all through the war—the first war, I mean—so, up to the age of five, I never saw much of him, and what I saw did not worry me. Sometimes I woke and there was a big figure in khaki peering down at me in the candlelight. Sometimes in the early morning I heard the slamming of the front door and the clatter of nailed boots down the cobbles of the lane. These were Father's entrances and exits. Like Santa Claus he came and went mysteriously.

In fact, I rather liked his visits, though it was an uncomfortable squeeze between Mother and him when I got into the big bed in the early morning. He smoked, which gave him a pleasant musty smell, and shaved, an operation of astounding interest. Each time he left a trail of

souvenirs—model tanks and Gurkha knives with handles made of bullet cases, and German helmets and cap
badges and button-sticks, and all sorts of military equipment—carefully stowed away in a long box on top of the
wardrobe, in case they ever came in handy. When his
back was turned, Mother let me get a chair and rummage
through his treasures. She didn't seem to think so highly
of them as he did.

The war was the most peaceful period of my life. The
window of my attic faced southeast. My mother had cur-
tained it, but that had small effect. I always woke with
the first light and, with all the responsibilities of the previous day melted, feeling myself rather like the sun,
ready to illumine and rejoice. Life never seemed so simple and clear and full of possibilities as then. I put my
feet out from under the clothes—I called them Mrs. Left
and Mrs. Right—and invented dramatic situations for
them in which they discussed the problems of the day. At
least Mrs. Right did; she was very demonstrative, but I
hadn't the same control of Mrs. Left, so she merely con-
tented herself with nodding agreement.

They discussed what Mother and I should do during
the day, what Santa Claus should give a fellow for
Christmas, and what steps should be taken to brighten
the home. There was that little matter of the baby, for instance. Mother and I could never agree about that. Ours
was the only house in the terrace without a new baby,
and Mother said we couldn't afford one till Father came
back from the war because they cost seventeen and six.
That showed how simple she was. The Geneys up the
road had a baby, and everyone knew they couldn't afford
seventeen and six. It was probably a cheap baby, and
Mother wanted something really good, but I felt she was
too exclusive. The Geneys' baby would have done us fine.

Having settled my plans for the day, I got up, put a
chair under the attic window, and lifted the frame high
enough to stick out my head. The window overlooked the

front gardens of the terrace behind ours, and beyond these it looked over a deep valley to the tall, red-brick houses terraced up the opposite hillside, which were all still in shadow, while those on our side of the valley were all lit up, though with long strange shadows that made them seem unfamiliar; rigid and painted.

After that I went into Mother's room and climbed into the big bed. She woke and began to tell me of her schemes. By this time, though I never seem to have noticed it, I was petrified in my nightshirt, and I thawed as I talked until, the last frost melted, I fell asleep beside her and woke again only when I heard her below in the kitchen, making the breakfast.

After breakfast we went into town; heard Mass at St. Augustine's and said a prayer for Father, and did the shopping. If the afternoon was fine we either went for a walk in the country or a visit to Mother's great friend in the convent, Mother St. Dominic. Mother had them all praying for Father, and every night, going to bed, I asked God to send him back safe from the war to us. Little, indeed, did I know what I was praying for!

One morning, I got into the big bed, and there, sure enough, was Father in his usual Santa Claus manner, but later, instead of uniform, he put on his best blue suit, and Mother was as pleased as anything. I saw nothing to be pleased about, because, out of uniform, Father was altogether less interesting, but she only beamed, and explained that our prayers had been answered, and off we went to Mass to thank God for having brought Father safely home.

The irony of it! That very day when he came in to dinner he took off his boots and put on his slippers, donned the dirty old cap he wore about the house to save him from colds, crossed his legs, and began to talk gravely to Mother, who looked anxious. Naturally, I disliked her looking anxious, because it destroyed her good looks, so I interrupted him.

"Just a moment, Larry!" she said gently.

This was only what she said when we had boring visitors, so I attached no importance to it and went on talking.

"Do be quiet, Larry!" she said impatiently. "Don't you hear me talking to Daddy?"

This was the first time I had heard those ominous words, "talking to Daddy," and I couldn't help feeling that if this was how God answered prayers, he couldn't listen to them very attentively.

"Why are you talking to Daddy?" I asked with as great a show of indifference as I could muster.

"Because Daddy and I have business to discuss. Now, don't interrupt again!"

In the afternoon, at Mother's request, Father took me for a walk. This time we went into town instead of out the country, and I thought at first, in my usual optimistic way, that it might be an improvement. It was nothing of the sort. Father and I had quite different notions of a walk in town. He had no proper interest in trams, ships, and horses, and the only thing that seemed to divert him was talking to fellows as old as himself. When I wanted to stop he simply went on, dragging me behind him by the hand; when he wanted to stop I had no alternative but to do the same. I noticed that it seemed to be a sign that he wanted to stop for a long time whenever he leaned against a wall. The second time I saw him do it I got wild. He seemed to be settling himself forever. I pulled him by the coat and trousers, but, unlike Mother who, if you were too persistent, got into a wax and said: "Larry, if you don't behave yourself, I'll give you a good slap," Father had an extraordinary capacity for amiable inattention. I sized him up and wondered would I cry, but he seemed to be too remote to be annoyed even by that. Really, it was like going for a walk with a mountain! He either ignored the wrenching and pummelling entirely, or else glanced down with a grin of amusement from his peak. I had never met anyone so absorbed in himself as he seemed.

At teatime, "talking to Daddy" began again, complicated this time by the fact that he had an evening paper, and every few minutes he put it down and told Mother something new out of it. I felt this was foul play. Man for man, I was prepared to compete with him any time for Mother's attention, but when he had it all made up for him by other people it left me no chance. Several times I tried to change the subject without success.

"You must be quiet while Daddy is reading, Larry," Mother said impatiently.

It was clear that she either genuinely liked talking to Father better than talking to me, or else that he had some terrible hold on her which made her afraid to admit the truth.

"Mummy," I said that night when she was tucking me up, "do you think if I prayed hard God would send Daddy back to the war?"

She seemed to think about that for a moment.

"No, dear," she said with a smile. "I don't think he would."

"Why wouldn't he, Mummy?"

"Because there isn't a war any longer, dear."

"But, Mummy, couldn't God make another war, if He liked?"

"He wouldn't like to, dear. It's not God who makes wars, but bad people."

"Oh!" I said.

I was disappointed about that. I began to think that God wasn't quite what he was cracked up to be.

Next morning I woke at my usual hour, feeling like a bottle of champagne. I put out my feet and invented a long conversation in which Mrs. Right talked of the trouble she had with her own father till she put him in the Home. I didn't quite know what the Home was but it sounded the right place for Father. Then I got my chair and stuck my head out of the attic window. Dawn was just breaking, with a guilty air that made me feel I had caught it in the act. My head bursting with stories and schemes, I stumbled in next door, and in the half-darkness scrambled into the big bed. There was no room at Mother's side so I had to get between her and Father. For the time being I had forgotten about him, and for several minutes I sat bolt upright, racking my brains to know what I could do with him. He was taking up more than his fair share of the bed, and I couldn't get comfortable, so I gave him several kicks that made him grunt and stretch. He made room all right, though. Mother woke and felt for me. I settled back comfortably in the warmth of the bed with my thumb in my mouth.

"Mummy!" I hummed, loudly and contentedly.

"Sssh! dear," she whispered. "Don't wake Daddy!"

This was a new development, which threatened to be even more serious than "talking to Daddy." Life without my early-morning conferences was unthinkable.

"Why?" I asked severely.

"Because poor Daddy is tired."

This seemed to me a quite inadequate reason, and I was sickened by the sentimentality of her "poor Daddy." I never liked that sort of gush; it always struck me as insincere.

"Oh!" I said lightly. Then in my most winning tone: "Do you know where I want to go with you today, Mummy?"

"No, dear," she sighed.

"I want to go down to the Glen and fish for thornybacks with my new net, and then I want to go out to the Fox and Hounds, and—"

"Don't-wake-Daddy!" she hissed angrily, clapping her hand across my mouth.

But it was too late. He was awake, or nearly so. He grunted and reached for the matches. Then he stared incredulously at his watch.

"Like a cup of tea, dear?" asked Mother in a meek, hushed voice I had never heard her use before. It sounded almost as though she were afraid.

"Tea?" he exclaimed indignantly. "Do you know what the time is?"

"And after that I want to go up the Rathcooney Road," I said loudly, afraid I'd forgot something in all those interruptions.

"Go to sleep at once, Larry!" she said sharply.

I began to snivel. I couldn't concentrate, the way that pair went on, and smothering my early-morning schemes was like burying a family from the cradle.

Father said nothing, but lit his pipe and sucked it, looking out into the shadows without minding Mother or me. I knew he was mad. Every time I made a remark Mother hushed me irritably. I was mortified. I felt it wasn't fair; there was even something sinister in it. Every time I had pointed out to her the waste of making two beds when we could both sleep in one, she had told me it was healthier like that, and now here was this man, this stranger, sleeping with her without the least regard for her health!

He got up early and made tea, but though he brought Mother a cup he brought none for me.

"Mummy," I shouted, "I want a cup of tea, too."

"Yes, dear," she said patiently. "You can drink from Mummy's saucer."

That settled it. Either Father or I would have to leave the house. I didn't want to drink from Mother's saucer; I wanted to be treated as an equal in my own home, so, just to spite her, I drank it all and left none for her. She took that quietly, too.

But that night when she was putting me to bed she said gently:

"Larry, I want you to promise me something."

"What is it?" I asked.

"Not to come in and disturb poor Daddy in the morning. Promise?"

"Poor Daddy" again! I was becoming suspicious of everything involving that quite impossible man.

"Why?" I asked.

"Because poor Daddy is worried and tired and he doesn't sleep well."

"Why doesn't he, Mummy?"

"Well, you know, don't you, that while he was at the war Mummy got pennies from the Post Office?"

"From Miss MacCarthy?"

"That's right. But now, you see, Miss MacCarthy hasn't any more pennies, so Daddy must go out and find us some. You know what would happen if he couldn't?"

"No," I said, "tell us."

"Well, I think we might have to go out and beg for them like the poor old woman on Fridays. We wouldn't like that, would we?"

"No," I agreed. "We wouldn't."

"So you'll promise not to come and wake him?"

"Promise."

Mind you, I meant that. I knew pennies were a serious matter, and I was all against having to go out and beg like the old woman on Fridays. Mother laid out all my toys in a complete ring round the bed so that, whatever way I got out, I was bound to fall over one of them.

When I woke I remembered my promise all right. I got up and sat on the floor and played—for hours, it seemed to me. Then I got my chair and looked out the attic window for more hours. I wished it was time for Father to wake; I wished someone would make me a cup of tea. I didn't feel in the least like the sun; instead, I was bored and so very, very cold! I simply longed for the warmth and depth of the big featherbed.

At last I could stand it no longer. I went into the next room. As there was still no room at Mother's side I climbed over her and she woke with a start.

"Larry," she whispered, gripping my arm very tightly, "what did you promise?"

"But I did, Mummy, " I wailed, caught in the very act. "I was quiet for ever so long."

"Oh, dear, and you're perished!" she said sadly, feeling me all over. "Now, if I let you stay will you promise not to talk."

"But I want to talk, Mummy," I wailed.

"That has nothing to do with it," she said with a firmness that was new to me. "Daddy wants to sleep. Now, do you understand that?"

I understood it only too well. I wanted to talk, he wanted to sleep—whose house was it, anyway?

"Mummy," I said with equal firmness, "I think it would be healthier for Daddy to sleep in his own bed."

That seemed to stagger her, because she said nothing for a while.

"Now, once and for all," she went on, "you're to be perfectly quiet or go back to your own bed. Which is it to be?"

The injustice of it got me down. I had convicted her out of her own mouth of inconsistency and unreasonableness, and she hadn't even attempted to reply. Full of spite, I gave Father a kick, which she didn't notice but which made him grunt and open his eyes in alarm.

"What time is it?" he asked in a panic-stricken voice, not looking at Mother but at the door, as if he saw someone there.

"It's early yet," she replied soothingly. "It's only the child. Go to sleep again. . . . Now, Larry," she added, getting out of bed, "you've wakened Daddy and you must go back."

This time, for all her quiet air, I knew she meant it, and knew that my principal rights and privileges were as good as lost unless I asserted them at once. As she lifted me, I gave a screech, enough to wake the dead, not to mind Father. He groaned.

"That damn child! Doesn't he ever sleep?"

"It's only a habit, dear," she said quietly, though I could see she was vexed.

"Well, it's time he got out of it," shouted Father, beginning to heave in the bed. He suddenly gathered all the bedclothes around him, turned to the wall, and then looked back over his shoulder with nothing showing only two small, spiteful, dark eyes. The man looked very wicked.

To open the bedroom door, Mother had to let me down, and I broke free and dashed for the farthest corner, screeching. Father sat bolt upright in bed.

"Shut up, you little puppy!" he said in a choking voice.

I was so astonished that I stopped screeching. Never, never had anyone spoken to me in that tone before. I looked at him incredulously and saw his face convulsed with rage. It was only then that I realized how God had codded me, listening to my prayers for the safe return of this monster.

"Shut up, you!" I bawled, beside myself.

"What's that you said?" shouted Father, making a wild leap out of the bed.

"Mick, Mick!" cried Mother. "Don't you see the child isn't used to you?"

"I see he's better fed than taught," snarled Father, waving his arms wildly. "He wants his bottom smacked."

All his previous shouting was as nothing to these obscene words referring to my person. They really made my blood boil.

"Smack your own!" I screamed hysterically. "Smack your own! Shut up! Shut up!"

At this he lost his patience and let fly at me. He did it with the lack of conviction you'd expect of a man under Mother's horrified eyes, and it ended up as a mere tap, but the sheer indignity of being struck at all by a stranger, a total stranger who had cajoled his way back from the war into our big bed as a result of my innocent intercession, made me completely dotty. I shrieked and shrieked, and danced in my bare feet, and Father, looking awkward and hairy in nothing but a short gray army shirt, glared down at me like a mountain out for murder. I think it must have been then that I realized he was jealous too. And there stood Mother in her nightdress, looking as if her heart was broken between us. I hoped she felt as she looked. It seemed to me that she deserved it all.

From that morning out my life was a hell. Father and I were enemies, open and avowed. We conducted a series of skirmishes against one another, he trying to steal my time with Mother and I his. When she was sitting on my bed, telling me a story, he took to looking for some pair of old boots which he alleged he had left behind him at the beginning of the war. While he talked to Mother I played loudly with my toys to show my total lack of concern. He created a terrible scene one evening when he came in from work and found me at his box, playing with his regimental badges, Gurkha knives and button-sticks. Mother got up and took the box from me.

"You mustn't play with Daddy's toys unless he lets you, Larry," she said severely. "Daddy doesn't play with yours."

For some reason Father looked at her as if she had struck him and then turned away with a scowl.

"Those are not toys," he growled, taking down the box again to see had I lifted anything. "Some of those curios are very rare and valuable."

But as time went on I saw more and more how he managed to alienate Mother and me. What made it worse was that I couldn't grasp his method or see what attraction he had for Mother. In every possible way he was less winning than I. He had a common accent and made noises at his tea. I thought for a while that it might be the newspapers she was interested in, so I made up bits of news of my own to read to her. Then I thought it might be the smoking, which I personally thought attractive, and took his pipes and went round the house dribbling into them till he caught me. I even made noises at my tea, but Mother only told me I was disgusting. It all seemed to hinge round that unhealthy habit of sleeping together, so I made a point of dropping into their bedroom and nosing round, talking to myself, so that they wouldn't know I was watching them, but they were never up to anything that I could see. In the end it beat me. It seemed to depend on being grown-up and giving people rings, and I realized I'd have to wait.

But at the same time I wanted him to see that I was only waiting, not giving up the fight. One evening when he was being particularly obnoxious, chattering away well above my head, I let him have it.

"Mummy," I said, "do you know what I'm going to do when I grow up?"

"No, dear," she replied. "What?"

"I'm going to marry you," I said quietly.

Father gave a great guffaw out of him, but he didn't take me in. I knew it must only be pretense. And Mother, in spite of everything, was pleased. I felt she was probably relieved to know that one day Father's hold on her would be broken.

"Won't that be nice?" she said with a smile.

"It'll be very nice," I said confidently. "Because we're going to have lots and lots of babies."

"That's right, dear," she said placidly. "I think we'll have one soon, and then you'll have plenty of company."

I was no end pleased about that because it showed that in spite of the way she gave into Father she still considered my wishes. Besides, it would put the Geneys is their place.

It didn't turn out like that, though. To begin with, she was very preoccupied—I suppose about where she would get the seventeen and six—and though Father took to staying out late in the evenings it did me no particular good. She stopped taking me for walks, became as touchy as blazes, and smacked me for nothing at all. Sometimes I wished I'd never mentioned the confounded baby—I seemed to have a genius for bringing calamity on myself.

And calamity it was! Sonny arrived in the most appalling hullabaloo—even that much he couldn't do without a fuss—and from the first moment I disliked him. He was a difficult child—so far as I was concerned he was always difficult—and demanded far too much attention. Mother was simply silly about him, and couldn't see when he was only showing off. As company he was worse than useless. He slept all day, and I had to go round the house on tiptoe to avoid waking him. It wasn't any longer a question of not waking Father. The slogan now was "Don't wake Sonny!" I couldn't understand why the child wouldn't sleep at the proper time, so whenever Mother's back was turned I woke him. Sometimes to keep him awake I pinched him as well. Mother caught me at it one day and gave me a most unmerciful flaking.

One evening, when Father was coming home from work, I was playing trains in the front garden. I let on not to notice him; instead, I pretended to be talking to myself, and said in a loud voice: "If another bloody baby comes into this house, I'm going out."

Father stopped dead and looked at me over his shoulder.

"What's that you said?" he asked sternly

"I was only talking to myself," I replied, trying to conceal my panic. "It's private."

He turned and went in without a word. Mind you, I intended it as a solemn warning, but its effect was quite different. Father started being quite nice to me. I could understand that, of course. Mother was quite sickening about Sonny. Even at mealtimes she'd get up and gawk at him in the cradle with an idiotic smile, and tell Father to do the same. He was always polite about it, but he looked so puzzled you could see he didn't know what she was talking about. He complained of the way Sonny cried at night, but she only got cross and said that Sonny never cried except when there was something up with him—which was a flaming lie, because Sonny never had anything up with him, and only cried for attention. It was really painful to see how simpleminded she was. Father wasn't attractive, but he had a fine intelligence. He saw through Sonny, and now he knew that I saw through him as well.

One night I woke with a start. There was someone beside me in the bed. For one wild moment I felt sure it must be mother, having come to her senses and left Father for good, but then I heard Sonny in convulsions in the next room, and Mother saying: "There! There! There!" and I knew it wasn't she. It was Father. He was lying beside me, wide awake, breathing hard and apparently as mad as hell.

After a while it came to me what he was mad about. It was his turn now. After turning me out of the big bed, he had been turned out himself. Mother had no consideration now for anyone but that poisonous pup, Sonny. I couldn't help feeling sorry for Father. I had been through it all myself, and even at that age I was magnanimous. I began to stroke him down and say: "There! There!" He wasn't exactly responsive.

"Aren't you asleep either?" he snarled.

"Ah, come on and put your arm around us, can't you?" I said, and he did, in a sort of way. Gingerly, I suppose, is how you'd describe it. He was very bony but better than nothing.

At Christmas he went out of his way to buy me a really nice model railway.

To Understand

1. Early in the story, Larry compares his father to Santa Claus. Explain how this description allows a reader to understand how Larry views his father.

2. At what places in the story does Larry misunderstand the relationship and roles of his parents? What purpose do these places have for a reader's understanding of the story?

3. How does life change for Larry when his younger brother, Sonny, is born?

4. Would you consider Larry a spoiled child? Point to particular places in the story to support your answer.

To Write

1. Write about the ways in which your childhood relationship to your parent of the opposite sex compares with Larry's relationship to his mother.

Gwendolyn Brooks

A Song in the Front Yard

The author of more than twenty volumes of poetry and many other books, Gwendolyn Brooks is one of America's most-loved poets. She received the Pulitzer Prize for Annie Allen *and many other honors and awards including being named Poet Laureate for the State of Illinois and Consultant in Poetry to the Library of Congress. Before her death in December of 2000, she used her poetry to recognize the African-American experience in all its complexity. In the following poem, the speaker, who is seeking "a good time today," is feeling overprotected by her mother.*

Before Reading: Consider the safe paths to avoid trouble that parents, teachers, and others often want children to follow. Think about the various ways children respond to these adults' wishes.

I've stayed in the front yard all my life.
I want to peek at the back
Where it's rough and untended and hungry weeds grow.
A girl gets sick of a rose.

I want to go in the back yard now
And maybe down the alley,
To where the charity children play.
I want a good time today.
They do some wonderful things.
They have some wonderful fun.
My mother sneers, but I say it's fine
How they don't have to go in at a quarter to nine.
My mother, she tells me that Johnnie Mae
Will grow up to be a bad woman.

That George will be taken to Jail soon or late
(On account of last winter he sold our back gate).

But I say it's fine. Honest, I do.
And I'd like to be a bad woman, too,
And wear the black stockings of night-black lace
And strut down the street with paint on my face.

To Understand

1. What would you say is the speaker's age in this poem? What, overall, does she want?
2. What is the difference between the front yard and the back yard? Why does the speaker "want to go in the back yard. . ."?
3. Explain the role of the mother who first appears in the third stanza. What influence does she have on her daughter?

To Write

1. Imagine being a child again and living in your childhood home. Write a list of things you wanted. Then write a paragraph explaining the list. What does the list say about who you were as a child?

Sandra Cisneros

Eleven

Sandra Cisneros is one of the most widely recognized Chicana writers in America. Winner of the Before Columbus American Book Award for her frequently taught first book, The House on Mango Street, *Cisneros writes both fiction and poetry and has won numerous awards including two National Endowment for the Arts Fellowships. As in many of her stories, the following piece from* Woman Hollering Creek *focuses on a young person who struggles to understand what seems like a confusing world.*

Before Reading: Think about when you turned eleven. What was particularly wonderful or challenging about that age? As you read, ask yourself if your feelings or emotions were anything like those of Rachel, the main character in this story.

What they don't understand about birthdays and what they never tell you is that when you're eleven, you're also ten, and nine, and eight, and seven, and six, and five, and four, and three, and two, and one. And when you wake up on your eleventh birthday you expect to feel eleven, but you don't. You open your eyes and everything's just like yesterday, only it's today. And you don't feel eleven at all. You feel like you're still ten. And you are—underneath the year that makes you eleven.

Like some days you might say something stupid, and that's the part of you that's still ten. Or maybe some days you might need to sit on your mama's lap because you're scared, and that's the part of you that's five. And maybe one day when you're all grown up maybe you will need to cry like if you're three, and that's okay. That's what I tell

Mama when she's sad and needs to cry. Maybe she's feeling three.

Because the way you grow old is kind of like an onion or like the rings inside a tree trunk or like my little wooden dolls that fit one inside the other, each year inside the next one. That's how being eleven years old is.

You don't feel eleven. Not right away. It takes a few days, weeks even, sometimes even months before you say Eleven when they ask you. And you don't feel smart eleven, not until you're almost twelve. That's the way it is.

Only today I wish I didn't have only eleven years rattling inside me like pennies in a tin Band-Aid box. Today I wish I was one hundred and two instead of eleven because if I was one hundred and two I'd have known what to say when Mrs. Price put the red sweater on my desk. I would've known how to tell her it wasn't mine instead of just sitting there with that look on my face and nothing coming out of my mouth.

"Whose is this?" Mrs. Price says, and she holds the red sweater up in the air for all the class to see. "Whose? It's been sitting in the coatroom for a month."

"Not mine," says everybody. "Not me."

"It has to belong to somebody," Mrs. Price keeps saying, but nobody can remember. It's an ugly sweater with red plastic buttons and a collar and sleeves all stretched out like you could use it for a jump rope. It's maybe a thousand years old and even if it belonged to me I wouldn't say so.

Maybe because I'm skinny, maybe because she doesn't like me, that stupid Sylvia Saldívar says, "I think it belongs to Rachel." An ugly sweater like that, all raggedy and old, but Mrs. Price believes her. Mrs. Price takes the sweater and puts it right on my desk, but when I open my mouth nothing comes out.

"That's not, I don't, you're not . . . Not mine," I finally say in a little voice that was maybe me when I was four.

"Of course it's yours," Mrs. Price says. "I remember you wearing it once." Because she's older and the teacher, she's right and I'm not.

Not mine, not mine, not mine, but Mrs. Price is already turning to page thirty-two, and math problem number four. I don't know why but all of a sudden I'm feeling sick inside, like the part of me that's three wants to come out of my eyes, only I squeeze them shut tight and bite down on my teeth real hard and try to remember today I am eleven, eleven. Mama is making a cake for me tonight, and when Papa comes home everybody will sing Happy birthday, happy birthday to you.

But when the sick feeling goes away and I open my eyes, the red sweater's still sitting there like a big red mountain. I move the red sweater to the corner of my desk with my ruler. I move my pencil and books and eraser as far from it as possible. I even move my chair a little to the right. Not mine, not mine, not mine.

In my head I'm thinking how long till lunchtime, how long till I can take the red sweater and throw it over the schoolyard fence, or leave it hanging on a parking meter, or bunch it up into a little ball and toss it in the alley. Except when math period ends Mrs. Price says loud and in front of everybody, "Now, Rachel, that's enough," because she sees I've shoved the red sweater to the tippy-tip corner of my desk and it's hanging all over the edge like a waterfall, but I don't care.

"Rachel," Mrs. Price says. She says it like she's getting mad. "You put that sweater on right now and no more nonsense."

"But it's not—"

"Now!" Mrs. Price says.

This is when I wish I wasn't eleven, because all the years inside of me—ten, nine, eight, seven, six, five, four, three, two and one—are pushing at the back of my eyes when I put one arm through one sleeve of the sweater that smells like cottage cheese, and then the other arm through the other and stand there with my arms apart like if the sweater hurts me and it does, all itchy and full of germs that aren't even mine.

That's when everything I've been holding in since this morning, since when Mrs. Price put the sweater on my desk, finally lets go, and all of a sudden I'm crying in front of everybody. I wish I was invisible, but I'm not. I'm eleven and it's my birthday today and I'm crying like I'm three in front of everybody. I put my head down on the desk and bury my face in my stupid clown-sweater arms. My face all hot and spit coming out of my mouth because I can't stop the little animal noises from coming out of me, until there aren't any more tears left in my eyes, and it's just my body shaking like when you have the hiccups, and my whole head hurts like when you drink milk too fast.

But the worst part is right before the bell rings for lunch. That stupid Phyllis Lopez, who is even dumber than Sylvia Saldívar, says she remembers the red sweater is hers! I take it off right away and give it to her, only Mrs. Price pretends like everything's okay.

Today I'm eleven. There's a cake Mama's making for tonight, and when Papa comes home from work we'll eat it. There'll be candles and presents and everybody will sing Happy birthday, happy birthday to you, Rachel, only it's too late.

I'm eleven today. I'm eleven, ten, nine, eight, seven, six, five, four, three, two, and one, but I wish I was a hundred and two. I wish I was anything but eleven, because I want today to be far away already, far away like a run-away balloon, like a tiny *o* in the sky, so tiny-tiny you have to close your eyes to see it.

To Understand

1. Explain what Rachel is saying about being eleven, how it is possible for her to be all the ages leading up to eleven and eleven at the same time.

2. Why is Rachel unable to explain to Mrs. Price that the red sweater isn't hers? How is this incident related to her age?

3. How does Rachel feel at the end of the story?

To Write

1. Write about an age that was particularly difficult for you. State in general why it was difficult; then offer a couple of examples of how you struggled at this time.

Stuart Dybek

Death of the Right Fielder

Stuart Dybek is the author of two books of short stories,
Childhood and Other Neighborhoods *and* The Coast of
Chicago. *In "Death of the Right Fielder," Dybek's setting is
commonplace, a baseball field, but his fanciful story is
anything but ordinary.*

Before Reading: Think about the various positions in the sport of
baseball: pitcher, catcher, short stop, right fielder, and so on. Which
positions are the most and least prestigious? Which positions do young
players most want to play?

After too many balls went out and never came back
we went out to check. It was a long walk—he always
played deep. Finally we saw him, from the distance re-
sembling the towel we sometimes threw down for second
base.

It was hard to tell how long he'd been lying there,
sprawled on his face. Had he been playing infield, his
presence, or lack of it, would, of course, have been noticed
immediately. The infield demands communication—the
constant, reassuring chatter of team play. But he was remote, clearly an outfielder (the temptation is to say
out*sider*). The infield is for wisecrackers, pepper-pots,
gum-poppers; the outfield is for loners, onlookers, brooders
who would rather study clover and swat gnats than holler.
People could pretty much be divided between infielders
and outfielders. Not that one always has a choice. He didn't
necessarily choose right field so much as accept it.

There were several theories as to what killed him.
From the start the most popular was that he'd been shot.
Perhaps from a passing car, possibly by the gang that

called themselves the Jokers, who played sixteen-inch softball on the concrete diamond with painted bases in the center of the housing project, or by the Latin Lords, who didn't play sports, period. Or maybe some pervert with a telescopic sight from a bedroom window, or a mad sniper from a water tower, or a terrorist with a silencer from the expressway overpass, or maybe it was an accident, a stray slug from a robbery, or shoot-out, or assassination attempt miles away.

No matter who pulled the trigger it seems more plausible to ascribe his death to a bullet than to natural causes like, say, a heart attack. Young deaths are never natural; they're all violent. Not that kids don't die of heart attacks. But he never seemed the type. Sure, he was quiet, but not the quiet of someone always listening for the heart murmur his family repeatedly warned him about since he was old enough to play. Nor could it have been leukemia. He wasn't a talented enough athlete to die of that. He'd have been playing center, not right, if leukemia was going to get him.

The shooting theory was better, even though there wasn't a mark on him. Couldn't it have been, as some argued, a high-powered bullet traveling with such velocity that its hole fuses behind it? Still, not everyone was satisfied. Other theories were formulated, rumors became legends over the years: he'd had an allergic reaction to a bee sting, been struck by a single bolt of lightening from a freak, instantaneous electrical storm, ingested too strong a dose of insecticide from the grass blades he chewed on, sonic waves, radiation, pollution, etc. And a few of us liked to think it was simply that chasing a sinking liner, diving to make a shoestring catch, he broke his neck.

There *was* a ball in the webbing of his mitt when we turned him over. His mitt had been pinned under his body and was coated with an almost luminescent gray film. There was the same gray on his black, high-top gym shoes, as if he'd been running through lime, and along the bill of his baseball cap—the blue felt one with the red *C* which he always denied stood for the Chicago Cubs. He may have been a loner, but he didn't want to be identified with a loser. He lacked the sense of humor for that, lacked the perverse pride that sticking for losers season after season breeds, and the love. He was just an ordinary guy, .250 at the plate, and we stood above him not knowing what to do next. By then the guys from the other outfield positions had trotted over. Someone, the shortstop probably, suggested team prayer. But no one could think of a team prayer. So we all just stood there silently bowing our heads, pretending to pray while the shadows moved darkly across the outfield grass. After a while the entire diamond was swallowed and the field lights came on.

In the bluish squint of those lights he didn't look like someone we'd once known—nothing looked quite right— and we hurriedly scratched a shallow grave, covered him over, and stamped it down as much as possible so that the next right fielder, whoever he'd be, wouldn't trip. It could be just such a juvenile, seemingly trivial stumble that would ruin a great career before it had even begun, or hamper it years later the way Mantle's was hampered by bum knees. One can never be sure the kid beside him isn't another Roberto Clemente; and who can ever know how many potential Great Ones have gone down in the obscurity of their neighborhoods? And so, in the catcher's phrase, we "buried the grave" rather than contribute to any further tragedy. In all likelihood the next right fielder, whoever he'd be, would be clumsy too, and if there was a mound to trip over he'd find it and break *his* neck, and soon right field would get the reputation as haunted, a kind of sandlot Bermuda Triangle, inhabited by phantoms calling for ghostly fly balls, where no one but the most desperate outcasts, already on the verge of suicide, would be willing to play.

Still, despite our efforts, we couldn't totally disguise it. A fresh grave is stubborn. It's outline remains visible—a scuffed bald spot that might have been confused for an aberrant pitcher's mound except for the bat jammed in the earth with the mitt and blue cap fit over it. Perhaps we didn't want to eradicate it completely—a part of us was resting there. Perhaps we wanted the new right fielder, whoever he'd be, to notice and wonder about who played there before him, realizing he was now the only link between past and future that mattered. A monument, epitaph, flowers, wouldn't be necessary.

As for us, we walked back, but by then it was too late—getting onto supper, getting onto the end of summer vacation, time for other things, college, careers, settling down and raising a family. Past thirty-five the talk starts about being over the hill, about a graying Phil Niekro in his forties still fanning them with the knuckler as if it's some kind of miracle, about Pete Rose still going in head first at forty, beating the odds. And maybe the talk is right. One remembers Willie Mays, forty-two years old and a Met, dropping that can-of-corn fly in the '73 Series, all that grace stripped away and with it the conviction, leaving a man confused and apologetic about the boy in him. It's sad to admit it ends so soon, but everyone knows those are the lucky ones. Most guys are washed up by seventeen.

To Understand

1. While reading you will have noticed that this story has no main characters (other than the dead right fielder) to follow and that nobody is given a name. Why has Dybek chosen to write the story in this way?

2. What opinion do the narrator and the other players have of the position of right field? How is this opinion important to the story?

3. Why does the team bury their teammate right out in the outfield?

4. The narrator speculates at length about what killed the right fielder. What does this speculation tell you about the kind of story this is?

To Write

1. In paragraph 2, the narrator says, "People could pretty much be divided between infielders and outfielders." Given those two categories, how would you classify yourself? Start by brainstorming the characteristics of both infielders and outfielders; then write about why you are like one or the other.

2. Go back to the story's last sentence, "Most guys are washed up by seventeen." Would you agree with this assertion as it pertains to baseball—as it pertains to other aspects of life? Write about this statement in relation to one or two aspects of human development—sports related or not.

Sharon Olds

Rite of Passage

In 1984 Sharon Olds won the Lamont Poetry Prize and the National Book Critics Circle Award for The Dead and the Living, *from which this poem is taken. Her other books include* The Gold Cell, The Wellspring, *and* Blood, Tin, Straw. *A native of California, she serves as chair of New York University's Creative Writing Program and was New York State Poet from 1998–2000.*

Before Reading: Think about childhood birthday parties. How do you, as an adult, feel about these parties and the typical actions or behavior of the children attending them?

As the guests arrive at my son's party
they gather in the living room—
short men, men in first grade
with smooth jaws and chins.
Hands in pockets, they stand around
jostling, jockeying for place, small fights
breaking out and calming. One says to another
How old are you? Six. I'm seven. So?
They eye each other, seeing themselves
tiny in the other's pupils. They clear their
throats a lot, a room of small bankers,
they fold their arms and frown. *I could beat you
up,* a seven says to a six,
the dark cake, round and heavy as a
turret, behind them on the table. My son,
freckles like specks of nutmeg on his cheeks,
chest narrow as the balsa keel of a
model boat, long hands
cool and thin as the day they guided him

out of me, speaks up as a host
for the sake of the group.
We could easily kill a two-year-old,
he says in his clear voice. The other
men agree, they clear their throats
like Generals, they relax and get down to
playing war, celebrating my son's life.

To Understand:

1. Why does the speaker refer to her son and his young friends as "men," as "bankers," and as "Generals"?
2. What do you conclude from the boys' brave speech: *"How old are you? Six. I'm seven. So?"* *"I could beat you / up,"* *"We could easily kill a two-year old"*?
3. What is the speaker's attitude in this poem? How does she feel about the behavior of the boys at her son's party?

To Write

1. Describe a birthday party (or another similar event) of your youth. How did you and your friends act? How was your behavior seen by adults?
2. Explain how, in your experience, young boys are like men or young girls are like women.

Annie Dillard

The Chase*

Winner of the Pulitzer Prize in general non-fiction for her Pilgrim at Tinker Creek, *Annie Dillard is nationally respected for both her prose and poetry. Her other books include* Ticket for a Prayer Wheel, The Writing Life, *and* An American Childhood, *from which this selection is excerpted. She teaches at Wesleyan University in Connecticut. In the following essay, Dillard writes about throwing snowballs at passing cars and how this activity got her and some friends in trouble.*

Before Reading: Recall any mischievous play you engaged in as a child. Compare how it made you feel to how Dillard felt with her friends.

Some boys taught me to play football. This was fine sport. You thought up a new strategy for every play and whispered it to the others. You went out for a pass, fooling everyone. Best, you got to throw yourself mightily at someone's running legs. Either you brought him down or you hit the ground flat out on your chin, with your arms empty before you. It was all or nothing. If you hesitated in fear, you would miss and get hurt; you would take a hard fall while the kid got away, or you would get kicked in the face while the kid got away. But if you flung yourself wholeheartedly at the back of his knees—if you gathered and joined body and soul and pointed them diving fearlessly—then you likely wouldn't get hurt, and you'd stop the ball. Your fate,

---

*This excerpt has been titled "The Chase" by the editor. It is untitled in its original form.

and your team's score, depended on your concentration and courage. Nothing girls did could compare with it.

Boys welcomed me at baseball, too, for I had, through enthusiastic practice, what was weirdly known as a boy's arm. In winter, in the snow, there was neither baseball nor football, so the boys and I threw snowballs at passing cars. I got in trouble throwing snowballs, and have seldom been happier since.

On one weekday morning after Christmas, six inches of new snow had just fallen. We were standing up to our boot tops in snow on a front yard on trafficked Reynolds Street, waiting for cars. The cars traveled Reynolds Street slowly and evenly; they were targets all but wrapped in red ribbons, cream puffs. We couldn't miss.

I was seven; the boys were eight, nine, and ten. The oldest two Fahey boys were there—Mikey and Peter—polite blond boys who lived near me on Lloyd Street, and who already had four brothers and sisters. My parents approved Mikey and Peter Fahey. Chickie McBride was there, a tough kid, and Billy Paul and Mackie Kean too, from across Reynolds, where the boys grew up dark and furious, grew up skinny, knowing, and skilled. We had all drifted from our houses that morning looking for action, and had found it here on Reynolds Street.

It was cloudy but cold. The cars' tires laid behind them on the snowy street a complex trail of beige chunks like crenellated castle walls, I had stepped on some earlier; they squeaked. We could not have wished for more traffic. When a car came, we all popped it one. In the intervals between cars we reverted to the natural solitude of children.

I started making an iceball—a perfect iceball, from perfectly white snow, perfectly spherical, and squeezed perfectly translucent so no snow remained all the way through. (The Fahey boys and I considered it unfair actually to throw an iceball at somebody, but it had been known to happen.)

I had just embarked on the iceball project when we heard tire chains come clanking from afar. A black Buick was moving toward us down the street. We all spread out, banged together some regular snowballs, took aim, and when the Buick drew nigh, fired.

A soft snowball hit the driver's windshield right before the driver's face. It made a smashed star with a hump in the middle.

Often, of course, we hit our target, but this time, the only time in all of life, the car pulled over and stopped. Its wide black door opened; a man got out of it, running. He didn't even close the car door.

He ran after us, and we ran away from him, up the snowy Reynolds sidewalk. At the corner, I looked back; incredibly, he was still after us. He was in city clothes: a suit and tie, street shoes. Any normal adult would have quit, having sprung us into flight and made his point. This man was gaining on us. He was a thin man, all action. All of a sudden, we were running for our lives.

Wordless, we split up. We were on our turf; we could lose ourselves in the neighborhood backyards, everyone for himself. I paused and considered. Everyone had vanished except Mikey Fahey, who was just rounding the corner of a yellow brick house. Poor Mikey, I trailed him. The driver of the Buick sensibly picked the two of us to follow. The man apparently had all day.

He chased Mikey and me around the yellow house and up a backyard path we knew by heart: under a low tree, up a bank, through a hedge, down some snowy steps, and across the grocery store's delivery driveway. We smashed through a gap in another hedge, entered a scruffy backyard and ran around its back porch and tight between houses to Edgerton Avenue; we ran across Edgerton to an alley and up our own sliding woodpile to the Hall's front yard; he kept coming. We ran up Lloyd Street and wound through mazy backyards toward the steep hilltop at Willard and Lang.

He chased us silently, block after block. He chased us silently over picket fences, through thorny hedges, between houses, around garbage cans, and across streets. Every time I glanced back, choking for breath, I expected he would have quit. He must have been as breathless as we were. His jacket strained over his body. It was an immense discovery, pounding into my hot head with every sliding, joyous step, that this ordinary adult evidently knew what I thought only children who trained at football knew: that you have to fling yourself at what you're doing, and you have to point yourself, forget yourself, aim, dive.

Mikey and I had nowhere to go, in our own neighborhood or out of it, but away from this man who was chasing us. He impelled us forward; we compelled him to follow our route. The air was cold; every breath tore my throat. We kept running, block after block; we kept improvising, backyard after backyard, running a frantic course and choosing it simultaneously, failing always to find small places or hard places to slow him down, and discovering always, exhilarated, dismayed, that only bare speed could save us—for he would never give up, this man—and we were losing speed.

He chased us through the backyard labyrinths of ten blocks before he caught us by our jackets. He caught us and we all stopped.

We three stood staggering, half blinded, coughing, in an obscure hilltop backyard: a man in his twenties, a boy, a girl. He had released our jackets, our pursuer, our captor, our hero: he knew we weren't going anywhere. We all played by the rules. Mikey and I unzipped our jackets. I pulled off my sopping mittens. Our tracks multiplied in the backyard's new snow. We had been breaking new snow all morning. We didn't look at each other. I was cherishing my excitement. The man's lower pants were wet; his cuffs were full of snow, and there was a prow of snow beneath them on his shoes and socks. Some trees bordered the little flat backyard, some messy winter trees. There was no one around: a clearing in the grove, and we the only players.

It was a long time before he could speak. I had some difficulty at first recalling why we were there. My lips felt frozen; I couldn't see out of the sides of my eyes; I kept coughing.

"You stupid kids," he began perfunctorily.

We listened perfunctorily indeed, if we listened at all, for the chewing out was redundant, a mere formality, and beside the point. The point was that he had chased us passionately without giving up, and so he had caught us. Now he came down to earth. I wanted the glory to last forever.

But how could the glory have lasted forever? We could have run through every backyard in North America until we got to Panama. But when he trapped us at the lip of the Panama Canal, what precisely could he have done to prolong the drama of the chase and cap its glory? I brooded about this for the next few years. He could only have fried Mikey Fahey and me in boiling oil, say, or dismembered us piecemeal, or staked us to anthills. None of which I really wanted, and none of which any adult was likely to do, even in the spirit of fun. He could only chew us out there in the Panamanian jungle, after months or years of exalting pursuit. He could only begin, "You stupid kids," and continue in his ordinary Pittsburgh accent with his normal righteous anger and the usual common sense.

If in that snowy backyard the driver of the black Buick had cut off our heads, Mikey's and mine, I would have died happy, for nothing has required so much of me since as being chased all over Pittsburgh in the middle of winter— running terrified, exhausted—by this sainted, skinny, furious redheaded man who wished to have a word with us. I don't know how he found his way back to his car.

To Understand

1. Why did the young Dillard enjoy playing football and baseball—and throwing snowballs—with the boys? How is this important in the story?

2. Dillard says she has "seldom been happier since" her experience of being chased by the man. Why did this event make her happy? Describe how she felt during the chase.

3. What was Dillard's reaction to what the man said after he caught her and the boys? Is this how you expected her to react?

To Write:

1. Dillard says her "immense discovery" about the man who had been chasing her was "that this ordinary adult evidently knew what I thought only children who trained at football knew: that you have to fling yourself at what you're doing, you have to point yourself, forget yourself, aim, dive." Explain how the man who chased the kids embodied this quality, and relate how this way of approaching a situation can be applied to other activities.

Regina Barreca

Nighttime Fires

Regina Barreca is Professor of English Literature and Feminist Theory at the University of Connecticut. Her best-selling books include They Used to Call Me Snow White, But I Drifted; Perfect Husbands (and Other Fairy Tales); *and* Sweet Revenge: The Wicked Delights of Getting Even. *She writes a column for the* Hartford Courant, *her work has appeared in many national magazines, and as an expert on the media she has appeared on several national television shows including* Oprah. *She has also written scholarly works as well as poetry, a selection of which we have here.*

Before Reading: Ask yourself why people are fascinated with tragedy in other people's lives. Why do we slow down on the highway to peer at an auto accident? Why does television news focus so much on tragedy?

When I was five in Louisville
we drove to see the nighttime fires. Piled seven of us,
all pajamas and running noses, into the Olds,
drove fast toward smoke. It was after my father
lost his job, so not getting up in the morning
gave him time: awake past midnight, he read old news-
     papers
with no news, tried crosswords until he split the pencil
between his teeth, mad. When he heard
the wolf whine of the siren, he woke my mother,
and she pushed and shoved
us all into waking. Once roused we longed for burnt wood
and a smell of flames high into the pines. My old man
     liked

driving us to rich neighborhoods best, swearing in a good
   mood
as he followed fire engines that snaked like dragons
and split the silent streets. It was festival, carnival.

If there were a Cadillac or any car
in a curved driveway, my father smiled a smile
from a secret, brittle heart.
His face lit up in the heat given off by destruction
like something was being made, or was being set right.
I bent my head back to see where sparks
ate up the sky. My father who never held us
would take my hand and point to the falling cinders that
covered the ground like snow, or, excited, show us
the swollen collapse of a staircase. My mother
watched my father, not the house. She was happy
only when we were ready to go, when it was finally over
and nothing else could burn.
Driving home, she would sleep in the front seat
as we huddled behind. I could see his quiet face in the
rearview mirror, eyes like hallways filled with smoke.

To Understand

1. Explain how important it is that the father has lost his job.

2. Why does the father smile "if there were a Cadillac or any car/ in a curved driveway"? What is it about that kind of car or that kind of driveway to make him react that way?

3. How does the mother feel about this nighttime excursion, driving to see other people's houses destroyed by fire? Characterize the father's relationship with the rest of the family.

4. How does the speaker feel about this activity? Point to particular parts of the poem to explain your answer.

To Write

1. Describe an unusual activity in your family, and explain the importance of the activity to both you and your family.

James Laughlin

Junk Mail

James Laughlin published many of the 20th century's most famous writers—including Vladimir Nabokov, Henry Miller, F. Scott Fitzgerald, and William Carlos Williams—under the publishing company he founded, New Directions. A poet and fiction writer himself, his own books include The Collected Poems of James Laughlin. *In the following poem, Laughlin describes the eccentric behavior of one elderly man.*

Before Reading: Consider what you know of elderly people who have begun to lose their mental faculties. (Also, notice that this is the kind of poem in which the title leads directly into the first line—in one sentence.)

is a pleasure to at least
one person a dear old man

in our town who is drift-
ing into irreality he

walks each morning to the
post office to dig the

treasure from his box he
spreads it out on the lob

by counter and goes through
it with care and delight.

To Understand

1. Why does the old man look at his junk mail "with care and delight"? What are we readers to conclude about this?
2. What does it mean that the old man "is drift- / ing into irreality"?
3. Why is the word "treasure" appropriate for describing junk mail in this poem?

To Write

1. Describe in detail one behavior of an elderly person you know or have known. Make clear how you want your readers to think about this behavior.

Toshio Mori

The Woman Who Makes Swell Doughnuts

Toshio Mori was born in Oakland, California. During World War II, he and his family were shipped off to a relocation camp in Topaz, Utah along with 8,000 other Japanese-Americans who were suspected of being dangerous to national security. Publication of his first novel, Yokohama, California, *was delayed seven years because of this, yet despite the hardship Mori pressed on with his writing, publishing short stories and other novels,* Women from Hiroshima *and* The Brothers Murata.

Before Reading: Think about under what circumstances elderly people are respected and valued in our society. When are they not?

There is nothing I like to do better than to go to her house and knock on the door and when she opens the door, to go in. It is one of the experiences I will long remember—perhaps the only immortality that I will ever be lucky to meet in my short life—and when I say experience I do not mean the actual movement, the motor of our lives. I mean by experience the dancing of emotions before our eyes and inside of us, the dance that is still but is the roar and the force capable of stirring the earth and the people.

Of course, she, the woman I visit, is old and of her youthful beauty there is little left. Her face of today is course with hard water and there is no question that she has lived her life: given birth to six children, worked side by side with her man for forty years, working in the fields, working in the house, caring for the grandchildren, facing

the summers and winters and also the springs and au-
tumns, running the household that is completely her
little world. And when I came on the scene, when I discovered her in her little house on Seventh Street, all of
her life was behind, all of her task in this world was
tabbed, looked into, thoroughly attended, and all that is
before her in life and the world, all that could be before
her now was to sit and be served; duty done, work done,
time clock punched; old-age pension or old-age security;
easy chair; soft serene hours till death take her. But this
was not of her, not the least bit of her.

When I visit her she takes me to the coziest chair in
the living room, where are her magazines and books in
Japanese and English. "Sit down," she says, "Make yourself comfortable. I will come back with some hot doughnuts just out of oil."

And before I can turn a page of a magazine she is back
with a plateful of hot doughnuts. There is nothing I can
do to describe her doughnut; it is in a class by itself, without words, without demonstration. It is a doughnut, just
a plain doughnut just out of oil but it is different, unique.
Perhaps when I am eating her doughnuts I am really eating her; I have this foolish notion in my head many times
and whenever I catch myself doing so I say, that is not so,
that is not true. Her doughnuts really taste swell, she is
the best cook I have ever known, Oriental dishes or
American dishes.

I bow humbly that such a room, such a house exists in
my neighborhood so I may dash in and out when my spirit
wanes, when hell is loose. I sing gratefully that such a simple and common experience becomes an event, an event of
necessity and growth. It is an event that is part of me, an
addition to the elements of earth, water, fire, and air, and I
seek the day when it will become a part of everyone.

All her friends, old and young, call her Mama. Everybody calls her Mama. That is not new, it is logical. I suppose there is in every block of every city in America a

woman who can be called Mama by her friends and the strangers meeting her. This is commonplace, it is not new and the old sentimentality may be the undoing of the moniker. But what of a woman who isn't a mama but is, and instead of priding in the expansion of her little world, takes her little circle, living out her days in the little circle, perhaps never to be exploited in a biography or on everybody's tongue, but enclosed, shut, excluded from the world news and newsreels; just sitting, just moving, just alive, planting the plants in the fields, caring for the children and the grandchildren and baking the tastiest doughnuts this side of the next world.

When I sit with her I do not need to ask deep questions, I do not need to know Plato or The Sacred Books of the East or dancing. I do not need to be on guard. But I am on guard and foot-loose because the room is alive.

"Where are the grandchildren?" I say. "Where are Mickey, Tadao, and Yaeko?"

"They are out in the yard," she says. "I say to them, play, play hard, go out there and play hard. You will be glad later for everything you have done with all your might."

Sometimes we sit many minutes in silence. Silence does not bother her. She says silence is the most beautiful symphony, she says the air breathed in silence is sweeter and sadder. That is about all we talk of. Sometimes I sit and gaze out the window and watch the Southern Pacific trains rumble by and the vehicles whizz with speed. And sometimes she catches me doing this and she nods her head and I know she understands that I think the silence in the room is great, and also the roar and the dust of the outside is great, and when she is nodding I understand that she is saying that this, her little room, her little circle, is a depot, a pause, for the weary traveler, but outside, outside of her little world there is dissonance, hugeness of another kind, and the travel to do. So she has her little house, she bakes the grandest doughnuts, and inside of her she houses a little depot.

Most stories would end with her death, would wait till she is peacefully dead and peacefully at rest but I cannot wait that long. I think she will grow, and her hot doughnuts just out of the oil will grow with softness and touch. And I think it would be a shame to talk of her doughnuts after she is dead, after she is formless.

Instead I take today to talk of her and her wonderful doughnuts when the earth is something to her, when the people from all parts of the earth may drop in and taste the flavor, her flavor, which is everyone's and all flavor; talk to her, sit with her, and also taste the silence of her room and the silence that is herself; and finally go away to hope and keep alive what is alive in her, on earth and in men, expressly myself.

To Understand

1. What does Mori get out of his visits with this elderly woman who makes doughnuts?

2. Mori says "it is logical" that everyone calls the woman Mama. Explain why he sees this as logical.

3. Of his visits to the woman's house, Mori says, "I sing gratefully that such a simple and common experience becomes an event, an event of necessity and growth." How does Mori grow through these visits?

4. The woman says that "silence is the most beautiful symphony." Explain why she and Mori value silence.

To Write

1. Write about an elderly person that you particularly value—and why you value that person. To start, list three or four main reasons you appreciate that person. If the elderly person is a part of your family, list reasons other than the fact that you are related.

Maxine Kumin

Henry Manley, Living Alone, Keeps Time

Winner of the Pulitzer Prize in poetry for Up Country:
Poems of New England, *Maxine Kumin has served as Poet
Laureate of New Hampshire and Consultant in Poetry to
the Library of Congress. Her publications include eleven
books of poetry, four novels, a collection of short stories,
numerous children's books, and a memoir. This poem is
one of several Kumin has written about the same character, Henry Manley.*

Before Reading: Consider the special challenges for elderly people
who live alone.

Sundowning,
the doctor calls it, the way
he loses words when the light fades.
The way the names of his dear ones
fall out of his eyeglass case.
Even under the face of his father
in an oval on the wall
he cannot say *Catherine, Vera, Paul*
but goes on loving them out of place.
Window, wristwatch, cup, knife
are small prunes that drop from his pockets.
Terror sweeps him from room to room.
Knowing how much he weighed once
he knows how much he has departed his life.
Especially he knows how the soul
can slip out of the body unannounced

like that helium-filled balloon
he opened his fingers on, years back.

Now it is dark. He undresses
and takes himself off to bed
as loose in his skin as a puppy,
afraid the blankets will untuck,
afraid he will flap up, unblessed.
Instead, proper nouns return to his keeping.
The names of faces are put back
in his sleeping mouth. At first light
he gets up, grateful once more
for how coffee smells. Sits stiff
at the bruised porcelain table
saying them over, able
to with only the slightest catch.
Coffee. Coffee cup. Watch.

To Understand

1. What parts of the poem suggest Henry Manley's diminished mental capabilities?

2. How are things different for Henry Manley in the morning than at night?

3. What is the significance of the italicized lists in the eighth and tenth lines and in the final line?

To Write

1. Write about how we readers should respond to Henry Manley: with sympathy, with understanding, with admiration, or with some other response.

David Ignatow

Pricing

*David Ignatow was the author of many books of poems in-
cluding, most recently,* Living Is What I Wanted: Last
Poems, *published in 1999. His many awards included two
Guggenheim fellowships and a National Institute of Arts
and Letters award. Ignatow taught at various universities
and edited several prestigious literary publications including* American Poetry Review, Beloit Poetry Journal, *and*
Chelsea Magazine. *He was also president of the Poetry
Society of America from 1980–1984. He died in 1997.*

Before Reading: Think about how funeral arrangements are typical-
ly made in a family. Who makes the arrangements when an elderly
person dies?

The grave needed a stone marker.
We picked Flint Rock from New England,
four feet high and three feet wide,
to cover two bodies lying side by side,
my mother and eventually my father.
He stood examining it with us,
his son and two sons-in-law,
in the marble store, and made no comment
other than the weary, grim look
of an old man who has lost his wife,
his only companion, and himself soon to go,
alone now, living among strangers,
though they were his kin.
An old man shuts himself off.
Later after the purchase, as I drove the car,
he tried to say something
to convey his mood and failed,

saying something hackneyed, conscious of it,
and said nothing further, until at home
finally with his daughter he discussed
the price and the stone's color
and its width.

To Understand

1. Explain the line, "An old man shuts himself off." How does this apply to the father in the poem?
2. Consider the poem's title, and explain how it might be interpreted.
3. Why isn't the father able to discuss his purchase until he is at home with his daughter?

To Write

1. Write about the various tasks that surviving family members (or sometimes friends) need to do when a loved one dies. What challenges do they face?
2. Imagine yourself in this father's place. Describe how you feel as you pick out the stone marker.

Growing Up/Growing Old: Ideas for Writing

1. Write a paper in which you explain what, in your opinion, is one of the greatest challenges in growing up for young people today.

2. We frequently hear parents tell their children, "You have it easy. You should have seen what I went through when I was growing up." Do you agree that your childhood was easier than that of your parents? Write a paper in which you compare one particular aspect of your childhood to that same aspect of at least one of your parents.

3. The *To Write* assignment following the Sandra Cisneros essay "Eleven" asks you to write about an age that was particularly difficult for you. Now generalize and argue how one particular age or school grade is difficult for most young people. Be sure to clearly identify the age or grade, and offer sufficient examples to illustrate your point.

4. Adults will sometimes tell high school students, "These are the best years of your lives." Yet we know that our high school years can be physically and emotionally confusing and difficult. Do you agree that, for most people, the high school years are the best they'll have? Write a paper in which you argue your position on this question.

5. The media will sometimes present a story about abuse of the elderly in convalescent homes or other care facilities. Do you know anyone, a family member perhaps, who has lived in such a place? Write a paper about this person and the quality of care he or she has received.

6. Some family experts will argue that young people in our country today have difficulty interacting with their elderly family members. Reasons vary from not living in proximity to the elderly relatives to not being taught to be respectful or to value these same people. Write a paper about how the young people in your family interact with their grandparents, great aunts, or great uncles.

7. Sometimes young people will see the elderly as being in the way and beyond their years of use. Write a paper in which you argue for the opposite, that the elderly are valuable to us as individuals or to us as a society. Focus on one or two

specific kinds of contributions elderly people make, and be sure to offer examples of elderly people you have known.

8. Write a profile of one particular elderly person you know. Don't rely entirely on past experiences or conversations. To discover new information about your subject, interview this person with prepared questions. After that, ask yourself what main impression you would like to give your readers of this person. Let this impression be the focus or thesis of your paper.

4

Learning and Teaching

Learning and Teaching

The selections in this unit are about learning and teaching. Many, naturally, have school as their setting with students and teachers as characters. However, our schools are just one place at which we learn. We learn our entire lives; some will argue that we learn in the womb, before we are born. We learn up until the time we die. We learn without even trying to learn, and sometimes we teach without intending to do so. Those who study human behavior understand that our species is unique in its capacity to learn. Because we are human, we are capable of learning and applying the Pythagorean theorem. We can learn the basic elements that make up the Earth and its atmosphere. We can learn about outer space as well as the complexities of the human brain. Yet without even intending to do so, we also learn a number of everyday skills and lessons: how not to offend a person, how to please a person, how to open a conversation, and how to avoid conflict. The number of ways in which we learn is countless. We learn, obviously, to better ourselves, yet sometimes we learn things that do us harm. As we all know, our learning is frequently a result of making mistakes.

Learning and teaching, then, are universal to human experience. Because of this, they enter our literature frequently. Professional writers know that one element of a good story is that a character will undergo some kind of change. Since learning and teaching are all about changing one's skills or outlook, writers will frequently find these subjects as fruitful areas for their own writing.

The selections in this chapter include:

- a poem about a Sikh immigrant who struggles with the difficulty her son has in fitting in at his American school;
- an essay about a girl who escapes her troubled house to go to a place that makes her feel more comfortable— school;
- a poem about a man who instructs his granddaughter about traditional manners;
- a short story about a woman who tries to teach some inner-city African American children a lesson about money and about human rights.

You, too, have the experiences and observations to make good writing about learning and teaching. You have been a student, and you have had many teachers in and out of class. Conscious of it or not, you have *been* a teacher for others. Use the *To Write* questions following each selection in the chapter as well as the *Ideas for Writing* section at the end of the chapter to help you with your own writing in this area.

Thomas Lux

You Go To School To Learn

Thomas Lux is the author of more than 15 books of poems, including his recent The Street of Clocks. *His awards include three National Endowment for the Arts grants and a Guggenheim fellowship. In this poem Lux questions the reasons people go to school and the subjects schools are teaching.*

Before Reading: Ask yourself how many times over the years you've wondered why you are going to school. Have your reasons changed? Have you always been clear about why you've gone?

You go to school to learn
to read and add, to someday
make some money. It—money—makes
sense: you need
a better tractor, an addition
to the gameroom, you prefer
to buy your beancurd by the barrel.
There's no other way to get the goods
you need. Besides, it keeps people busy
working—for it.
It's sensible and, therefore, you go
to school to learn (and the teacher,
having learned, gets paid to teach you) how
to get it. Fine. But:
you're taught away from poetry
or, say, dancing ("That's nice, dear,
but there's no dough in it"). No poem
ever bought a hamburger, or not too many. It's true,
and so, every morning—it's still dark!—
you see them, the children, like angels

being marched off to execution,
or banks. Their bodies luminous
in headlights. Going to school.

To Understand

1. According to the speaker, what is the main reason we go to school?

2. What does the speaker mean when he says we are "taught away from poetry / or, say, dancing"?

3. How are children going to school "like angels / being marched off to execution, / or banks"?

4. Examine Lux's use of light and dark images at the end of the poem. How do they contribute to your understanding of the piece?

To Write

1. Write about your purpose for going to school. Is it to "make some money," or is it for another reason?

2. Write about the degree to which "poetry / or, say, dancing," or fine arts such as music or painting, should be taught in school.

Chitra Banerjee Divakaruni

Yuba City School

Born in India, Chitra Banerjee Divakaruni came to the United States when she was nineteen. She writes both poetry and fiction and has published two short story collections, three poetry collections, and three novels, including her recent Vine of Desire. *The following poem from* Leaving Yuba City *chronicles the difficulty for a young Sikh immigrant— and for his mother—of fitting in at an American school.*

Before Reading: Ask yourself what difficulties immigrant families (both children and parents) have in learning to succeed in the American school system.

From the black trunk I shake out
my one American skirt, blue serge
that smells of mothballs. Again today
Jagjit came crying from school. All week
the teacher has made him sit
in the last row, next to the boy
who drools and mumbles,
picks at the spotted milk-blue skin
of his face, but knows to pinch, sudden-sharp,
when she is not looking.

The books are full of black curves,
dots like the eggs the boll-weevil lays
each monsoon in furniture-cracks
in Ludhiana. Far up front the teacher makes word-
    sounds
Jagjit does not know. They float
from her mouth-cave, he says,
in discs, each a different color.

Candy pink for the girls in their lace dresses,
matching shiny shoes. Silk-yellow for the boys beside them,
crisp blonde hair, hands raised
in all the right answers. Behind them
the Mexicans, whose older brothers,
he tells me, carry knives,
whose catcalls and whizzing rubber bands clash, mid-air,
with the teacher's voice,
its sharp purple edge.
For him the words are a muddy red,
flying low and heavy,
and always the one he has learned to understand:
idiot idiot idiot.

I heat the iron over the stove. Outside
evening blurs the shivering
in the eucalyptus. Jagjit's shadow
disappears into the hole he is hollowing
all afternoon. The earth, he knows, is round,
and if he can tunnel all the way through,
he will end up in Punjab,
in his grandfather's mango orchard, his grandmother's songs
lighting on his head, the old words glowing
like summer fireflies.

In the playground, Jagjit says, invisible hands
snatch at his turban, expose
his uncut hair, unseen feet trip him from behind,
and when he turns, ghost laughter
all around his bleeding knees.
He bites down on his lip to keep in
the crying. They are
waiting for him to open his mouth,
so they can steal his voice.

I test the iron with little drops of water
that sizzle and die. Press down
on the wrinkled cloth. The room fills
with a smell like singed flesh.
Tomorrow in my blue skirt I will go
to see the teacher, my tongue
a stiff embarrassment in my mouth,
my few English phrases. She will pluck them from me,
nail shut my lips. My son will keep sitting
in the last row
among the red words that drink his voice.

Note
uncut hair: the boy in the poem is a Sikh immigrant, whose religion forbids the cutting of his hair.

To Understand

1. Who is speaking this poem? Describe her predicament. How large an issue is language for Jagjit?

2. Why does the teacher make Jagjit sit in the last row? What does this suggest about her treatment of him?

3. Review the way the speaker (the mother) describes both written and spoken words. How do these descriptions help you understand what Jagjit experiences?

4. In the last stanza, the mother says the teacher will "pluck" her "few English phrases" from her. Explain what the mother fears.

To Write

1. Write about a time you felt like an outsider—at school, in a club, or in some other situation. How did others treat you?

Dorianne Laux

Books

Dorianne Laux is the author of three books of poetry, most recently Smoke, *from which this poem is taken. Laux teaches in the creative writing program at the University of Oregon, but before her life in poetry, she worked as a maid, a gas station manager, a sanatorium cook, and a donut-holer. She has won two National Endowment for the Arts fellowships among other awards.*

Before Reading: Think about typical reactions students have to finishing high school.

You're standing on the high school steps,
the double door swung closed behind you
for the last time, not the last time you'll ever

be damned or praised by your peers, spoken of
in whispers, but the last time you'll lock your locker,
zip up your gym bag, put on your out-of-style jacket,

your too-tight shoes. You're about to be
done with it: the gum, the gossip, the worship
of a boy in the back row, histories of wheat and war,

cheat sheets, tardies, the science of water,
negative numbers and compound fractions.
You don't know it yet but what you'll miss

is the books, heavy and fragrant and frayed,
the pages greasy, almost transparent, thinned
at the edges by hundreds of licked thumbs.

What you'll remember is the dumb joy
of stumbling across a passage so perfect
it drums in your head, drowns out

the teacher and the lunch bell's ring. You've stolen
A Tree Grows in Brooklyn from the library.
Lingering on the steps, you dig into your bag

to touch its heat: stolen goods, willfully taken,
in full knowledge of right and wrong.
You call yourself a thief. There are worse things,

you think, fingering the cover, tracing
the embossed letters like someone blind.
This is all you need as you take your first step
toward the street, joining characters whose lives
might unfold at your touch. You follow them into
the blur of the world. Into whoever you're going to be.

To Understand

1. Look at the details in the second and third stanzas: "your out-of-style jacket, / your too-tight shoes . . . the gum, the gossip." What do these details tell you about the experiences of this person in high school?

2. Notice that Laux uses the pronoun "you." Is she really addressing you, the reader? What effect does this point of view have?

3. The speaker says about stealing a book, "There are worse things. . . ." Describe the frame of mind of this character.

To Write

1. Write about the way you felt upon finishing high school (or grammar school if you prefer). Start by listing several emotions that describe how you felt, and give examples of what caused those emotions.

Lynda Barry

The Sanctuary of School

Growing up in Seattle, Washington, Lynda Barry was the first member of her family to attain a higher education. Now she is a professional writer and artist with books including My Perfect Life, The Freddie Stories, Cruddy: An Illustrated Novel, *and* The Good Times Are Killing Me. *She also writes and draws the syndicated comic strip* Ernie Pook's Comeek.

Before Reading: Ask yourself whether most children feel that school is a safe place.

I was seven years old the first time I snuck out of the house in the dark. It was winter and my parents had been fighting all night. They were short on money and long on relatives who kept "temporarily" moving into our house because they had nowhere else to go.

My brother and I were used to giving up our bedroom. We slept on the couch, something we actually liked because it put us that much closer to the light of our lives, our television.

At night when everyone was asleep, we lay on our pillows watching it with the sound off. We watched Steve Allen's mouth moving. We watched Johnny Carson's mouth moving. We watched movies filled with gangsters shooting machine guns into packed rooms, dying soldiers hurling a last grenade and beautiful women crying at windows. Then the sign-off finally came and we tried to sleep.

The morning I snuck out, I woke up filled with a panic about needing to get to school. The sun wasn't quite up yet but my anxiety was so fierce that I just got dressed, walked quietly across the kitchen and let myself out the back door.

It was quiet outside. Stars were still out. Nothing moved and no one was in the street. It was as if someone had turned the sound off on the world.

I walked the alley, breaking thin ice over puddles with my shoes. I didn't know why I was walking to school in the dark. I didn't think about it. All I knew was a feeling of panic, like the panic that strikes kids when they realize they are lost.

That feeling eased the moment I turned the corner and saw the dark outline of my school at the top of the hill. My school was made up of about 15 nondescript portable classrooms set down on a fenced concrete lot in a rundown Seattle neighborhood, but it had the most beautiful view of the Cascade Mountains. You could see them from anywhere on the playfield and you could see them from the windows of my classroom—Room 2.

I walked over to the monkey bars and hooked my arms around the cold metal. I stood for a long time just looking across Rainier Valley. The sky was beginning to whiten and I could hear a few birds.

In a perfect world my absence at home would not have gone unnoticed. I would have had two parents in panic to locate me, instead of two parents in a panic to locate an answer to the hard question of survival during a deep financial and emotional crisis.

But in an overcrowded and unhappy home, it's incredibly easy for any child to slip away. The high levels of frustration, depression and anger in my house made my brother and me invisible. We were children with the sound turned off. And for us, as for the steadily increasing number of neglected children in this country, the only place where we could count on being noticed was at school.

"Hey there, young lady. Did you forget to go home last night?" It was Mr. Gunderson, our janitor, whom we all loved. He was nice and he was funny and he was old with white hair, thick glasses and an unbelievable number of keys. I could hear them jingling as he walked across the playfield. I felt incredibly happy to see him.

He let me push his wheeled garbage can between the different portables as he unlocked each room. He let me turn on the lights and raise the window shades and I saw my school slowly come to life. I saw Mrs. Holman, our school secretary, walk into the office without her orange lipstick on yet. She waved.

I saw the fifth-grade teacher, Mr. Cunningham, walking under the breezeway eating a hard roll. He waved.

And I saw my teacher, Mrs. Claire LeSane, walking toward us in a red coat and calling my name in a very happy and surprised way, and suddenly my throat got tight and my eyes stung and I ran toward her crying. It was something that surprised us both.

It's only thinking about it now, 28 years later, that I realize I was crying from relief. I was with my teacher, and in a while I was going to sit at my desk, with my crayons and pencils and books and classmates all around me, and for the next six hours I was going to enjoy a thoroughly secure, warm and stable world. It was a world I absolutely relied on. Without it, I don't know where I would have gone that morning.

Mrs. LeSane asked me what was wrong and when I said "Nothing," she seemingly left it at that. But she asked me if I would carry her purse for her, an honor above all honors, and she asked me if I wanted to come into Room 2 early and paint.

She believed in the natural healing power of painting and drawing for troubled children. In the back of her room there was always a drawing table and an easel with plenty of supplies, and sometimes during the day she would come up to you for what seemed like no good reason and quietly ask you if you wanted to go to the back table and "make some pictures for Mrs. LeSane." We all had a chance at it—to sit apart from the class for a while to paint, draw and silently work out impossible problems on 11 × 17 sheets of newsprint.

Drawing came to mean everything to me. At the back table in Room 2, I learned to build myself a life preserver that I could carry into my home.

We all know that a good education system saves lives, but the people of this country are still told that cutting the budget for public schools is necessary, that poor salaries for teachers are all that we can manage and that art, music, and all creative activities must be the first to go when times are lean.

Before- and after-school programs are cut and we are told that public schools are not made for baby-sitting children. If parents are neglectful temporarily or permanently, for whatever reason, it's certainly sad, but their unlucky children must fend for themselves. Or slip through the cracks. Or wander in a dark night alone.

We are told in a thousand ways that not only are public schools not important, but that the children who attend them, the children who need them most, are not important either. We leave them to learn from the blind eye of a television, or to the mercy of "a thousand points of light" that can be as far away as stars.

I was lucky. I had Mrs. LeSane. I had Mr. Gunderson. I had an abundance of art supplies. And I had a particular brand of neglect in my home that allowed me to slip away and get to them. But what about the rest of the kids who weren't as lucky? What happened to them?

By the time the bell rang that morning I had finished my drawing and Mrs. LeSane pinned it up on the special bulletin board she reserved for drawings from the back table. It was the same picture I always drew—a sun in the corner of a blue sky over a nice house with flowers all around it.

Mrs. LeSane asked us to please stand, face the flag, place our right hands over our hearts and say the Pledge of Allegiance. Children across the country do it faithfully.

I wonder now when the country will face its children and say a pledge right back.

To Understand

1. Why does the young Barry leave her house in the morning and go to school?

2. What exactly does Barry value in making artwork for Mrs. LeSane?

3. What is Barry saying about the American public education system? How would she like the system to change?

To Write

1. When you were a child, did you consider school a sanctuary, a burdensome place, or something else? Explain.

Carol Lem

Office Hour

The author of several books of poems, Carol Lem teaches writing at East Los Angeles College. "Office Hour" won an award in the "Poetry in the Windows" contest sponsored by the Arroyo Arts Collective of Highland Park.

Before Reading: Ask yourself how important it is to visit your instructors during their office hours.

after Philip Levine

My student says he wrote a poem
about me, but not as I am, not
this tired maestra talking to the blackboard
deafened by the echo of her own voice
but as a poet blowing her bamboo flute
on a hill. My student, a Chicano, is sitting
in my office, his eyes focused
on shelves of books, "Do you read all these?"
I don't say these are only textbooks,
my real books are at home, nor do I name
all the poets I love. He can take in
only a few now—Baca, Soto, Rodriguez.
The fluorescent lights above us
hum a broken tune, something like
"America the Beautiful" or "Time on My Hands."
It is late. Everyone has gone home
to shore up their other lives, and East L.A.
is quiet again. What a dream—
a teacher and a student meeting at the edge
of a battle zone where drivebys and tortillas,
quinceañeras and someone's mijito cycling a future

on blood-stained sidewalks go on.
"I want to write," he says, "but I can't leave
my turf." I don't say you won't
even when you're a thousand miles from here.
What a dream—a young Chicano
crosses the border to me, a Chinese,
three decades away, to give me a poem,
knowing we are both Americans with a song
to pass on, even if it's still out of tune.
We hear the music in the attention of this hour.
What a dream—When I drove home
the 10 East was jammed with trucks and exhaust
and the San Gabriel mountains a vague vision.
That hill will have to stay in a poem
for a while. But think, without
the blaring horns and broken glass, without
these messages of hope spread across my desk
and the shadow who fills the barrel
of this pen, I could have missed it all.

To Understand

1. What is the significance of the songs the speaker mentions,
"America the Beautiful" and "Time on My Hands"?

2. What response does the speaker have when her student says,
" 'I want to write' . . . 'but I can't leave my turf' "? Explain her
response.

3. How does the speaker feel about this meeting with her student? Point to particular lines to support your answer.

4. In the final line the speaker says, "I could have missed it all."
What is it that she could have missed?

To Write

1. Write about one teacher with whom you have worked closely.
Explain what made you comfortable or confident enough to
work with this person. If you haven't worked closely with an
instructor, write about why you haven't.

Elizabeth Wong

The Struggle to Be an All-American Girl

Elizabeth Wong was raised in Chinatown and grew up to be an important American playwright. In 1991, her play Letters to a Student Revolutionary *premiered off Broadway, and since then it has been produced across the nation. A few of her other plays are* The Concubine Spy, China Doll, *and* The Happy Prince. *Wong has worked as a reporter for several newspapers, as a writer for Walt Disney Studios, and as a staff writer for the ABC sitcom* All-American Girl.

Before Reading: Think about the things that your parents wanted you to learn and that you resisted. What were they? Why didn't you want to learn these things?

It's still there; the Chinese school on Yale Street where my brother and I used to go. Despite the new coat of paint and the high wire fence, the school I knew ten years ago remains remarkably, stoically the same.

Every day at 5 p.m., instead of playing with our fourth- and fifth-grade friends or sneaking out to the empty lot to hunt ghosts and animal bones, my brother and I had to go to Chinese school. No amount of kicking, screaming, or pleading could dissuade my mother, who was solidly determined to have us learn the language of our heritage.

Forcibly, she walked us the seven long, hilly blocks from our home to school, depositing our defiant, tearful faces before the stern principal. My only memory of him is that he swayed on his heels like a palm tree, and he always clasped his impatient, twitching hands behind his back. I recognized him as a repressed maniacal child killer, and knew that if we ever saw his hands, we'd be in big trouble.

We all sat in little chairs in an empty auditorium. The room smelled like Chinese medicine, an imported faraway mustiness. Like ancient mothballs or dusty closets. I hated that smell. I favored crisp new scents. Like the soft French perfume that my American teacher wore in public school.

There was a stage far to the right, flanked by an American flag and the flag of the Nationalist Republic of China, which was also red, white, and blue, but not as pretty.

Although the emphasis at the school was mainly language—speaking, reading, writing—the lessons always began with an exercise in politeness. With the entrance of the teacher, the best student would tap a bell and everyone would get up, kowtow, and chant, "*Sing sun ho*," the phonetic for "How are you, teacher?"

Being ten years old, I had better things to learn than ideographs copied painstakingly in lines that ran right to left from the tip of a *moc but*, a real ink pen that had to be held in an awkward way if blotches were to be avoided. After all, I could do the multiplication tables, name the satellites of Mars, and write reports on *Little Women* and *Black Beauty*. Nancy Drew, my favorite book heroine, never spoke Chinese.

The language was a source of embarrassment. More times than not, I had tried to dissociate myself from the nagging, loud voice that followed me wherever I wandered in the nearby American supermarket outside Chinatown. The voice belonged to my grandmother, a fragile woman in her seventies, who could outshout the best of the street vendors. Her humor was raunchy, her Chinese rhythmless, patternless. It was quick, it was loud, it was unbeautiful. It was not like the quiet, lilting romance of French or the gentle refinement of the American. South Chinese sounded pedestrian. Public.

In Chinatown, the comings and goings of hundreds of Chinese on their daily tasks sounded chaotic and frenzied. I did not want to be thought of as mad, as talking gibberish. When I spoke English, people nodded at me, smiled sweetly, said encouraging words. Even the people in my culture would cluck and say that I'd do well in life. "My, doesn't she move her lips fast," they'd say, meaning that I'd be able to keep up with the world outside Chinatown.

My brother was even more fanatical than I about speaking English. He was especially hard on my mother, criticizing her, often cruelly, for her pidgin speech—smatterings of Chinese scattered like chop suey in her conversation. "It's not 'What it is,' Mom," he'd say in exasperation. "It's 'What *is*, what *is*, what *is!*'" Sometimes, Mom might leave out an occasional "the" or "a," or perhaps a verb of being. He would stop her in mid-sentence: "Say it again, Mom. Say it right." When he tripped over his own tongue, he'd blame it on her: "See, Mom, it's all your fault. You set a bad example."

What infuriated my mother most was when my brother cornered her on her consonants, especially *r*. My father had played a cruel joke on Mom by assigning her an American name that her tongue wouldn't allow her to say. No matter how hard she tried, "Ruth" always ended up "Luth" or "Roof."

After two years of writing with a *moc but* and reciting words with multiples of meanings, I finally was granted a cultural divorce. I was permitted to stop Chinese school.

I thought of myself as multicultural. I preferred tacos to egg rolls; I enjoyed Cinco de Mayo more than Chinese New Year. At last, I was one of you; I wasn't one of them.

Sadly, I still am.

To Understand

1. Why does Elizabeth Wong object to attending Chinese school? Point to particular places in the essay to support your answer.

2. How does Wong feel about speaking Chinese versus speaking English?

3. Explain Wong's final sentences, "At last, I was one of you; I wasn't one of them," and finally, "Sadly, I still am." Why is she sad?

To Write

1. Does your family have a strong ethnic or cultural identity? Write about the degree to which your parents wanted you to retain an identity as you were growing up.

2. Is it important for children who are raised bilingual to retain the language of their parents? If you are bilingual, you may want to use your own experiences as a guide here, but think about the many others who grow up speaking two languages. What are the benefits of being bilingual? The drawbacks?

Elizabeth Bishop

Manners

One of America's most important poets, Elizabeth Bishop won nearly every poetry award in America including the National Book Award for Questions of Travel, *the National Book Critics Circle Award for* Geography III, *and the Pulitzer Prize for* Poems: North and South. *Living in many places including Massachusetts, Nova Scotia, Brazil, and Key West, Florida, her travels influenced her writing greatly. Bishop was a chancellor of the Academy of American Poets and a Consultant to the Library of Congress. She died in 1979.*

Before Reading: Consider Bishop's title. What situations does the word "manners" bring to mind?

for a child of 1918

My grandfather said to me
as we sat on the wagon seat,
"Be sure to remember to always
speak to everyone you meet."

We met a stranger on foot.
My grandfather's whip tapped his hat.
"Good day, sir. Good day. A fine day."
And I said it and bowed where I sat.

Then we overtook a boy we knew
with his big pet crow on his shoulder.
"Always offer everyone a ride;
don't forget that when you get older,"

my grandfather said. So Willy
climbed up with us, but the crow

gave a "Caw!" and flew off. I was worried.
How would he know where to go?

But he flew a little way at a time
from fence post to fence post, ahead;
and when Willy whistled he answered.
"A fine bird," my grandfather said,

"and he's well brought up. See, he answers
nicely when he's spoken to.
Man or beast, that's good manners.
Be sure that you both always do."

When automobiles went by,
the dust hid the people's faces,
but we shouted "Good day! Good day!
Fine day!" at the top of our voices.

When we came to Hustler Hill,
he said that the mare was tired,
so we all got down and walked,
as our good manners required.

To Understand

1. Considering the date mentioned in the subtitle, how important are the various modes of transportation in the poem: horse and wagon, walking, and automobiles?
2. What qualities does the grandfather admire in a person?
3. How important are the relative ages of the characters in this poem? Explain?

To Write

1. Consider the grandfather's advice about manners in this poem. Would it be good advice for the children of today? Write about whether you would advise children to follow his wisdom, and give thorough reasons to explain your answer.

William Saroyan

The Two-Twenty
Low Hurdle Race

*William Saroyan was born in Fresno, California, in 1908,
the son of Armenian immigrants. Inspired by his Armenian background, he gained international fame for his
books and plays. From his first book,* The Daring Young
Man on the Flying Trapeze, *to his Pulitzer Prize-winning
play,* The Time of Your Life, *he established great popular-
ity for his work. The following story is a chapter from his
novel,* The Human Comedy, *which was made into a movie
that won an Academy Award for Best Writing Original
Screen Story. Saroyan died in 1981.*

Before Reading: As this story begins, Homer Macauley, the protago-
nist, has been held after class by his teacher, Miss Hicks, for arguing
with another student, Hubert Ackley the Third. Later, Homer is mistreated by his track coach. Ask yourself what power a student has if a
teacher or coach mistreats him or her.

The boys' athletic coach of Ithaca High stood in the office of the principal—a man whose last name was Ek, a
circumstance duly reported by Mr. Robert Ripley in a
daily newspaper cartoon entitled "Believe It or Not." Mr.
Ek's first name was Oscar and not worthy of notice.

"Miss Hicks," the principal said to the coach, "is the
oldest and best teacher we have ever had at this school.
She was my teacher when I attended Ithaca High, and
she was your teacher too, Mr. Byfield. I'm afraid I would-
n't care to go over her head about punishing a couple of
unruly boys."

"Hubert Ackley the Third is *not* an unruly boy," the coach said. "Homer Macauley—yes. Hubert Ackley—no. He is a perfect little gentleman."

"Well, he comes from a well-to-do family, at any rate. But if Miss Hicks has asked him to stay in after school, then *in* it is. Perhaps he *is* a perfect little gentleman. But Miss Hicks is the teacher of the ancient history class and she has never been known to punish anyone who has not deserved to be punished. Hubert Ackley will have to run the race some other time."

The matter was surely closed now, the principal felt. The coach turned and left the office. He did not go to the athletic field, however. He went to the ancient history classroom instead. There he found Homer and Hubert and Miss Hicks. He bowed to the old teacher and smiled.

"Miss Hicks," he said, "I have spoken to Mr. Ek about this matter." The implication of his remark was that he had been given authorization to come and liberate Hubert Ackley III. Homer Macauley, however, leaped to his feet as if it were *he* who was to be liberated.

"Not you," the coach said. "Mr. Ackley."

"What do you mean?" the ancient history teacher said.

"Mr. Ackley is to get into his track suit immediately and run the two-twenty low hurdles. We're waiting for him."

"Oh yeah?" Homer said. He was overflowing with righteous indignation. "Well what about Mr. *Macauley?*" There was no reply from the coach, who walked out of the room followed by a somewhat troubled and confused young man—Hubert Ackley III.

"Did you see that, Miss Hicks?" Homer said.

The ancient history teacher was so upset she could barely speak. At last she managed to whisper, "Mr. Byfield is a liar." Homer was amazed to see Miss Hicks so angry. It made him feel that she was just about the best teacher ever.

"I have taught ancient history at Ithaca High for thir-ty-five years. I have known hundreds of Ithaca boys and girls. I have taught your brother Marcus and your sister Bess, and if you have younger brothers or sisters at home I shall someday teach them, too."

"Just a brother, Ulysses. How *was* Marcus in school?"

"Marcus and Bess were both good students—honest and civilized. Yes, *civilized*. The behavior of ancient peoples had made them civilized from birth. Like yourself, Marcus sometimes spoke out of turn, but he was never a liar. That man came here and deliberately lied to me—just as he lied to me time and again when he sat in this classroom as a boy. He has learned nothing except to toady to those he feels are superior. The two-twenty low hurdles! *Low* indeed!" The ancient history teacher blew her nose and wiped her eyes.

"Don't feel bad, Miss Hicks," Homer said. "I never knew teachers are human beings like everybody else—and *better,* too. I'll stay in, Miss Hicks. You can punish me."

"I didn't keep you in to punish you," the teacher said. "I have always kept in only those who have meant the most to me. I still don't believe I'm mistaken about Hubert Ack-ley. I was going to send both of you to the field after a mo-ment, anyway. You were not *kept* in for punishment, but for education. I watch the growth of spirit in the children who come to my class. You apologized to Hubert Ackley. And even though it embarassed him to do so, because your apology made him unworthy, he graciously accepted your apology. I kept you in after school because I wanted to talk to both of you—one of you from a good well-to-do family, the other from a good poor family. Getting along in this world will be even more difficult for him than for you. I wanted you to know one another a little better. It is very important. I wanted to talk to *both* of you."

"I guess I like Hubert," Homer said, "only he seems to think he's better than the other boys."

"I know how you feel, but every man in the world *is* better than someone else. And not as good as someone *else*. Joseph Terranova is brighter than Hubert, but Hubert is just as honest in his own way. In a democratic state every man is the equal of every other man up to the point of exertion, and after that every man is free to exert himself as he chooses. I am eager for my boys and girls to exert themselves about behaving with honor. What my children appear to be on the surface is no matter to me. I am fooled neither by gracious manner nor by bad manner. I am interested in what is truly beneath each kind of manners. Whether one of my children is rich or poor, brilliant or slow, genius or simple-minded, is no matter to me, if there is humanity in him—if he has a heart—if he lives truth and honor—if he respects both his inferiors and his superiors. If the children in my classroom are human, I do not want them to be alike in their *manner* of being human. If they are not corrupt, it does not matter to me how they differ from one another. I want each of my children to be himself. I don't want you to be like somebody else just to please me or to make my work easier. I would soon be weary of a classroom full of perfect little ladies and gentlemen. I want my children to be *people*—each one separate—each one special—each one a pleasant and exciting variation of all the others. I wanted Hubert Ackley here to listen to this with you—to understand with you that if at the present you do not like him and he does not like you, that is perfectly natural. I wanted him to know that each of you will begin to be truly human when, in spite of your natural dislike of one another, you still respect one another. That is what it means to be civilized—that is what we are to learn from a study of ancient history. I'm glad I've spoken to you, rather than to anyone else I know. When you leave this school—long after you have forgotten *me*—I shall be watching for you in the world." Again Miss Hicks blew her nose and touched her handkerchief to her eyes. "Run along to the athletic field, now."

The second son of the Macauley family of Santa Clara Avenue in Ithaca, California, got up from his desk and walked out of the room.

On the athletic field Hubert Ackley and the three boys who had already raced with him that day were taking their places in the lanes for the two-twenty low hurdle race. Homer reached the fifth lane just as the man with the pistol lifted his arm to start the race. Homer went to his mark with the others. He felt good, but very angry and he believed that nothing in the world would be able to keep him from winning this race—the wrong kind of shoes, the wrong kind of clothes for running, no practice, or anything else. He would just naturally win the race.

Hubert Ackley, in the lane next to Homer's lane, turned to him and said, "*You* can't run this race—like *that*."

"No?" Homer said. "Wait and see."

Mr. Byfield, sitting in the grandstand, asked himself, "Who's that starting in the outside lane without track clothes?" Then he remembered who it was.

He decided to stop the race so he could remove the fifth runner, but it was too late. The gun had been fired and the runners were running. Homer and Hubert took the first hurdle a little ahead of the others, each of them clearing nicely. Homer moved a little ahead of Hubert on the second hurdle and kept moving ahead on the third, fourth, fifth, sixth, seventh, and eighth hurdles. But close behind was Hubert Ackley.

Homer reached the ninth hurdle precisely when the coach of Ithaca High also reached it, coming in the opposite direction, so that Homer hurdled straight into the outstretched arms of the athletic coach and the man and the boy fell to the ground. Hubert Ackley stopped running and stopped the other runners. "Stay where you are," he shouted. "Let him get up." Homer got to his feet, and the race resumed.

Everyone in the grandstand, even Helen Eliot, was amazed at what had happened. Now, the ancient history teacher was at the finish line of the race.

"Come on, Homer!" she said. "Come on, Hubert! Hurry, Sam!—George!—Henry!"

At the next to last hurdle Hubert caught up with Homer. "Sorry," he said.

"Go ahead," Homer said.

Hubert Ackley moved a little ahead of Homer and now there was no longer very far to go. Homer kicked the last hurdle, but he almost caught up with Hubert. The finish of the race was so close no one could tell who actually won it. Sam, George, and Henry came in soon after.

Furious and bitter, and a little shocked by the fall he had taken, the coach of Ithaca High came running toward the group which Miss Hicks had gathered around her.

"Macauley!" he shouted from a distance of fifteen yards.

When he reached the group he stood panting for breath and glaring at Homer Macauley.

Then he said, "For the remainder of this semester you will take no part in any school athletic activities."

"Yes, sir," Homer said.

"Now go to my office and stay there."

"Your office?" Homer suddenly remembered that he had to be at work at four o'clock. "What time is it?" he said.

Hubert Ackley looked at his wristwatch. "A quarter to four."

"Go to my office!" Byfield shouted.

"But you don't understand, Mr. Byfield," Homer said. "I've got to go somewhere, and I just can't be late."

Joe Terranova came into the group. "Why should he go to your office? He didn't do anything wrong."

The poor coach had already suffered too much. "You keep your dirty little wop mouth shut!" he shouted. Then he pushed the boy, who went sprawling. But even before he touched the ground, Joe shouted: "W-O-P?"

On his feet again, Joe tackled Byfield as if they were in a football game.

Mr. Ek came running, breathless and bewildered.

"Gentlemen!" he said. "Boys, boys!" He dragged Joe Terranova off the athletic coach, who did not get to his feet.

"Mr. Byfield," the principal said, "what is the meaning of this unusual behavior?"

Speechless, Byfield pointed at Miss Hicks.

"Mr. Byfield owes Joe Terranova an apology," she said.

"Is that so? Is that so, Mr. Byfield?" Mr. Ek said.

"Joe's people *are* from Italy, that's quite true, but they are not to be referred to as wops," Miss Hicks said.

Joe Terranova said, "He doesn't need to apologize to me. If he calls me names, I'll bust him in the mouth. If he beats me up, I'll get my brothers."

"Joseph," Miss Hicks said. "You must allow Mr. Byfield to apologize. You must give him the privilege of once again trying to be an American."

"Yes, that's so," the principal said. "This is America, and the only foreigners here are those who forget that this *is* America." He turned to the man who was still sprawled on the ground. "Mr. Byfield," he commanded.

The athletic coach of Ithaca High School got to his feet. To no one in particular he said, "I apologize," and hurried away.

Joe Terranova and Homer Macauley went off together. Joe walked well, but Homer limped. He had hurt his left leg when Byfield had tried to stop him.

Miss Hicks and Mr. Ek turned to the thirty or forty boys and girls who had gathered around. They were of many types and many nationalities.

"All right, now," Miss Hicks said. "Go along home to your families," and as the boys and girls were all a little bewildered, she added, "Brighten up, brighten up—this is nothing."

"Yes," the principal said, "brighten up, every one of you, please."

The children broke into groups and walked away.

To Understand

1. Why does Miss Hicks make Homer and Hubert stay after class? What does she hope to accomplish by keeping them in?

2. Miss Hicks wants her students to be "civilized." What does she mean by this?

3. What kind of person is Mr. Byfield? Explain your answer with information from the story.

4. In the end, Mr. Ek and Miss Hicks tell the gathered boys and girls to "brighten up." Why do they do this?

To Write

1. Write about a time when you felt mistreated by a teacher. What happened? What were you able to do, if anything, to remedy the situation?

2. Write about a time when a teacher supported you. What in particular did the teacher do to help you?

Ann Darr

Advice I Wish Someone Had Given Me

Ann Darr's many books include Do You Take This Woman;
Gussie, Mad Hannah & Me; *and* Love in the Past Tense.
*She has worked as both an Air Force pilot and a radio per-
sonality. In this poem Darr takes on the general subject of
advice about how to live one's life.*

Before Reading: Consider the poem's title. What kind of advice have
you received about how to carry out your life?

Be strange if it is necessary, be
quiet, kindly as you can without
feeling the heel marks on your head.
Be expert in some way that pleasures
you, story-telling, baking, bed;
marvel at the marvelous
in leaves, stones, intercepted light;
put truth and people in their right-
full angle in the sun . . . find the shadow,
what it falls upon.
Trust everyone a little, no one much.
Care carefully.
Thicken your skin to hints and hurts, be
allergic to the soul scrapers.

To Understand

1. This poem contains many pieces of advice. Do they have anything in common? Is there any general advice that would link
all of these suggestions together?

2. Is there any one piece of advice that at first is unclear to you? Focus on that one. What do you think Darr is saying there?

3. Who are the "soul scrapers" mentioned in the final line?

To Write

1. Write your own poem or paragraph under the title, "Advice I Wish Someone Had Given Me."

2. Evaluate one piece of advice given in the poem. How good of advice is it? Explain your answer with examples.

Toni Cade Bambara

The Lesson

*The author of several books of fiction—*Gorilla, My Love; The Seabirds are Still Alive; The Salt Eaters; *and* If Blessing Comes—*Toni Cade Bambara has devoted herself to civil rights and has often focused her writing on the unique struggles of African-American women. Nobel Prize-winning author Toni Morrison says of Bambara's work that "nothing distracts from the sheer satisfaction her storytelling provides." In this story Bambara looks at the subject of opportunity for inner city African-American children.*

Before Reading: Ask yourself if all people in this country have the same opportunity to become educated, to get good jobs, and to share in our nation's wealth.

Back in the days when everyone was old and stupid or young and foolish and me and Sugar were the only ones just right, this lady moved on our block with nappy hair and proper speech and no makeup. And quite naturally we laughed at her, and laughed the way we did at the junk man who went about his business like he was some big-time president and his sorry-ass horse his secretary. And we kinda hated her too, hated the way we did the winos who cluttered up our parks and pissed on our handball walls and stank up our hallways and stairs so you couldn't halfway play hide-and-seek without a god-damn gas mask. Miss Moore was her name. The only woman on the block with no first name. And she was black as hell, cept for her feet, which were fish-white and spooky. And she was always planning these boring-ass things for us to do, us being my cousin, mostly, who lived on the block cause we all moved North the same time and to the same apartment then spread out gradual to breathe. And our parents would yank our heads into some kinda shape and crisp up our clothes so we'd be presentable for travel with Miss Moore, who always looked like she was going to church, though she never did. Which is just one of the things the grownups talked about when they talked behind her back like a dog. But when she came calling with some sachet she'd sewed up or some gingerbread she'd made or some book, why then they'd all be too embarrassed to turn her down and we'd get handed over all spruced up. She'd been to college and said it was only right that she should take responsibility for the young one's education, and she not even related by marriage or blood. So they'd go for it. Specially Aunt Gretchen. She been screwed into the go-along for so long, it's a blood-deep natural thing with her. Which is how she got saddled with me and Sugar and Junior in the first place while our mothers were in a la-de-da apartment up the block having a good ole time.

So this one day Miss Moore rounds us all up at the mailbox and it's puredee hot and she's knockin herself out about arithmetic. And school suppose to let up in summer I heard, but she don't never let up. And the starch in my pinafore scratching the shit outta me and I'm really hating this nappy-head bitch and her goddamn college degree. I'd much rather go to the pool or to the show where it's cool. So me and Sugar leaning on the mailbox being surly, which is a Miss Moore word. And Flyboy checking out what everybody brought for lunch. And Fat Butt already wasting his peanut-butter-and-jelly sandwich like the pig he is. And Junebug punchin on Q.T.'s arm for potato chips. And Rosie Giraffe shifting from one hip to the other waiting for somebody to step on her foot or ask her if she from Georgia so she can kick ass, preferably Mercedes'. And Miss Moore asking us do we know what money is, like we a bunch of retards. I mean real money, she say, like it's only poker chips or monopoly papers we lay on the grocer. So right away I'm tired of this and say so. And would much rather snatch Sugar and go to the Sunset and terrorize the West Indian kids and take their hair ribbons and their money too. And Miss Moore files that remark away for next week's lesson on brotherhood, I can tell. And finally I say we oughta get to the subway cause it's cooler and besides we might meet some cute boys. Sugar done swiped her mama's lipstick, so we ready.

So we heading down the street and she's boring us silly about what things cost and what our parents make and how much goes for rent and how money ain't divided up right in this country. And then she gets to the part about we all poor and live in the slums, which I don't feature. And I'm ready to speak on that, but she steps out in the street and hails two cabs just like that. Then she hustles half the crew in with her and hands me a five-dollar bill and tells me to calculate 10 percent tip for the driver. And we're off. Me and Sugar and Junebug and Flyboy hangin out the window and hollering to everybody, putting lipstick on each other cause Flyboy a faggot anyway, and making farts with our sweaty armpits. But I'm mostly trying to figure out how to spend this money. But they all fascinated with the meter ticking and Junebug starts laying bets as to how much it'll read when Flyboy can't hold his breath no more. Then Sugar lays bets as to how much it'll be when we get there. So I'm stuck. Don't nobody want to go for my plan, which is to jump out at the next light and run off to the first bar-b-que we can find. Then the driver tells us to get the hell out cause we there already. And the meter reads eighty-five cents. And I'm stalling to figure out the tip and Sugar says give him a dime. And I decide he don't need it as bad as I do, so later for him. But then he tries to take off with Junebug foot still in the door so we talk about his mama something ferocious. Then we check out that we on Fifth Avenue and everybody dressed up in stockings. One lady in a fur coat, hot as it is. White folks crazy.

"This is the place," Miss Moore say, presenting it to us in the voice she uses at the museum. "Let's look in the windows before we go in."

"Can we steal?" Sugar asks very serious like she's getting the ground rules squared away before she plays. "I beg your pardon," say Miss Moore, and we fall out. So she leads us around the windows of the toy store and me and Sugar screamin, "This is mine, that's mine, I gotta have that, that was made for me, I was born for that," till Big Butt drowns us out.

"Hey, I'm goin to buy that there."

"That there? You don't even know what it is, stupid."

"I do so," he say punchin on Rosie Giraffe. "It's a microscope."

"Watcha gonna do with a microscope, fool?"

"Look at things."

"Like what, Ronald?" asks Miss Moore. And big Butt ain't got the first notion. So here go Miss Moore gabbing about the thousands of bacteria in a drop of water and the somethinorother in a speck of blood and the million and one living things in the air around us is invisible to the naked eye. And what she say that for? Junebug go to town on that "naked" and we rolling. Then Miss Moore ask what it cost. So we all jam into the window smudgin it up and the price tag say $300. So then she ask how long it would take for Big Butt and Junebug to save up their allowances. "Too long," I say. "Yeh," adds Sugar, "outgrown it by that time." And Miss Moore say no, you never outgrow learning instruments. "Why, even medical students and interns and," blah, blah, blah. And we ready to choke Big Butt for bringing it up in the first damn place.

"This here costs four hundred eighty dollars," say Rosie Giraffe. So we pile up all over her to see what she pointin out. My eyes tell me it's a chunk of glass cracked with something heavy, and different color inks dripped into the splits, then the whole thing put into a oven or something. But for $480 it don't make sense.

"That's a paperweight made of semi-precious stones fused together under tremendous pressure," she explains slowly, with her hands doing the mining and all the factory work.

"So what's a paperweight?" asks Rosie Giraffe.

"To weigh paper with, dumbbell," say Flyboy, the wise man from the East.

"Not exactly," say Miss Moore, which is what she say when you warm or way off too. "It's to weigh paper down so it won't scatter and make your desk untidy." So right away me and Sugar curtsy to each other and then to Mercedes who is more the tidy type.

"We don't keep paper on top of the desk in my class," say Junebug, figuring Miss Moore crazy or lyin one.

"At home, then," she say. "Don't you have a calendar and pencil case and a blotter and a letter-opener on your desk at home where you do your homework?" And she know damn well what our homes look like cause she nosys around in them every chance she gets.

"I don't even have a desk," say Junebug. "Do we?"

"No. And I don't get no homework neither," says Big Butt.

"And I don't even have a home," say Flyboy like he do at school to keep the white folks off his back and sorry for him. Send this poor kid to camp posters, is his specialty.

"I do," says Mercedes. "I have a box of stationery on my desk and a picture of my cat. My godmother bought me the stationery and the desk. There's a big rose on each sheet and envelopes smell like roses."

"Who wants to know about your smelly-ass stationery," say Rosie Giraffe fore I can get my two cents in.

"It's important to have a work area all your own so that ..."

"Will you look at this sailboat, please," say Flyboy, cuttin her off and pointin to the thing like it was his. So once again we tumble all over each other to gaze at this magnificent thing in the toy store which is just big enough to sail maybe two kittens across the pond if you strap them to the posts tight. We all start reciting the price tag like we in assembly. "Handcrafted sailboat of fiberglass at one thousand one hundred ninety-five dollars."

"Unbelievable," I hear myself say and am really stunned. I read it again for myself just in case the group recitation put me in a trance. Same thing. For some reason this pisses me off. We look at Miss Moore and she lookin at us, waiting for I dunno what.

"Who'd pay all that when you can buy a sailboat set for a quarter at Pop's, a tube of glue for a dime, and a ball of string for eighty cents? It must have a motor and a whole lot else besides," I say. "My sailboat cost me about fifty cents."

"But will it take water?" say Mercedes with her smart ass.

"Took mine to Ally Pond Park once," say Flyboy. "String broke. Lost it. Pity."

"Sailed mine in Central Park and it keeled over and sank. Had to ask my father for another dollar."

"And you got the strap," laugh Big Butt. "The jerk didn't even have a string on it. My old man wailed on his behind."

Little Q.T. was staring hard at the sailboat and you could see he wanted it bad. But he too little and somebody'd just take it from him. So what the hell. "This boat for kids, Miss Moore?"

"Parents silly to buy something like that just to get all broke up," say Rosie Giraffe.

"That much money it should last forever," I figure.

"My father'd buy it for me if I wanted it."

"Your father, my ass," say Rosie Giraffe getting a chance to finally push Mercedes.

"Must be rich people shop here," say Q.T.

"You are a very bright boy," say Flyboy. "What was your first clue?" And he rap him on the head with the back of his knuckles, since Q.T. the only one he could get away with. Though Q.T. liable to come up behind you years later and get his licks in when you half expect it.

"What I want to know is," I say to Miss Moore though I never talk to her, I wouldn't give the bitch that satisfaction, "is how much a real boat costs? I figure a thousand'd get you a yacht any day."

"Why don't you check that out," she says, "and report back to the group?" Which really pains my ass. If you gonna mess up a perfectly good swim day least you could do is have some answers. "Let's go," she say like she got something up her sleeve. Only she don't lead the way. So me and Sugar turn the corner to where the entrance is, but when we get there I kinda hang back. Not that I'm scared, what's there to be afraid of, just a toy store. But I feel funny, shame. But what I got to be shamed about? Got as much right to go in as anybody. But somehow I can't seem to get hold of the door, so I step away from Sugar to lead. But she hangs back too. And I look at her and she looks at me and this is ridiculous. I mean, damn, I have never ever been shy about doing nothing or going nowhere. But then Mercedes steps up and then Rosie Giraffe and Big Butt crowd in behind and shove, and next thing we all stuffed into the doorway with only Mercedes squeezing past us, smoothing out her jumper and walking right down the aisle. Then the rest of us tumble in like a glued-together jigsaw done all wrong. And people lookin at us. And it's like the time me and Sugar crashed into the Catholic church on a dare. But once we got in there and everything so hushed and holy and the candles and the bowin and the handkerchiefs on all the drooping heads, I just couldn't go through with the plan. Which was for me to run up to the altar and do a tap dance while Sugar played the nose flute and messed around in the holy water. And Sugar kept givin me the elbow. Then later teased me so bad I tied her up in the shower and turned it on and locked her in. And she'd be there till this day if Aunt Gretchen hadn't finally figured I was lyin about the boarder takin a shower.

Same thing in the store. We all walkin on tiptoe and hardly touchin the games and puzzles and things. And I watched Miss Moore who is steady watchin us like she waitin for a sign. Like Mama Drewery watches the sky and sniffs the air and takes note of just how much slant is in the bird formation. Then me and Sugar bump smack into each other, so busy gazing at the toys, specially the sailboat. But we don't laugh and go into our fat-lady bump-stomach routine. We just stare at the price tag. Then Sugar run a finger over the whole boat. And I'm jealous and want to hit her. Maybe not her, but I sure want to punch somebody in the mouth.

"Watcha bring us here for, Miss Moore?"

"You sound angry, Sylvia. Are you mad about something?" Givin me one of them grins like she tellin a grown-up joke that never turns out to be funny. And she's lookin very closely at me like maybe she planning to do my portrait from memory. I'm mad but I won't give her that satisfaction. So I slouch around the store bein very bored and say, "Let's go."

Me and Sugar at the back of the train watchin the tracks whizzin by large then small then getting gobbled up in the dark. I'm thinkin about this tricky toy I saw in the store. A clown that somersaults on a bar then does chin-ups just cause you yank lightly at his leg. Cost $35. I could see me askin my mother for a $35 birthday clown. "You wanna who that costs what?" she say, cocking her head to the side to get a better view of the hole in my head. Thirty-five dollars could buy new bunk beds for Junior and Gretchen's boy. Thirty-five dollars and the whole household could go visit Granddaddy Nelson in the country. Thirty-five dollars would pay for the rent and the piano bill too. Who are these people that spend that much for performing clowns and $1000 for toy sailboats? What kinda work they do and how they live and how come we ain't in on it? Where we are is who we are, Miss Moore always pointin out. But it don't necessarily have to be that way, she always adds then waits for somebody to say that poor people have to wake up and demand their share of the pie and don't none of us know what kind of pie she talkin about in the first damn place. But she ain't so smart cause I got her four dollars from the taxi and she sure ain't gettin it. Messin up my day with this shit. Sugar nudges me in the pocket and winks.

Miss Moore lines us up in front of the mailbox where we started from, seems like years ago, and I got a headache for thinkin so hard. And we lean all over each other so we can hold up under the draggy-ass lecture she always finishes us off with at the end before we thank her for borin us to tears. But she just looks at us like she readin tea leaves. Finally she say, "Well, what did you think of F.A.O. Schwarz?"

Rosie Giraffe mumbles, "White folks crazy."

"I'd like to go there again when I get my birthday money," says Mercedes, and we shove her out the pack so she has to lean on the mailbox by herself.

"I'd like a shower. Tiring day," say Flyboy.

Then Sugar surprises me by sayin, "You know, Miss Moore, I don't think all of us here put together eat in a year what that sailboat costs." And Miss Moore lights up like somebody goosed her. "And?" she say, urging Sugar on. Only I'm standin on her foot so she don't continue.

"Imagine for a minute what kind of society it is in which some people can spend on a toy what it would cost to feed a family of six or seven. What do you think?"

"I think," say Sugar pushing me off her feet like she never done before, cause I whip her ass in a minute, "that this is not much of a democracy if you ask me. Equal chance to pursue happiness means an equal crack at the dough, don't it?" Miss Moore is beside herself and I am disgusted by Sugar's treachery. So I stand on her foot one more time to see if she'll shove me. She shuts up, and Miss Moore looks at me, sorrowfully I'm thinkin. And somethin weird is goin on, I can feel it in my chest.

"Anybody else learn anything today?" lookin dead at me. I walk away and Sugar has to run to catch up and don't even seem to notice when I shrug her arm off my shoulder.

"Well, we got four dollars anyway," she says.

"Uh hunh."

"We could go to Hascombs and get half a chocolate layer and then go to the Sunset and still have plenty money for potato chips and ice cream sodas."

"Un hunh."

"Race you to Hascombs," she say.

We start down the block and she gets ahead which is O.K. by me cause I'm going over to the West End and then over to the Drive to think this day through. She can run if she want to and even run faster. But ain't nobody gonna beat me at nuthin.

To Understand

1. Describe the conditions in which Sylvia and her friends live. Point to details in the story to help you with your description.

2. When the children finally enter the door of F.A.O. Schwarz, they pile up, showing reluctance about going in. Explain this behavior. Why don't they walk in boldly?

3. How do the kids treat Miss Moore? Do they respect her attempts to educate them?

4. Has Sylvia learned any part of what Miss Moore has intended as "the lesson"? What specifically in the story leads you to your answer?

To Write

1. Write on the following question Miss Moore asks: "Imagine for a minute what kind of society it is in which some people can spend on a toy what it would cost to feed a family of six or seven. What do you think?"

2. Write about whether you believe you have had "an equal crack at the dough," as Sugar puts it. Have you had more opportunity than some people? Less?

Learning and Teaching: Ideas for Writing

1. Who was the best (or worst) teacher you have ever had? Write a paper describing this person, highlighting the main qualities that made this teacher excellent or poor.

2. Write a paper about the person *other than a teacher* who has taught you the most. This person might be a parent, grandparent, neighbor, or friend. Start by listing what this person has taught you, and brainstorm examples of how these lessons have benefited you.

3. Throughout your schooling you have learned math, English, history, social science, and so on. What other lessons or skills have you learned in school in addition to those subjects you studied in class? Write a paper about the other things you've learned, and offer examples of these lessons.

4. Imagine your audience as the parents of preschool children. Write a paper in which you offer these parents advice about how they can best help their kids throughout elementary school. Start by coming up with three to five specific suggestions; then determine how those suggestions can be brought together under one overall piece of advice—your main idea.

5. In their many years of going to school, students face countless challenges, both in and out of the classroom. Write a paper about one main challenge that most or many students will face at some point during their education. Clearly explain what the challenge is, and offer specific examples of how you and others have faced it.

6. Outside of school, we have many occasions for learning about life. Write about one kind of occasion that offers many people an opportunity to learn a life lesson. Start by listing such occasions—a relative's serious illness, a life-changing trip, a move to a different part of the country or world, a tragic accident, and so on—and choose one to explain how a person learns from it. Be sure to offer examples to illustrate the lesson.

7. How important is it to get a college education? Write a paper arguing for the benefits of going to college. The trick here will be in offering reasons that go beyond the obvious—to

make more money. Start by brainstorming reasons with classmates or friends; ask your instructors, too. Then choose the most convincing reasons and organize your argument around those.

5

The Emotional Side

The Emotional Side

Has anyone ever said to you, "Don't get emotional over that"? Perhaps you were grieving the breakup of a relationship, suffering over a poor test score in biology, or aching because your favorite team lost an important game. In these cases "getting emotional" means showing the pain you're feeling. We are sometimes warned not to do this because it makes others feel our pain (and that isn't pleasant for them), because it suggests that we are weak, or because the pain seems unnecessary to that person. We are encouraged to "grin and bear it," as the expression goes. Some of us, likewise, have been taught to avoid displaying positive emotions. While others laugh loudly, talking about how much fun they are having, seemingly ready to burst from the joy they are feeling, these people stand stoic and silent, only a small grin on their faces.

Regardless of how we learn to show or hide our grief, joy, pride, anger, greed, envy, or love, these emotions—whether shown or not—are some of the most powerful reactions we have to our surroundings and to other people. It makes sense, then, that our literature celebrates this emotional side of ourselves. Writers know, in fact, that a story or poem should almost always provoke an emotional reaction within readers for it to be successful. If readers feel nothing, then the piece fails. Some literature, however, goes beyond the act of stirring readers' emotions. These works show striking emotional displays by their characters or narrators. We read them to experience both the characters emotions and our own.

In this chapter you will find

- a poem in which a woman expresses her strength and pride by discussing just one part of her body—her hips;
- an essay in which a young man recalls the shame he felt for living in substandard housing;
- a poem about a homesteader's love and devotion in the midst of extreme circumstances;
- a story about high school love and what became of it thirty years later at a class reunion.

You will notice that several of the selections in this chapter have love as a dominant emotion. However, also notice how the kind of love changes from piece to piece. Literature, if it is good, does not oversimplify the emotions it presents. Love is not neatly packaged into red hearts, Cupids, or picturesque sunsets the way it is in Valentine's Day cards. Neither should your reactions to the works be oversimplified. Allow yourself to experience the complex mix of emotions that the characters are feeling. When you do your own writing for this unit, remember that one person's emotional reactions to anything will differ (if only slightly) from the next person's. As you have in other parts of this book, use the *To Write* questions following each piece as well as the *Ideas for Writing* at the end of the chapter. These, as well as the poems and stories themselves, should give you many ideas to explore on paper.

✥✥✥✥✥

Linda Pastan

Marks

Linda Pastan's most recent books of poems are Carnival
Evening: New and Selected Poems 1968–1998 *and* The
Last Uncle. *From 1991–1994 she served as Poet Laureate
of Maryland. Her many awards include the Di Castagnola
Award, a Dylan Thomas Award, and a Pushcart Prize.
The following short poem humorously presents the feel-
ings a person has when being judged by others.*

Before Reading: Consider how frequently people judge one another
for both large and small things.

My husband gives me an A
for last night's supper,
an incomplete for my ironing,
a B plus in bed.
My son says I am average,
an average mother, but if
I put my mind to it
I could improve.
My daughter believes
in Pass/Fail and tells me
I pass. Wait 'til they learn
I'm dropping out.

To Understand

1. What is the effect of the speaker using letter grades and other
   language that suggests academic evaluation to show how she
   is being judged?

2. What emotions is the speaker feeling? Read this poem out
   loud. What tone of voice works best to convey her emotions?

3. What does the speaker's final sentence suggest? What do you think she is planning to do?

To Write

1. Sometimes we feel as if we are being judged or graded by people other than our instructors. Explain what some of these "marks" might be for you, who would give them, and your reaction to them.

Lucille Clifton

Homage to My Hips

Lucille Clifton is one of America's most loved African-American poets. Her publications include nine books of poems (most recently Blessing the Boats: New and Selected Poems 1988–2000), *a memoir, and more than sixteen children's books. She has served as Chancellor of the Academy of American Poets and has won an Emmy Award from the American Academy of Television Arts and Sciences among many other awards. Frequently anthologized, "Homage to My Hips" is an excellent example of Clifton's trademark persona, a persona described by Jocelyn Moody in the* Oxford Companion to African American Literature *as "at once both plain and extraordinary."*

Before Reading: Think about what, for you, suggests power or confidence in a person.

these hips are big hips.
they need space to
move around in.
they don't fit into little
petty places. these hips
are free hips.
they don't like to be held back.
these hips have never been enslaved,
they go where they want to go
they do what they want to do.
these hips are mighty hips.
these hips are magic hips.
I have known them
to put a spell on a man and
spin him like a top!

To Understand

1. What words or phrases suggest that this poem is about more than "hips"?

2. List the adjectives the speaker uses to describe her hips. What impression do they give?

3. Describe the speaker's voice and the emotion in it.

To Write

1. The speaker's hips seem to be a source of power. What part of you would be your source of power—hands, arms, eyes, or other? Explain.

Randall Williams

Daddy Tucked the Blanket

Randall Williams has been a writer and editor for several magazines and newspapers including the Birmingham News, Southern Exposure, *and the* Alabama Journal. *Active in his community, he has worked at the Southern Poverty Law Center and is second vice president on the Board of Directors of the Montgomery Improvement Association. As an editor and publisher, he has recently co-founded NewSouth Books. Williams first published the following essay in* The New York Times. *In it he reflects on the emotions he felt growing up in substandard housing.*

Before Reading: Consider how much of our identity comes from the physical surroundings in which we live.

About the time I turned 16, my folks began to wonder why I didn't stay home any more. I always had an excuse for them, but what I didn't say was that I had found my freedom and was getting out.

I went through four years of high school in semirural Alabama and became active in clubs and sports; I made a lot of friends and became a regular guy, if you know what I mean. But one thing was irregular about me; I managed those four years without ever having a friend visit at my house.

I was ashamed of where I lived. I had been ashamed for as long as I had been conscious of class.

We had a big family. There were several of us sleeping in one room, but that's not so bad if you get along, and we always did. As you get older, though, it gets worse.

Being poor is a humiliating experience for a young person trying hard to be accepted. Even now—several years removed—it is hard to talk about. And I resent the weakness of these words to make you feel what it was really like.

We lived in a lot of old houses. We moved a lot because we were always looking for something just a little better than what we had. You have to understand that my folks worked harder than most people. My mother was always at home, but for her that was a full-time job—and no fun, either. But my father worked his head off from the time I can remember in construction and shops. It was hard, physical work.

I tell you this to show that we weren't shiftless. No matter how much money Daddy made, we never made much progress up the social ladder. I got out thanks to a college scholarship and because I was a little more articulate than the average.

I have seen Daddy wrap copper wire through the soles of his boots to keep them together in the wintertime. He couldn't buy new boots because he had used the money for food and shoes for us. We lived like hell, but we went to school well-clothed and with a full stomach.

It really is hell to live in a house that was in bad shape 10 years before you moved in. And a big family puts a lot of wear and tear on a new house, too, so you can imagine how one goes downhill if it is teetering when you move in. But we lived in houses that were sweltering in summer and freezing in winter. I woke every morning for a year and a half with plaster on my face where it had fallen out of the ceiling during the night.

This wasn't during the Depression; this was in the late 60's and early 70's.

When we boys got old enough to learn trades in school, we would try to fix up the old houses we lived in. But have you ever tried to paint a wall that crumbled when a roller went across it? And bright paint emphasized the holes in the wall. You end up more frustrated than when you began, especially when you know that at best you might come up with only enough money to improve one of the six rooms in the house. And we might move out soon after, anyway.

The same goes for keeping a house like that clean. If you have a house full of kids and the house is deteriorating, you'll never keep it clean. Daddy used to yell at Mama about that, but she couldn't do anything. I think Daddy knew it inside, but he had to have an outlet for his rage somewhere, and at least yelling isn't as bad as hitting, which they never did to each other.

But you have a kitchen which has no counter space and no hot water, and you will have dirty dishes stacked up. That sounds like an excuse, but try it. You'll go mad from the sheer sense of futility. It's the same thing in a house with no closets. You can't keep clothes clean and rooms in order if they have to be stacked up with things.

Living in a bad house is generally worse on girls. For one thing, they traditionally help their mother with the housework. We boys could get outside and work in the field or cut wood or even play ball and forget about living conditions. The sky was still pretty.

But the girls got the pressure, and as they got older it became worse. Would they accept dates knowing they had to "receive" the young man in a dirty hallway with broken windows, peeling wallpaper and a cracked ceiling? You have to live it to understand it, but it creates a shame which drives the soul of a young person inward.

I'm thankful none of us ever blamed our parents for this, because it would have crippled our relationships. As it worked out, only the relationship between our parents was damaged. And I think the harshness which they expressed to each other was just an outlet to get rid of their anger at the trap their lives were in. It ruined their marriage because they had no one to yell at but each other. I know other families where the kids got the abuse, but we were too much loved for that.

Once I was about 16 and Mama and Daddy had had a particularly violent argument about the washing machine, which had broken down. Daddy was on the back porch—that's where the only water faucet was—trying to fix it and Mama had a washtub out there washing school clothes for the next day and they were screaming at each other.

Later that night everyone was in bed and I heard Daddy get up from the couch where he was reading. I looked out from my bed across the hall into their room. He was standing right over Mama and she was already asleep. He pulled the blanket up and tucked it around her shoulders and just stood there and tears were dropping off his cheeks and I thought I could faintly hear them splashing against the linoleum rug.

Now they're divorced.

I had courses in college where housing was discussed, but the sociologists never put enough emphasis on the impact living in substandard housing has on a person's psyche. Especially children's.

Small children have a hard time understanding poverty. They want they same things children from more affluent families have. They want the same things they see advertised on television, and they don't understand why they can't have them.

Other children can be incredibly cruel. I was in elementary school in Georgia—and this is interesting because it is the only thing I remember about that particular school—when I was about eight or nine.

After Christmas vacation had ended, my teacher made each student describe all his or her Christmas presents. I became more and more uncomfortable as the privilege passed around the room toward me. Other children were reciting the names of dolls they had been given, the kinds of bicycles and the grandeur of their games and toys. Some had lists which seemed to go on and on for hours.

It took me only a few second to tell the class that I had gotten for Christmas a belt and a pair of gloves. And then I was laughed at—because I cried—by a roomful of children and a teacher. I never forgave them, and that night I made my mother cry when I told her about it.

In retrospect, I am grateful for that moment, but I remember wanting to die at the time.

To Understand

1. What details does Williams use to show his family's poverty? List them.

2. Describe the relationships within the Williams family: the children with each other, the children with their parents, and the parents with each other. How did the family's poverty affect these relationships?

3. What emotions does the writer show in this piece? Point to places in the essay where these emotions are revealed.

4. Consider the essay's final sentence. Explain how or why the writer could be grateful for the humiliating event he had just described.

To Write

1. Write about an experience or circumstance that caused you to feel embarrassment or shame. Include, as Williams does, vivid details to show the source of your feelings. Then explain how you overcame these feelings.

Andre Dubus

Leslie in California

The author of many books of fiction, Andre Dubus received the PEN / Malamud Award, the Rea Award for Excellence in short fiction, the Jean Stein Award from the American Academy of Arts and Letters, and the MacArthur Genius Award. In 1986, while stopping to assist a disabled motorist, Dubus, a former Marine Corps captain, was struck by another car but managed to save the life of the woman he was helping. As a result of the accident, both of his legs were severely injured, one requiring amputation above the knee. His book of essays, Broken Vessels, *records his recollections of the accident and its aftermath. "Leslie in California" and other short stories can be found in his* Selected Stories. *Dubus died in 1999.*

Before Reading: Ask yourself what feelings a woman has when she is being physically abused by her husband or boyfriend. As you read, ask yourself if Leslie's emotional reactions are typical for someone in her circumstances.

When the alarm rings the room is black and gray; I smell Kevin's breath and my eye hurts and won't open. He gets out of bed, and still I smell beer in the cold air. He is naked and is dressing fast. I get up shivering in my nightgown and put on my robe and go by flashlight to the kitchen, where there is some light from the sky. Birds are singing, or whatever it is they do. I light the gas lantern and set it near the stove, and remember New England mornings with the lights on and a warm kitchen and catching the school bus. I won't have to look at my eye till the sun comes up in the bathroom. Dad was happy about us going to California; he talked about the sourdough bread and fresh fruit and vegetables all year. I put water on the stove and get bacon and eggs and milk from the ice chest. A can of beer is floating, tilting, in the ice and water; the rest are bent in the paper bag for garbage. I could count them, know how many it takes. I put on the bacon and smoke a cigarette, and when I hear him coming I stand at the stove so my back is to the door.

'Today's the day,' he says.

They are going out for sharks. They will be gone for five days, maybe more, and if he comes back with money we can have electricity again. For the first three months out here he could not get on a boat, then yesterday he found one that was short a man, so last night he celebrated.

'Hey, hon.'

I turn the bacon. He comes to me and hugs me from behind, rubbing my hips through the robe, his breath sour beer with mint.

'Let me see your eye.'

I turn around and look up at him, and he steps back. His blonde beard is damp, his eyes are bloodshot, and his mouth opens as he looks.

'Oh, hon.'

He reaches to touch it, but I jerk my face away and turn back to the skillet.

'I'll never do that again,' he says.

The bacon is curling brown. Through the window above the stove I can see the hills now, dark humps against the sky. Dad liked the Pacific, but we are miles inland and animals are out there with the birds; one morning last week a rattlesnake was on the driveway. Yesterday some men went hunting a bobcat in the hills. They say it killed a horse, and they are afraid it will kill somebody's child, but they didn't find it. How can a bobcat kill a horse? My little sister took riding lessons in New England; I watched her compete, and I was afraid, she was so small on that big animal jumping. Dad told me I tried to pet some bobcats when I was three and we lived at Camp Pendleton. He was the deer camp duty officer one Sunday, and Mom and I brought him lunch. Two bobcats were at the edge of the camp; they wanted the deer hides by the scales, and I went to them saying here, kitty, here, kitty. They just watched me, and Dad called me back.

'It wasn't you,' Kevin says. 'You know it wasn't you.'

'Who was it?'

My first words of the day and my voice sounds like dry crying. I clear my throat and grip the robe closer around it.

'I was drunk,' he says. 'You know. You know how rough it's been.'

He harpoons fish. We came across country in an old Ford he worked on till it ran like it was young again. We took turns driving and sleeping and only had to spend motel money twice. That was in October, after we got married on a fishing boat, on a clear blue Sunday on the Atlantic. We had twenty-five friends and the two families and open-faced sandwiches and deviled eggs, and beer and wine. On the way out to sea we got married, then we fished for cod and drank, and in the late afternoon we went to Dad's for a fish fry with a fiddle band. Dad has a new wife, and Mom was up from Florida with her boy friend. Out here Kevin couldn't get on a boat, and I couldn't even waitress. He did some under-the-table work: carpenter, mechanic, body work, a few days here, a few there. Now it's February, a short month.

'Hon,' he says behind me.

'It's three times.'

'Here. Let me do something for that eye.'

I hear him going to the ice chest, the ice moving in there to his big hands. I lay the bacon on the paper towel and open the door to poor out some of the grease; I look at the steps before I go out. The grease sizzles and pops on the wet grass, and there's light at the tops of the hills.

'Here,' he says, and I shut the door. I'm holding a skillet with a pot holder, and I see he's wearing his knife, and I think of all the weapons in a house: knives, cooking forks, ice picks, hammers, skillets, cleavers, wine bottles, and I wonder if I'll be one of those women. I think of this without fear, like I'm reading in the paper about somebody else dead in her kitchen. He touches my eye with ice wrapped in a dish towel.

'I have to do the eggs.'

I break them into the skillet and he stands behind me, holding the ice on my eye. His arm is over mine, and I bump it as I work the spatula.

'Not now,' I say.

I lower my face from the ice; for a while he stands behind me, and I watch the eggs and listen to the grease and his breathing and the birds, then he goes to the chest and I hear the towel and ice drop in.

'After, okay?' he says. 'Maybe the swelling will go down. Jesus, Les. I wish I wasn't going.'

'The coffee's dripped.'

He pours two cups, takes his to the table, and sits with a cigarette. I know his mouth and throat are dry, and probably he has a headache. I turn the eggs and count to four, then put them on a plate with bacon. I haven't had a hangover since I was sixteen. He likes carbohydrates when he's hung over; I walk past him, putting the plate on the table, seeing his leg and arm and shoulder, but not his face, and get a can of pork and beans from the cupboard. From there I look at the back of his head. He has a bald spot the size of a quarter. Then I go to the stove and heat the beans on a high flame, watching them, drinking coffee and smoking.

'We'll get something,' he says between bites. 'They're out there.'

Once, before I met him, he was in the water with a swordfish. He had harpooned it, and they were bringing it alongside, it was thrashing around in the water, and he tripped on some line and fell in with it.

'We'll get the lights back on,' he says. 'Go out on the town, buy you something nice. A sweater, a blouse, okay? But I wish I wasn't going today.'

'I wish you didn't hit me last night.' The juice in the beans is bubbling. 'And the two before that.'

'I'll tell you one thing, hon. I'll never get that drunk again. It's not even me anymore. I get drunk like that, and somebody crazy takes over.'

I go to his plate and scoop all the beans on his egg yellow. The coffee makes me pee, and I leave the flashlight and walk through the living room that smells of beer and ashtrays and is grey now, so I can see a beer can on the arm of a chair. I sit in the bathroom where it is darkest, and the seat is cold. I hear a car coming up the road, shifting down and turning into the driveway, then the horn. I wash my hands without looking in the mirror; in the gas light of the kitchen, and the first light from the sky, he's standing with his bag and harpoon.

'Oh, hon,' he says, and holds me tight. I put my arms around him, but just touching his back. 'Say it's okay.'

I nod, my forehead touching his chest, coming up, touching, coming up.

'That's my girl.'

He kisses me and puts his tongue in, then he's out the door, and I stand on the top step and watch him to the car. He waves and grins and gets in. I hold my hand up at the car as they back into the road, then are gone downhill past the house. The sun is showing red over the hills, and there's purple at their tops, and only a little green. They are always dry, but at night everything is wet.

I go through the living room and think about cleaning it, and open the front door and look out through the screen. The house has a shadow now, on the grass and dew. There are other houses up here, but I can't see any of them. The road goes winding up into the hills where the men hunted yesterday. I think of dressing and filling the canteen and walking, maybe all morning, I could make a sandwich and bring it in my jacket, and an orange. I open the screen and look up the road as far as I can see, before it curves around a hill in the sun. Blue is spreading across the sky. Soon the road will warm, and I think of rattlesnakes sleeping on it, and I shut the screen and look around the lawn where nothing moves.

To Understand

1. Explain why Leslie and Kevin have come to California.
2. Describe the conditions in which Leslie and Kevin live. Give details to support your assessment.
3. Explain how Leslie feels as a result of having been hit by Kevin. What clues do we have of her emotional state?
4. What kind of person is Kevin? How should we readers feel about his behavior the morning after he has hit Leslie?

To Write

1. Speculate about the future for Leslie and Kevin. The story takes place in the course of a morning, but what will life hold for them in a month, a year, or five years? Use particulars from the story to support your claims you make about their future.

Gary Soto

Oranges

Gary Soto's essay "Father" (as well as information about the author) can be found on page 30 in this book. In "Oranges," Soto presents an anecdote about young love, an emotion most readers can remember.

Before Reading: Recall how it felt, as a young person, when you were first attracted to someone else.

The first time I walked
With a girl, I was twelve,
Cold, and weighted down
With two oranges in my jacket.
December. Frost cracking
Beneath my steps, my breath
Before me, then gone,
As I walked toward
Her house, the one whose
Porch light burned yellow
Night and day, in any weather.
A dog barked at me, until
She came out pulling
At her gloves, face bright
With rouge. I smiled,
Touched her shoulder, and led
Her down the street, across
A used car lot and a line
Of newly planted trees,
Until we were breathing
Before a drugstore. We

Entered, the tiny bell
Bringing a saleslady
Down a narrow aisle of goods.
I turned to the candies
Tiered like bleachers,
And asked what she wanted—
Light in her eyes, a smile
Starting at the corners
Of her mouth. I fingered
A nickel in my pocket,
And when she lifted a chocolate
That cost a dime,
I didn't say anything.
I took the nickel from
My pocket, then an orange,
And set them quietly on
The counter. When I looked up,
The lady's eyes met mine,
And held them, knowing
Very well what it was all
About.

Outside,
A few cars hissing past,
Fog hanging like old
Coats between the trees.
I took my girl's hand
In mine for two blocks,
Then released it to let
Her unwrap the chocolate.
I peeled my orange
That was so bright against
The gray of December
That, from some distance,
Someone might have thought
I was making a fire in my hands.

To Understand

1. This poem is full of physical description. Choose two or three details and explain why they are significant to your understanding of the poem.

2. Explain what happens between the saleslady and the speaker.

3. What impression are we readers supposed to get from the poem's final images?

To Write

1. Write about a time in your youth when you first became aware of your feelings for someone else. Try to record specific details as Soto does in his poem.

Sherwood Anderson

Paper Pills

Sherwood Anderson's Winesburg Ohio, *from which this selection is taken, is one of the most influential books of short fiction in American literature. Its stories are set in the fictional small town of Winesburg, which Anderson based on his hometown of Clyde, Ohio. A veteran of the Spanish-American War, Anderson drew attention for his fierce commitment to writing, quitting his career as president of the Anderson Manufacturing Co. (and leaving his family) to devote his life to his stories. His stories are known for quirky characters, and "Paper Pills," in which a young woman chooses to marry an eccentric old doctor instead of younger suitors, is an example of this.*

Before Reading: Ask yourself why a young woman would marry someone much older than herself. You may know of a relationship like this. What does each person have to offer the other?

He was an old man with a white beard and huge nose and hands. Long before the time during which we will know him, he was a doctor and drove a jaded white horse from house to house through the streets of Winesburg. Later he married a girl who had money. She had been left a large, fertile farm when her father died. The girl was quiet, tall, and dark, and to many people she seemed very beautiful. Everyone in Winesburg wondered why she married the doctor. Within a year after the marriage she died.

The knuckles of the doctor's hands were extraordinarily large. When the hands were closed they looked like clusters of unpainted wooden balls as large as walnuts fastened together by steel rods. He smoked a cob pipe and after his wife's death sat all day in his empty office close by a window that was covered with cobwebs. He never opened the window. Once on a hot day in August he tried but found it stuck fast and after that he forgot all about it.

Winesburg had forgotten the old man, but in Doctor Reefy there were the seeds of something very fine. Alone in his musty office in the Heffner Block above the Paris Dry Goods Company's store, he worked ceaselessly, building up something that he himself destroyed. Little pyramids of truth he erected and after erecting knocked them down again that he might have the truths to erect other pyramids.

Doctor Reefy was a tall man who had worn one suit of clothes for ten years. It was frayed at the sleeves and little holes had appeared at the knees and elbows. In the office he wore also a linen duster with huge pockets into which he continually stuffed scraps of paper. After some weeks the scraps of paper became little hard round balls, and when the pockets were filled he dumped them out upon the floor. For ten years he had but one friend, another old man named John Spaniard who owned a tree nursery. Sometimes, in a playful mood, old Doctor Reefy took from his pockets a handful of the paper balls and threw them at the nursery man. "That is to confound you, you blithering old sentimentalist," he cried, shaking with laughter.

The story of Doctor Reefy and his courtship of the tall dark girl who became his wife and left her money to him is a very curious story. It is delicious, like the twisted little apples that grow in the orchards of Winesburg. In the fall one walks in the orchards and the ground is hard with frost underfoot. The apples have been taken from the trees by the pickers. They have been put in barrels and shipped to the cities where they will be eaten in apartments that are filled with books, magazines, furniture, and people. On the trees are only a few gnarled apples that the pickers have rejected. They look like the knuckles of Doctor Reefy's hands. One nibbles at them and they are delicious. Into a little round place at the side of the apple has been gathered all of its sweetness. One runs from tree to tree over the frosted ground picking the gnarled, twisted apples and filling his pockets with them. Only the few know the sweetness of the twisted apples.

The girl and Doctor Reefy began their courtship on a summer afternoon. He was forty-five then and already he had begun the practice of filling his pockets with the scraps of paper that became hard balls and were thrown away. The habit had been formed as he sat in his buggy behind the jaded white horse and went slowly along country roads. On the papers were written thoughts, ends of thoughts, beginnings of thoughts.

One by one the mind of Doctor Reefy had made the thoughts. Out of many of them he formed a truth that arose gigantic in his mind. The truth clouded the world. It became terrible and then faded away and the little thoughts began again.

The tall dark girl came to see Doctor Reefy because she was in the family way and had become frightened. She was in that condition because of a series of circumstances also curious.

The death of her father and mother and the rich acres of land that had come down to her had set a train of suitors on her heels. For two years she saw suitors almost every evening. Except two they were all alike. They talked to her of passion, and there was a strained eager quality in their voices and in their eyes when they looked at her. The two who were different were much unlike each other. One of them, a slender young man with white hands, the son of a jeweler in Winesburg, talked continually of virginity. When he was with her he was never off the subject. The other, a black-haired boy with large ears, said nothing at all but always managed to get her into the darkness, where he began to kiss her.

For a time the tall dark girl thought she would marry the jeweler's son. For hours she sat in silence listening as he talked to her and then she began to be afraid of something. Beneath his talk of virginity she began to think there was a lust greater than in all the others. At times it seemed to her that as he talked he was holding her body in his hands. She imagined him turning it slowly about in the white hands and staring at it. At night she dreamed that he had bitten into her body and that his jaws were dripping. She had the dream three times, then she became in the family way to the other one who said nothing at all but who in the moment of his passion actually did bite her shoulder so that for days the marks of his teeth showed.

After the tall dark girl came to know Doctor Reefy it seemed to her that she never wanted to leave him again. She went into his office one morning and without her saying anything he seemed to know what had happened to her.

In the office of the doctor there was a woman, the wife of the man who kept the bookstore in Winesburg. Like all old-fashioned country practitioners, Doctor Reefy pulled teeth, and the woman who waited held a handkerchief to her teeth and groaned. Her husband was with her and when the tooth was taken out they both screamed and blood ran down the woman's white dress. The tall dark girl did not pay any attention. When the woman and the man had gone the doctor smiled. "I will take you driving into the country with me," he said.

For several weeks the tall dark girl and the doctor were together almost every day. The condition that had brought her to him had passed in an illness, but she was like one who had discovered the sweetness of the twisted apples, she could not get her mind fixed again upon the round perfect fruit that is eaten in the city apartments. In the fall after the beginning of her acquaintanceship with him she married Doctor Reefy and in the following spring she died. During the winter he read to her all of the odds and ends of thoughts he had scribbled on the bits of paper. After he had read them he laughed and stuffed them away in his pockets to become round hard balls.

To Understand

1. What are readers to think of Dr. Reefy's little balls of paper with his thoughts written on them. What purpose do they serve for Dr. Reefy?

2. Why does the girl go to see Dr. Reefy?

3. Why does the girl choose Dr. Reefy instead of one of the other suitors? Describe each of the two young suitors, and convey their characteristics that turned her away.

4. Go back and read the parts about apples in paragraph five and in the last paragraph. What is Anderson trying to convey with his comments about "twisted" versus "perfect" apples?

5. Speculate about why the girl died.

To Write

1. Write a passage from the girl's point of view describing a time Dr. Reefy read for her his bit of wisdom. What does she think?

2. A relationship between two people of widely different ages is somewhat unusual. Write about any relationship or marriage that you consider unusual. Go into detail about what makes it unusual.

Robert Wrigley

Winter Love

Information about Robert Wrigley (along with his poem "A Photo of Immigrants, 1903") can be found on page 17. In the following narrative poem, Wrigley offers a traumatic and tragic love story developed from diary entries.

Before Reading: Imagine the romance of living in a winter cabin with the person you love. Imagine doing this in the late 19th century, without modern amenities, in fiercely cold conditions.

from the diary of D. D. Pye (1871–1900)

1

They talked about the cold, the cold
each one felt warm in and believed,
breath clouds so long before their faces
when they spoke—months,
indoors and out—that speech became
unwieldy, frozen, cloud talk
and vapors, a rim of ice
on the lip of the morning blanket.

They made love then, and she rose
and knelt above the chamber pot,
a fog of them rising round her thighs.
He threw back the hides and covers
so his mist in the cabin rafters
might meld and mix with hers.
Love, when they talked, was what
they said. Love, she said,

and he did too, wadding rags in the heaved log
walls, kindling in the swollen,
buckled stove. The wood into flames
unraveling was their music,
and the low reports outside
as trees exploded, frozen to their hearts.
One morning the hens were dead,
in each cloaca, a frost-tufted egg.

2

We know, for all the dead
weight of winter, they never wept
to be back in Pennsylvania, but loved, and lived
on the frozen deer he hauled back
from the snow-locked meadow, one flank
here and there worried by coyote,
hacked away and abandoned.
He never felt watched in the crystalline woods.

Over years now we see the blunder,
the misfortune: a gorgeous homestead
worthless in a trapped-out mountains,
giddy lovers awash in dreams. And winter,
the steel of it driven through their lives,
how it took hold when they touched it—
a kiss of ice in the frozen world
that held them longer than they held each other.

Until the day the fire took the cabin,
when the stove gave way to a last
overload of wood and they huddled
on the tramped-down path to the outhouse,
warmed in a way they had not been
in weeks, until that day the diary we read from,
in his crisp, formal hand, revealed
only joy, and the color of her eyes.

3

The lovers, see them now, those first few
miles in a snow so light it is never
entirely fallen, but a kind of frigid fog
swirling under the useless sun.
At camp that night, in the deep bowl
wind-scoured round a fir tree's butt,
there is terror in his words,
a darkness, malevolent and haunted.

And his love is numbed to stillness
after violent shivers, her breath fitful,
obscured to him by the wind above them
and the rumble of his heart.
He vows to change course. Damn
the distant town and houses. He knows
a spring that boils beyond the western ridgeline,
and if its heat is from hell,

if he must move aside Satan to sit there,
to lower his love in its curing waters,
if he must carry her all the snow-clogged miles,
then so be it, he will. That is all
we can read, but for one entry
one line without date, one
sentence scrawled dumbly, simply,
as though the cold at last had killed his will.

4

"She is gone." Only that, and the rest
of the story, pieced together by those
who found them, she floating naked
in the steaming waters, he hung from the spar
of a spring-killed tree, diary
beneath his clothes, frozen there,

a flimsy shield across his chest.
Nothing more, but what we imagine:

how the last morning she could not
walk, how piggyback he carried her,
wading through that sea of snow,
feeling against his neck her cheek
foolingly warmed by the touch of him,
the sweat and grunt and ache of how he walked;
his blackened fingers fumbling her
out of her clothes, his scream

at those same fingers when he held her
in the heat of the pool.
How he must have swayed with her
there, light in his arms
and caught already in the slow, unceasing turn
of the current—two lovers
dancing in the hot and buoyant waters,
below the cloud of steam that hides their breath.

To Understand

1. Reread the poem paying special attention to Wrigley's descriptions of the cold. How do these descriptions influence your emotional reaction to the poem?

2. What causes the lovers to leave the cabin? What went wrong?

3. What do you conclude about the love in this tragedy? Is there a message in this story?

To Write

1. Have you ever had to endure dangerously harsh weather conditions? Describe the most severe conditions to which you have ever been exposed.

2. Think about another story in which the characters show extreme devotion through their love. Briefly mention and describe the story; then compare and contrast it to Wrigley's poem.

Gerald W. Haslam

It's Over

For over thirty years, Gerald Haslam has been publishing fiction and nonfiction about the American West and about California in particular. Born in Bakersfield, California, and raised in Oildale, Haslam writes (frequently with great humor) about small town and rural characters. His recent books include Condor Dreams *and other fictions (from which this story is taken),* Workin' Man Blues: Country Music in California, *and* Straight White Male *(winner of the Western States Book Award). In this story, Haslam writes about a man who is reunited with a former girlfriend at a high school reunion.*

Before Reading: Think about high school reunions and the purpose they serve. If you are recently out of high school, do you think you will be eager to attend a reunion five, ten, or twenty years from now?

Over Wynonna's shoulder, I see Elaine chatting with friends, then I grin at the attractive woman standing directly in front of me and reply, "Sure, why not?"

"For old times sake," she adds. "Right, old-timer?"

"Right, old-timer," I chuckle, and we join other couples on the floor.

The first time I ever danced with Wynonna was in this same high school multipurpose room nearly thirty years ago. We were fourteen-year-old freshmen at an afternoon sock hop. There was a girls'-choice dance, and her cronies dared her to ask a boy. Saucy, she bounced to the stag line and without hesitation pulled me onto the floor.

We went steady for the next four years until she departed for college and a much larger world than Bakersfield promised, leaving me devastated by the certain knowledge that my plans—my assumptions—had been wrong and would never be realized. Shortly thereafter, I was drafted into the army and began the odyssey that would lead me from a dead-end job at a gas station to college, then graduate school. Nearly thirty years ago it had started in this very room. . .

It's over.
    All over,
        And soon somebody else
            will make a fuss over you
              but how about me?

As a singer purrs, my high school love and I move together, facing one another, bodies still familiar. Despite my casual smile, I am breathless. "Your wife is lovely, Nicky," Wynonna smiles. "She really is. I'd heard that, but she's even nicer and prettier than I expected."

"Elaine's a great gal."

"You've been lucky."

"Yeah, I have . . . we have. And you?" It is an unintentionally thoughtless question. She's been married three times, I know.

Without hesitation, she grins. "Mixed bag. All big shots, dot the o's, if you get my meaning." Her legal practice in Santa Barbara is elite, mutual friends have told me. Little wonder she encounters big shots, dotted o's or not.

"I'm sorry."

"*You're* sorry"; she raises her eyebrows. Her voice is thick with wine, and mine is too, I guess. We're well into the evening.

From the moment Wynonna entered the reunion—our class's twenty-fifth—I had fought not to stare at her: It had been so long and she looked so trim, so youthful, so . . . yes . . . so expensive. While she hugged old chums and laughed with them, I managed to exchange a quick handshake with her, a moment of eye contact, while I sensed the gaze of others on us, then drifted away to those old friends with whom Elaine and I remained close.

So many years ago, Wynonna and I had explored life's currents and channels, learned together some mysterious lessons that have not left me. We had, of course, invented sex—secret and overwhelming—and it became deliciously central to our relationship. But there had been another, less understandable, less escapable bonding: not sister and brother, something deeper and more enduring. It can still swoop my stomach at odd times.

"Do you remember our first dance, Nicky?" she asks. My wife—everyone else, in fact—calls me Nick.

"Yeah." She should ask if I remember breathing.

"You asked me right in this room when we were freshmen."

"No, it was girls' choice. You asked me."

"No, I didn't. *You* asked me," she giggles.

There had been hints late in our senior year—she had less time for dates, we had no more noon rendezvous, my phone calls went increasingly unanswered—signs that her interests were turning from me, and the plans we'd made, toward the universities that beckoned a top student. Although my job at the service station paid little, I had simply and naively assumed that we'd graduate, marry, and live happily ever after, as the popular songs promised.

One terrible Saturday afternoon Wynonna had emerged with an icy face from her house to greet me. She looked delicious in pink shorts and a white blouse while I stood on her porch, fresh from work, wearing an oil-stained shirt with "Nick" sewn on one pocket. I don't think I'd ever wanted to hold her more, but she curtly informed me that she would leave the following August to attend the University of California in Los Angeles. Our marriage would have to wait until after she graduated. Her tone told me far more, and that evening I picked a fistfight with a guy I didn't know.

"You have four kids now?" she asks.

"Two boys, Dan and Nick; two girls, Kelly and Kit."

"Do you worry about your girls? You sure made my folks worry about me—for good reason, as it turned out." Her laugh is deep and intimate.

"No, I really don't, not about *that* anyway. Or about my boys either. What we did all seems pretty innocent today . . . so—what's the word?—so *sincere*, so *earnest* . . ."

"Yes," she replies, and her eyes leave mine. Her voice has suddenly lost its happy edge.

"And your family?" I ask, changing the subject.

"I have one boy, Bradley, from my first marriage. He's at Dartmouth."

"Danny and Kelly are both attending Cal Poly."

"Oh," she says with—or do I merely imagine—the tiniest hint of condescension.

If we had actually married immediately after high school, I wouldn't have been drafted, wouldn't have qualified for the GI Bill and wouldn't have been able to attend college; I certainly wouldn't have become principal of the local junior high school. What either of us would have been doing now is anyone's guess. Whether I'd have been the first of a string of husbands, whether she'd be another frustrated housewife or ex-wife struggling through college in her forties, whether we'd be mired in debt and hopelessness and mutual disdain or be one of those rare and enchanting couples who somehow have managed to keep it all together—it's anybody's guess.

While the music sweeps, she says, "My folks were relieved to be rid of you." Her eyes still look away, her voice remains deep.

"Your folks? I thought they liked me."

"They said you were going nowhere, that you were irresponsible and didn't have any ambition. They even said you'd probably get tired of me and leave me."

"Your folks? They said that? I *really* thought they liked me." I have never heard this before and am both shocked and pained by it.

"Oh, they did. But they *loved* me, and they were ambitious for me. They wanted me to have chances they didn't have. You were an obstacle."

Still uncomfortable about what she has revealed, I reply, "Not much of one, as it turned out."

"They said you weren't dumb but that you weren't motivated."

"I was young and in love," I point out, having to clear my thickening throat.

"Yes," she says, her voice softer. We fall silent once more, and her head is suddenly on my shoulder, her cheek next to mine. "Do you remember when we broke up, Nicky?" she breathes into my ear.

"I remember that we unraveled like a bad braid."

"No. I mean what happened at Don and Donna's party?"

We had been at Don Smith and Donna Pasquinni's wedding reception, just before Wynonna left for UCLA. We had danced—the last time until tonight—then sipped champagne at a corner table while she delicately explained that, after talking with her mother, she had decided that each of us should date others while she was away at school. "Is that all?" I asked. "Do we do anything besides 'date'?"

"I wouldn't do *that* with anyone else." Her eyes glistened, and one hand reached across the table and took mine, but I was receiving another, darker message, the final shredding of my dream.

"Do you really want someone else's babies?" I demanded in a cracking voice. Irrational as it seems now, it was my heart's most honest cry. I'd sensed even before this conversation that other forces now determined her life and that I was powerless, but at least I could speak what I felt.

Her eyes flashed. "I didn't say *breed,* I said *date,*" she snapped, her rationality and resolve negating my plea.

A moment later, I stood and said, "I've gotta go."

"I want to stay till Donna throws her bouquet." Wynonna remained seated. My eyes were imploring, hers implacable.

"Fine," I said. "I'll see you." I turned and walked away, my heart crumbling, my pride intact. Yearning immediately dislodged my innards as I drove away, a desolation I would not fully escape for years, and I kept glancing at the rearview mirror hoping that she'd emerge from the increasingly distant doorway to join me, but she didn't. For the first time since childhood, I wept.

Wynonna's voice grows even softer, her breath warmer on my ear where her lips brush. "I wanted your baby, Nicky, I really did, but my folks put so much pressure on me. . ." I feel that odd-but-not-unfamiliar sensation of her warm tears wetting my cheek. There is a sigh so deep that I seem to feel her lighten, then she adds, "I still want it."

Our bodies are moving together, her breath lurching into my ear and that distant, familiar passion again dislodges my heart. I cannot breathe. I cannot move my head to reply. And I cannot allow the music to stop.

But it does.

To Understand

1. Nick mentions Wynonna's legal practice as well as his own profession as a junior high school principal. How important to the story are their respective careers?

2. Why were Wynonna's parents concerned about Nick? Were they justified in their worries?

3. What do you believe the writer wants us to conclude about Nick and Wynonna's young love and their feelings for each other thirty years later?

To Write

1. Write about the benefits and/or shortcomings of high school reunions. Do people always enjoy themselves at these events? Why do we have them?

William Matthews

Loyal

Before his death in 1997, William Matthews published eleven books of poetry including A Happy Childhood, *winner of the National Book Critics Circle Award, and* Selected Poems and Translations 1969–1991. *A twelfth collection,* After All: Last Poems, *was published posthumously. Matthews taught at several colleges and served as president of Associated Writing Programs and of the Poetry Society of America.*

Before Reading: Consider the one-word title. What is loyalty? Where do we find it?

They gave him an overdose
of anesthetic, and its fog
shut down his heart in seconds.
I tried to hold him, but he was
somewhere else. For so much of love
one of the principles is missing,
it's no wonder we confuse love
with longing. Oh I was thick
with both. I wanted my dog
to live forever and while I was
working on impossibilities
I wanted to live forever, too.
I wanted company and to be alone.
I wanted to know how they trash
a stiff ninety-five pound dog
and I paid them to do it
and not tell me. What else?
I wanted a letter of apology
delivered by decrepit hand,

by someone shattered for each time
I'd had to eat pure pain. I wanted
to weep, not "like a baby,"
in gulps and breath-stretching
howls, but steadily, like an adult,
according to the fiction
that there is work to be done,
and almost inconsolably.

To Understand

1. The speaker says, "it's no wonder we confuse love / with longing." What is the difference?
2. Notice how many sentences begin with "I wanted. . . ." Sum up what the speaker wants.
3. Near the end the speaker says he wants to weep "like an adult. . . ." What does he mean by this?

To Write

1. This poem illustrates how attached we can become to our pets. Write about why we have such strong feelings for animals.

Brian Doyle

Two on Two

Brian Doyle, editor of Portland Magazine *at the University of Portland (Oregon), is the author of four collections of essays, most recently* Leaping: Revelations & Epiphanies. *His essays appear in the* Best American Essays *anthologies of 1998, 1999, and 2003. His essay here begins as a fable, ends as a prayer, is deliberately written in the headlong fashion we tell tales to each other, and uses loss to sing of love.*

Before Reading: Ask yourself how important it is for parents to play with their children.

Once upon a time, a long time ago, I rambled through thickets of brawny power forwards and quicksilver cocksure guards and rooted ancient centers, trying to slide smoothly to the hoop, trying to find space in the crowd to get off my shot, trying to maneuver at high speed with the ball around corners and hips and sudden angry elbows, the elbows of 20 years of men in grade school high school college the park the playground the men's league the noon league the summer league game, men as high as the 7-foot center I met violently during a summer league game, men as able as the college and professional players I was hammered by in playgrounds, men as fierce as the fellow who once took off his sweats and laid his shotgun down by his cap before he trotted onto the court.

I got hurt, everyone does eventually; I got hurt enough to quit; back pains then back surgery then more surgeries; it was quit or walk, now I walk.

The game receded, fell away, a part of me sliding into the dark like a rocket stage no longer part of the mission.

Now I am married and here come my children; my
lovely dark and thoughtful daughter and then three
years later suddenly my squirming twin electric sons and
now my daughter is 4 and my sons are 1 each and yesterday my daughter and I played two on two against my
sons on the lovely burnished oak floor of our dining room,
the boys who just learned to walk staggering across the
floor like drunken sailors and falling at the slightest
touch, my daughter loud lanky in her orange socks sliding from place to place without benefit of a dribble but
there is no referee only me on my knees, dribbling behind
my back and trick dribbling through the plump legs of
the boys, their diapers sagging, my daughter shrieking
with glee, the boys confused and excited, and I am weeping weeping weeping, in love with my perfect magic children, with the feel of the bright red plastic tiny ball
spinning in my hands, my arms at home in the old motions, my head and shoulders snapping fakes on the boys,
who laugh; I pick up a loose ball near the dining room
table and shuffle so slowly so slowly on my knees toward
the toy basket 8 feet away, a mile, 100 miles, my children
brushing against my thighs and shoulders like dreams
like birds; Joe staggers toward me, reaches for the ball, I
wrap it around my back to my left hand, which picks up
rapid dribble, Joe loses balance and grabs my hair, Lily
slides by suddenly and cuts Joe cleanly away, he takes a
couple of hairs with him as he and Lily disappear in a
tangle of limbs and laughs, a terrific moving pick, I would
stop to admire it but here comes big Liam, lumbering
along toward the ball as alluring and bright as the sun;
crossover dribble back to my right hand, Liam drops like
a stone, he spins on his bottom to stay with the play, I
palm ball, show-fake and lean into short fallaway from 4
feet away, ball hits rim of basket and bounces straight up
in the air, Lily slides back into picture and grabs my
right hand but I lean east and with the left hand catch
and slam the ball into the basket all in one motion; and it

bounces off a purple plastic duck and rolls away again under the table, and I lie there on the floor as Joe pulls on my sock and Lily sits on my chest and Liam ever so gently so meticulously so daintily takes off my glasses, and I am happier than I have ever been, ever and ever, amen.

To Understand

1. The essay begins with the familiar "Once upon a time, a long time ago" and ends with "ever and ever, amen." What is the effect of this opening and closing?

2. The author starts by describing his experiences playing basketball with adults. How important is this description in relation to his account of playing with his children?

3. Describe Doyle's sentence style. Are these the kinds of sentences you would use in your academic writing? What effect do these sentences have on the rhythm of Doyle's writing and on his subject?

To Write

1. Write about how much your parents played with you. Whether they played with you a lot or a little, explain how that has influenced you as an adult.

The Emotional Side: Ideas for Writing

1. Write a paper about one person you know who seems to exemplify a particular emotion: love, greed, jealousy, or other. Be sure to clearly identify the emotion, and give examples of what this person has done to embody the emotion.

2. Write about a particular event that brought out a strong emotional response in you—a graduation, a wedding, the first day of school, a final exam, a trip to the doctor, a walk up a mountain, or other—and convey for your reader what components of that event caused the emotion for you. Go beyond simply telling what happened in the event by breaking the event down into certain aspects that led to what you felt.

3. Write a paper in which you define an emotion. You might title your paper "What is Greed?" or "What is Parental Love?" or "What is Shame?" Start by brainstorming examples that illustrate the emotion you've chosen; then formulate your definition based on the common qualities in your examples.

4. What emotion do you most dislike in others? Greed, envy, jealousy, hatred, pity? Write a paper identifying that emotion and explaining the reasons you so dislike it.

5. Write a paper explaining in what circumstances it is fine to allow our emotions to control our behavior. How would things be different if our reactions were always based on logic or function? To write this paper, think about situations in which emotional thinking is frequently not valued (in most academic classes, for instance) and, conversely, situations in which emotional reactions are considered normal (on a date or at a family reunion).

6

Work and Dreams

Work and Dreams

Think of the many ways the word *work* is used in our everyday speech. We go to work. We do homework, house work, field work, and yard work. We work on our cars, our backswings, our homes, and our relationships. One could argue that we spend most of our time in work-related activity. This may be why people have such varied emotional reactions to this word. Some people cringe at the mention of work; others feel pride at having done it. Some feel hard work is a necessary component in building character; others try to avoid it at all cost.

What *is* work? In physics, work is a force acted upon an object that causes that object to be displaced. It's a transfer of energy from one thing to another. Although that definition has its special applications in the world of science, it is also a nice starting point for thinking about what work is in everyday life. Every kind of work requires energy or effort to get something accomplished. This effort is something we've all experienced in various ways. Because it's universal, writers have explored this topic and have given us new ways to think about our work and what it means to us.

This chapter includes

- a poem exploring the nature of work;
- an essay in which the author argues against giving children chores;
- a short story in which an old man tells some children about the days of slavery in our country;
- a poem about women who work in a cannery;
- an essay in which the author recalls his childhood days as a migrant field worker

These essays, short stories, and poems will give you a context for thinking about the many kinds of work you do in your life. This context may or may not make your work easier, but you should come away from these readings with a stronger understanding of the many ways work is an integral part of nearly everything we do. You will also increase your understanding by writing about work. Use the *To Write* questions following the readings as well as the *Ideas for Writing* topics at the end of the chapter to further your thinking about work as it relates to your own life and what you have experienced.

Philip Levine

What Work Is

The son of Russian-Jewish immigrants, Philip Levine was born in Detroit, Michigan in 1928. His poems address the lives of the working class—from Detroit to Fresno, California, where he taught for many years at Fresno State University. His books of poems have won many awards including the Pulitzer Prize for The Simple Truth, *the National Book Award for* What Work Is *(from which the title poem is presented here), and the National Book Critics Circle Award for* Ashes: Poems New and Old. *One of the most highly regarded poets in America, Levine lives and writes in both New York and in Fresno. His most recent book is* The Mercy.

Before Reading: Think about the different ways the word "work" might be defined. As you read, try to understand what Levine is saying about work.

We stand in the rain in a long line
waiting at Ford Highland Park. For work.
You know what work is—if you're
old enough to read this you know what
work is, although you may not do it.
Forget you. This is about waiting,
shifting from one foot to another.
Feeling the light rain falling like mist
into your hair, blurring your vision
until you think you see your own brother
ahead of you, maybe ten places.
You rub your glasses with your fingers,
and of course it's someone else's brother,
narrower across the shoulders than
yours but with the same sad slouch, the grin

that does not hide the stubbornness,
the sad refusal to give in to
rain, to the hours wasted waiting,
to the knowledge that somewhere ahead
a man is waiting who will say, "No,
we're not hiring today," for any
reason he wants. You love your brother,
now suddenly you can hardly stand
the love flooding you for your brother,
who's not beside you or behind or
ahead because he's home trying to
sleep off a miserable night shift
at Cadillac so he can get up
before noon to study his German.
Works eight hours a night so he can sing
Wagner, the opera you hate most,
the worst music ever invented.
How long has it been since you told him
you love him, held his wide shoulders,
opened your eyes wide and said those words,
and maybe kissed his cheek? You've never
done something so simple, so obvious,
not because you're too young or too dumb,
not because you're jealous or even mean
or incapable of crying in
the presence of another man, no,
just because you don't know what work is.

To Understand

1. What is the speaker saying about brothers? What kind of relationship do the "you" character and his brother have?

2. Explain why early in the poem the speaker says, "You know what work is . . ." and in the final line makes the opposite statement.

3. What *is* work according to this poem? Give a summary definition, but try not to oversimplify.

4. What does this poem say about love?

To Write

1. Write a paragraph or more of your own using the title "What Work Is."

⚜

Paul Zimmer

Work

Paul Zimmer has written more than a dozen books of poems including The Great Bird of Love, Family Reunion: Selected and New Poems *(from which this poem is taken), and* Crossing to Sunlight: Selected Poems. *Zimmer lives on a rural farm in Wisconsin and has recently published a book of essays,* After the Fire. *In this poem, Zimmer presents what may be for some readers a surprising attitude about work.*

Before Reading: Ask yourself how most people feel about work. Who likes work? Who merely tolerates it? Who hates it?

To have done it thirty years
Without question! Yet I tell myself
I am grateful for all work;
At noon in my air-conditioned office
With a sandwich and a poem,
I try to recollect nature;
But a clerk comes in with papers
To be signed. I tell myself
The disruption does not matter;
It is all work: computer runs,
Contracts, invoices, poems; the same
As breaking shells, hunting woods,
Making pots or gathering grain.
Jazzmen even refer to sex as work.
Some primitive people believe
That death is work. When my wife asks
What I am doing, I always answer,
I am working, working, working.

Now I know I will spend the rest
Of my life trying for perfect work,
A work as rare as aurora borealis,
So fine it will make all other work
Seem true, that it will last as long
As words will last. At home
In my room, I mumble to myself
Over my poems; over supper I talk
To myself; as I carpenter or paint
Or carry the groceries up the steps
I am speaking words to myself.
"What are you doing?" my children ask.
I am working, working, working.

To Understand

1. What is the speaker's attitude toward work? Point to places in the poem that lead you to your answer.

2. The speaker says he will be "trying for perfect work" the rest of his life. What does he mean by this?

3. Throughout much of the poem, the speaker refers to writing poems as work. Explain how any kind of writing can be thought of as work.

To Write

1. The speaker says he is "grateful for all work." What is your attitude about work? Write about whether you are grateful for work and why.

Katherine Ann Porter

The Witness

Katherine Ann Porter's collections of stories include Flowering Judas; Pale Horse, Pale Rider; *and* The Leaning Tower *(which includes "The Witness"). She wrote one novel,* Ship of Fools, *and it was made into an Oscar-winning film starring Vivien Leigh. Her* Collected Stories *was awarded both the Pulitzer Prize and the National Book Award. Porter died in 1980.*

In the following story, the main character, Uncle Jimbilly, tells some children about how difficult life was for slaves in this country.

Before Reading: Consider what you know about slavery in the United States. Do slave times seem a long time ago? Where have you learned about slavery?

Uncle Jimbilly was so old and had spent so many years bowed over things, putting them together and taking them apart, making them over and making them do, he was bent almost in double. His hands were closed and stiff from gripping objects tightly, while he worked at them, and they could not open altogether even if a child took the thick black fingers and tried to turn them back. He hobbled on a stick; his purplish skull showed through patches in his wool, which had turned greenish gray and looked as if the moths had got at it.

He mended harness and put half soles on the other Negroes' shoes, he built fences and chicken coops and barn doors; he stretched wires and put in new window panes and fixed sagging hinges and patched up roofs; he repaired carriage tops and cranky plows. Also he had a gift for carving miniature tombstones out of blocks of wood;

give him almost any kind of piece of wood and he could turn out a tombstone, shaped like the real ones, with carving, and a name and date on it if they were needed. They were often needed, for some small beast or birds was always dying and having to be buried with proper ceremonies: the cart draped as a hearse, a shoe-box coffin with a pall over it, a profuse floral outlay, and, of course, a tombstone. As he worked, turning the long blade of his bowie knife deftly in circles to cut a flower, whittling and smoothing the back and sides, stopping now and then to hold it at arm's length and examine it with one eye closed, Uncle Jimbilly would talk in a low, broken, abstract murmur, as if to himself; but he was really saying something he meant one to hear. Sometimes it would be an incomprehensible ghost story; listen ever so carefully, at the end it was impossible to decide whether Uncle Jimbilly himself had seen the ghost, whether it was a real ghost at all, or only another man dressed like one; and he dwelt much on the horrors of slave times.

"Dey used to take 'em out and tie 'em down and whup 'em," he muttered, "wid gret big leather strops inch thick long as yo' ahm, wid round holes bored in 'em so's evey time dey hit 'em de hide and de meat done come off dey bones in little round chunks. And wen dey had whupped 'em wid de strop till dey backs was all raw and bloody, dey spread dry cawnshucks on dey backs and set 'em afire and pahched 'em and den dey poured vinega all ovah 'em . . . Yassuh. And den, the ve'y nex day dey'd got to git back to work in the fiels or dey'd do the same thing right ovah agin. Yassah. Dat was it. If dey didn't git back to work dey got it all right ovah agin."

The children—three of them: a serious, prissy older girl of ten, a thoughtful sad looking boy of eight, and a quick flighty little girl of six—sat disposed around Uncle Jimbilly and listened with faint tinglings of embarrassment. They knew, of course, that once upon a time Negroes had been slaves; but they had all been freed long ago and were

now only servants. It was hard to realize that Uncle Jimbilly had been born in slavery, as the Negroes were always
saying. The children thought that Uncle Jimbilly had got
over his slavery very well. Since they had known him, he
had never done a single thing that anyone told him to do.
He did his work just as he pleased and when he pleased. If
you wanted a tombstone, you had to be very careful about
the way you asked for it. Nothing could have been more
impersonal and faraway than his tone and manner of talking about slavery, but they wriggled a little and felt guilty.
Paul would have changed the subject, but Miranda, the little quick one, wanted to know the worst. "Did they act like
that to you, Uncle Jimbilly?" she asked.

"No, *mam*," said Uncle Jimbilly. "Now whut name you
want on dis one? Dey nevah did. Dey done 'em dat way
in the rice swamps. I always worked right here close to
the house or in town with Miss Sophia. Down in the
swamps . . ."

"Didn't they ever die, Uncle Jimbilly?" asked Paul

"Cose dey died," said Uncle Jimbilly, "cose dey died—
dey died," he went on pursing his mouth gloomily, "by de
thousands and tens upon thousands."

"Can you carve 'Safe in Heaven' on that, Uncle Jimbilly?"
asked Maria in her pleasant, mincing voice.

"To put over a tame jackrabbit, Missy?" asked Uncle
Jimbilly indignantly. He was very religious. "A heathen
like dat? No, *mam*. In de swamps dey used to stake 'em
out all day and all night, and all day and all night and all
day wid dey hans and feet tied so dey couldn't scretch
and let de muskeeters eat 'em alive. De muskeeters 'ud
bite 'em tell dey was all swole up like a balloon all over,
and you could heah 'em howlin and prayin all ovah the
swamp. Yassuh. Dat was it. And nary a drop of watah noh
a moufful of braid . . . Yassuh, dat's it. Lawd, day done it.
Hosanna! Now take dis yere tombstone and don' bother
me no more . . . or I'll . . ."

Uncle Jimbilly was apt to be suddenly annoyed and you never knew why. He was easily put out about things, but his threats were always so exorbitant that not even the most credulous child could be terrified by them. He was always going to do something quite horrible to somebody and then he was going to dispose of the remains in a revolting manner. He was going to skin somebody alive and nail the hide on the barn door, or he was just getting ready to cut off somebody's ears with a hatchet and pin them on Bongo, the crop-eared brindle dog. He was often all prepared in his mind to pull somebody's teeth and make a set of false teeth for Ole Man Ronk . . . Ole Man Ronk was a tramp who had been living all summer in the little cabin behind the smokehouse. He got his rations along with the Negroes and sat all day mumbling his naked gums. He had skimpy black whiskers which appeared to be set in wax, and angry red eyelids. He took morphine, it was said; but what morphine might be, or how he took it, or why, no one seemed to know . . . Nothing could have been more unpleasant than the notion that one's teeth might be given to Ole Man Ronk.

The reason why Uncle Jimbilly never did any of these things he threatened was, he said, because he never could get round to them. He always had so much other work on hand he never seemed to get caught up on it. But some day, somebody was going to get a mighty big surprise, and meanwhile everybody had better look out.

To Understand

1. Review the opening description of Uncle Jimbilly. What can you conclude about his character based on this description?

2. What kind of work does Uncle Jimbilly do? What should we readers conclude about this work?

3. How do the children respond to Uncle Jimbilly's stories about slave times? What does their perspective add to the story?

4. Near the end of the story we find that Uncle Jimbilly frequently makes idle threats to those around him, threats "so exorbitant that not even the most credulous child could be terrified by them." Why does he make these threats?

5. Consider the title. Who is witnessing in this story?

To Write

1. Think about some of the elderly people in your life—grandparents, great aunts, or great uncles. What kind of work did they do when they were young? Write about how, as a young person yourself, you viewed their work: with admiration, confusion, or disinterestedness.

Jane Smiley

The Case Against Chores

Jane Smiley's novel, A Thousand Acres, *won the Pulitzer Prize in 1980. Her other books include* The Age of Grief, The Greenlanders, Moo, *and* Horse Heaven. *She has written essays for many magazines and is publishing a nonfiction book on the life of Charles Dickens. Smiley taught for years at Iowa State University and now raises horses in California. In this essay, Smiley argues that chores teach children the wrong lessons about work.*

Before Reading: Recall the chores (if any) you did as a child. Do you think they were valuable activities?

I've lived in the upper Midwest for twenty-one years now, and I'm here to tell you that the pressure to put your children to work is unrelenting. So far I've squirmed out from under it, and my daughters have led a life of almost tropical idleness, much to their benefit. My son, however, may not be so lucky. His father was himself raised in Iowa and put to work at an early age, and you never know when, in spite of all my husband's best intentions, that early training might kick in.

Although "chores" are so sacred in my neck of the woods that almost no one ever discusses their purpose, I have over the years gleaned some of the reasons parents give for assigning them. I'm not impressed. Mostly the reasons have to do with developing good work habits or, in the absence of good work habits, at least habits of working. No such thing as a free lunch, any job worth doing is worth doing right, work before play, all of that. According to this reasoning, the world is full of jobs that no one wants to do. If we divide them up and get them over with, then we can go on with pastimes we like. If we do them "right," then we won't have to do them again. Lots of times, though, in a family, that *we* doesn't operate. The operative word is *you*. The practical result of almost every child labor scheme that I've witnessed is the child doing the dirty work and the parent getting the fun: Mom cooks and Sis does the dishes; the parents plan and plant the garden, the kids weed it. To me, what this teaches the child is the lesson of alienated labor; not to love the work but to get it over with; not to feel pride in one's contribution but to feel resentment at the waste of one's time.

Another goal of chores: the child contributes to the work of maintaining the family. According to this rationale, the child comes to understand what it takes to have a family, and to feel that he or she is an important, even indispensable member of it. But come on. Would you really want to feel loved primarily because you're the one who gets the floors mopped? Wouldn't you rather feel that your family's love simply exists all around you, no matter what your contribution? And don't the parents love their children anyway, whether the children vacuum or not? Why lie about it just to get the housework done? Let's be frank about the other half of the equation too. In this day and age, it doesn't take much work at all to manage a household, at least in the middle class—maybe four hours a week to clean the house and another four to throw the laundry into the washing machine, move it to the dryer, and fold it. Is it really good to set the sort of example my former neighbors used to set, of mopping the floor every two days, cleaning the toilets every week, vacuuming every day, dusting, dusting, dusting? Didn't they have anything better to do than serve their house?

Let me confess that I wasn't expected to lift a finger when I was growing up. Even when my mother had a full-time job, she cleaned up after me, as did my grandmother. Later there was a housekeeper. I would leave my room in a mess when I headed off for school and find it miraculously neat when I returned. Once in a while I vacuumed, just because I liked the pattern the Hoover made on the carpet. I did learn to run water in my cereal bowl before setting it in the sink.

Where I discovered work was at the stable, and, in fact, there is no housework like horsework. You've got to clean the horses' stalls, feed them, groom them, tack them up, wrap their legs, exercise them, turn them out, and catch them. You've got to clip them and shave them. You have to sweep the aisle, clean your tack and your boots, carry bales of hay and buckets of water. Minimal horsekeeping, rising just to the level of humaneness, requires many more hours than making a few beds, and horsework turned out to be a good preparation for the real work of adulthood, which is rearing children. It was a good preparation not only because it was similar in many ways but also because my desire to do it, and to do a good job of it, grew out of my love and interest in my horse. I can't say that cleaning out her bucket when she manured in it was any actual joy, but I knew she wasn't going to do it herself. I saw the purpose of my labor, and I wasn't alienated from it.

Probably to the surprise of some of those who knew me as a child, I have turned out to be gainfully employed. I remember when I was in seventh grade, one of my teachers said to me, strongly disapproving, "The trouble with you is you do only what you want to do!" That continues to be the trouble with me, except that over the years I have wanted to do more and more.

My husband worked hard as a child, out-Iowa-ing the Iowans, if such a thing is possible. His dad had him mixing cement with a stick when he was five, pushing wheelbarrows not long after. It's a long sad tale on the order of two miles to school and both ways uphill. The result is, he's a great worker, much better than I am, but all the while he's doing it he wishes he weren't. He thinks of it as work; he's torn between doing a good job and longing not to be doing it at all. Later, when he's out on the golf course, where he really wants to be, he feels a little guilty, knowing there's work that should have been done before he gave in and took advantage of the beautiful day.

Good work is not the work we assign children but the work they want to do, whether it's reading in bed (where would I be today if my parents had rousted me out and put me to scrubbing floors?) or cleaning their rooms or practicing the flute or making roasted potatoes with rosemary and Parmesan for the family dinner. It's good for a teenager to suddenly decide that the bathtub is so disgusting she'd better clean it herself. I admit that for the parent, this can involve years of waiting. But if she doesn't want to wait, she can always spend her time dusting.

To Understand

1. Review this essay and list Smiley's reasons for believing children should not be assigned chores.

2. How does Smiley's husband view the issue of children doing chores? What are Smiley's objections to his work ethic?

3. Smiley confesses that she did no chores as a child. How does this influence your reaction to her argument?

4. Smiley says, "Good work is not the work we assign children but the work they want to do." Explain what she means.

To Write

1. Do you agree with Smiley's argument? Offer specific reasons for your response, and address the ideas Smiley puts forth.

Francisco Jiminez

The Circuit

Francisco Jiminez has written The Circuit: Stories from the Life of a Migrant Child *and* Breaking Through. *The title essay from his first collection, the following story recounts how Jiminez and his family moved from field to field, with few possessions, working in agriculture—and, as a result, how Jiminez craved his education.*

Before Reading: Consider what you know about our country's migrant agricultural workers. What opportunities do they have? What obstacles do they face?

It was that time of year again. Ito, the strawberry sharecropper, did not smile. It was natural. The peak of the strawberry season was over and the last few days the workers, most of them braceros, were not picking as many boxes as they had during the months of June and July.

As the last days of August disappeared, so did the number of braceros. Sunday, only one—the best picker—came to work. I liked him. Sometimes we talked for our half-hour lunch break. That is how I found out he is from Jalisco, the same state in Mexico my family was from. That Sunday was the last time I saw him.

When the sun had tired and sunk behind the mountains, Ito signaled us that it was time to go home. "Ya esora," he yelled in his broken Spanish. Those were the words I waited for twelve hours a day, every day, seven days a week, week after week. And the thought of not hearing them again saddened me.

As we drove home Papá did not say a word. With both hands on the wheel, he stared at the dirt road. My older brother, Roberto, was also silent. He leaned his head back and closed his eyes. Once in a while he cleared from his throat the dust that blew in from outside.

Yes, it was that time of year. When I opened the front door to the shack, I stopped. Everything we owned was neatly packed in cardboard boxes. Suddenly I felt even more the weight of hours, days, weeks, and months of work. I sat down on a box. The thought of having to move to Fresno and knowing what was in store for me there brought tears to my eyes.

That night I could not sleep. I lay in bed thinking about how much I hated this move.

A little before 5 o'clock in the morning, Papá woke everyone up. A few minutes later, the yelling and screaming of my little brothers and sisters, for whom the move was a great adventure, broke the silence of dawn. Shortly, the barking of dogs accompanied them.

While we packed the breakfast dishes, Papá went outside to start the "Carcanchita." That was the name Papá gave his old '38 black Plymouth. He bought it in a used car lot in Santa Rosa in the winter of 1949. Papá was very proud of his little jalopy. He had the right to be proud of it. He spent a lot of time looking at other cars before buying this one. When he finally chose the "Carcanchita," he checked it thoroughly before driving it out of the car lot. He examined every inch of the car. He listened to the motor, tilting his head from side to side like a parrot, trying to detect any noises that spelled car trouble. After being satisfied with the looks and sounds of the car, Papá then insisted on knowing who the original owner was. He never did find out from the car salesman, but he bought the car anyway. Papá figured the original owner must have been an important man because behind the rear seat of the car he found a blue necktie.

Papá parked the car out in front and left the motor running. "Listo," he yelled. Without saying a word, Roberto and I began to carry the boxes out to the car. Roberto carried the two big boxes and I carried the two smaller ones. Papá then threw the mattress on top of the car roof and tied it with ropes to the front and rear bumpers.

Everything was packed except Mamá's pot. It was an old large galvanized pot she had picked up at an army surplus store in Santa María the year I was born. The pot had many dents and nicks, and the more dents and nicks it acquired the more Mamá liked it. "Mi olla," she used to say proudly.

I held the door open as Mamá carefully carried out her pot by both handles, making sure not to spill the cooled beans. When she got to the car, Papá reached out to help her with it. Roberto opened the rear car door and Papá gently placed it on the floor behind the front seat. All of us then climbed in. Papá sighed, wiped the sweat off his forehead with his sleeve, and said wearily: "Es todo."

As we drove away, I felt a lump in my throat. I turned around and looked at our little shack for the last time.

At sunset we drove into the labor camp near Fresno. Since Papá did not speak English, Mamá asked the camp foreman if he needed any more workers. "We don't need no more," said the foreman, scratching his head. "Check with Sullivan down the road. Can't miss him. He lives in a big white house with a fence around it."

When we got there, Mamá walked up to the house. She went through a white gate, past a row of rose bushes, up the stairs to the front door. She rang the doorbell. The porch light went on and a tall husky man came out. They exchanged a few words. After the man went in, Mamá clasped her hands and hurried back to the car. "We have work! Mr. Sullivan said we can stay there the whole season," she said, gasping and pointing to an old garage near the stables.

The garage was worn out by the years. It had no windows. The walls, eaten by termites, strained to support the roof full of holes. The dirt floor, populated by earth worms, looked like a gray road map. That night, by the light of a kerosene lamp, we unpacked and cleaned our new home. Roberto swept away the loose dirt, leaving the hard ground. Papá plugged up the holes in the walls with old newspapers and tin can tops. Mamá fed my little brothers and sisters. Papá and Roberto then brought in the mattress and placed it in the far corner of the garage. "Mamá, you and the little ones sleep on the mattress. Roberto, Panchito, and I will sleep outside under the trees," Papá said.

Early next morning Mr. Sullivan showed us where his crop was, and after breakfast, Papá, Roberto, and I headed for the vineyard to pick.

Around nine o'clock the temperature had risen to almost one hundred degrees. I was completely soaked in sweat and my mouth felt as if I had been chewing on a handkerchief. I walked over to the end of the row, picked up the jug of water we had brought, and began drinking. "Don't drink too much; you'll get sick," Roberto shouted. No sooner had he said that then I felt sick to my stomach. I dropped to my knees and let the jug roll off my hands. I remained motionless with my eyes glued on the hot sandy ground. All I could hear was the drone of insects. Slowly I began to recover. I poured water over my face and neck and watched the dirty water run down my arms to the ground.

I still felt a little dizzy when we took a break to eat lunch. It was past two o'clock and we sat underneath a large walnut tree that was on the side of the road. While we ate, Papá jotted down the number of boxes we had picked. Roberto drew designs on the ground with a stick. Suddenly I noticed Papá's face turn pale as he looked down the road. "Here comes the school bus," he whispered loudly in alarm. Instinctively, Roberto and I ran and hid in the vineyards. We did not want to get in trouble for not going to school. The neatly dressed boys about my age got off. They carried books under their arms.

After they crossed the street, the bus drove away. Roberto and I came out from hiding and joined Papá. "Tienen que tener cuidado," he warned us.

After lunch we went back to work. The sun kept beating down. The buzzing insects, the wet sweat, and the hot dry dust made the afternoon seem to last forever. Finally the mountains around the valley reached out and swallowed the sun. Within an hour it was too dark to continue picking. The vines blanketed the grapes, making it difficult to see the bunches. "Vamonos," said Papá, signaling to us that it was time to quit work. Papá then took out a pencil and began to figure out how much we had earned our first day. He wrote down numbers, crossed some out, and wrote down some more. "Quince," he murmured.

When we arrived home, we took a cold shower underneath a waterhose. We then sat down to eat dinner around some wooden crates that served as a table. Mamá had cooked a special meal for us. We had rice and tortillas with "carne con chile," my favorite dish.

The next morning I could hardly move. My body ached all over. I felt little control over my arms and legs.

This feeling went on every morning for days until my muscles finally got used to the work.

It was Monday, the first week of November. The grape season was over and I could go to school. I woke up early that morning and lay in bed, looking at the stars and savoring the thought of not going to work and of starting sixth grade for the first time that year. Since I could not sleep, I decided to get up and join Papá and Roberto at breakfast. I sat at the table across from Roberto, but I kept my head down. I did not want to look up and face him. I knew he was sad. He was not going to school today. He was not going tomorrow, or next week, or next month. He would not go until the cotton season was over, and that was sometime in February. I rubbed my hands together and watched the dry, acid-stained skin fall the to the floor in little rolls.

When Papá and Roberto left for work, I felt relief. I walked to the top of a small grade next to the shack and watched the "Carcanchita" disappear in the distance in a cloud of dust.

Two hours later, around eight o'clock, I stood by the side of the road waiting for school bus number twenty. When it arrived I climbed in. Everyone was busy either talking or yelling. I sat in an empty seat in the back.

When the bus stopped in front of the school, I felt very nervous. I looked out the bus window and saw boys and girls carrying books under their arms. I put my hands in my pant pockets and walked to the principal's office. When I entered I heard a woman's voice say: "May I help you?" I was startled. I had not heard English for months. For a few seconds I remained speechless. I looked at the lady who waited for an answer. My first instinct was to answer her in Spanish, but I held back. Finally, after struggling for English words, I managed to tell her that I wanted to enroll in the sixth grade. After answering many questions, I was led to the classroom.

Mr. Lema, the sixth grade teacher, greeted me and assigned me a desk. He then introduced me to the class. I was so nervous and scared at that moment when everyone's eyes were on me that I wished I were with Papá and Roberto picking cotton. After taking role, Mr. Lema gave the class the assignment for the first hour. "The first thing we have to do this morning is finish reading the story we began yesterday," he announced enthusiastically. He walked up to me, handed me an English book, and asked me to read. "We are on page 125," he said politely. When I heard this, I felt my blood rush to my head; I felt dizzy. "Would you like to read?" he asked hesitantly. I opened the book to page 125. My mouth was dry. My eyes began to water. I could not begin. "You can read later," Mr. Lema said understandingly.

For the rest of the reading period I kept getting angrier and angrier with myself. I should have read, I thought to myself.

During recess I went into the restroom and opened my English book to page 125. I began to read in a low voice, pretending I was in class. There were many words I did not know. I closed the book and headed back to the classroom.

Mr. Lema was sitting at his desk correcting papers. When I entered he looked up at me and smiled. I felt better. I walked up to him and asked if he could help me with the new words. "Gladly," he said.

The rest of the month I spent my lunch hours working on English with Mr. Lema, my best friend at school.

One Friday during lunch hour Mr. Lema asked me to take a walk with him to the music room. "Do you like music?" he asked me as we entered the building.

"Yes, I like corridos," I answered. He then picked up a trumpet, blew on it, and handed it to me. The sound gave me goose bumps. I knew that sound. I had heard it in many corridos. "How would you like to learn how to play it?" he asked. He must have read my face because before I could answer, he added, "I'll teach you how to play it during our lunch hours."

That day I could hardly wait to get home to tell Papá and Mamá the great news. As I got off the bus, my little brothers and sisters ran up to greet me. They were yelling and screaming. I thought they were happy to see me, but when I opened the door to our shack, I saw that everything we owned was neatly packed in cardboard boxes.

To Understand

1. Early in the essay, Jiminez says he "hated this move" to Fresno. Explain why he is upset about moving.

2. Describe the family's car, the "Carcanchita." How does this car help you to understand the family, especially the father?

3. List details from the essay that describe the family's living conditions. What do these details reveal about the way they lived?

4. What effect does Mr. Lema have on Jiminez?

5. Explain the essay's final image. Why does Jiminez end the essay at that point?

To Write

1. In this essay, Mr. Lema asks Jiminez to read for the class, and Jiminez can't get himself to try. How have you felt under similar circumstances? Write about your experiences of reading out loud in class. First, describe at least one such experience; then indicate your emotional response—terror or glee or something in between—and explain why you responded that way.

Lorna Dee Cervantes

Cannery Town in August

Lorna Dee Cervantes' first book of poems, Emplumada, *won the American Book Award. Her second book,* From the Cables *of* Genocide, *won the Patterson Prize for Poetry and the Latino Literature Award. She has edited the literary journals* Red Dirt *and* Mango. *Cervantes' poetry is celebrated for its social awareness and vivid commentary on the concerns of women and Latinos. In the following poem, she describes the effect of working in a cannery on the women who spend many hours there.*

Before Reading: Think about the lives of people who work in canneries, factories, or assembly plants. What is the work like?

All night it humps the air.
Speechless, the steam rises
from the cannery columns. I hear
the night bird rave about work
or lunch, or sing the swing shift
home. I listen, while bodyless
uniforms and spinach specked shoes
drift in monochrome down the dark
moon-possessed streets. Women
who smell of whiskey and tomatoes,
peach fuzz reddening their lips and eyes—
I imagine them not speaking, dumbed
by the can's clamor and drop
to the trucks that wait, grunting
in their headlights below.
They spotlight those who walk
like a dream, with no one

waiting in the shadows
to palm them back to living.

To Understand

1. Go back and take note of all the images Cervantes uses to describe the atmosphere and the people at the cannery. Which two or three images tell you most about life at the cannery? Why?

2. What has happened to the women in the poem? What is the author's attitude toward these women?

3. Explain the poem's final lines. How is it that the women need to come "back to living"?

To Write

1. Write about another kind of work that you believe is like the cannery jobs in this poem. Plan your writing by listing two or three ways the job you've chosen is like the cannery work in the poem.

David Ignatow

The Fisherwoman

For over fifty years, David Ignatow published many books of poems including The Gentle Weightlifter, Rescue the Dead, Poems: 1934–1969, *and* What I Wanted: Last Poems. *His awards include the William Carlos Williams Award, the Frost Medal, two Guggenheim fellowships, and the Bollingen Prize. He served as president of the Poetry Society of America and taught at several universities. Ignatow died in 1997.*

Before Reading: Ask yourself what jobs offer an opportunity for success and what jobs do not.

She took from her basket four fishes
and carved each into four slices
and scaled them with her long knife,
this fisherwoman, and wrapped them;
and took four more and worked
in this rhythm through the day,
each action ending on a package
of old newspapers; and when it came
to close, dark coming upon the streets,
she had done one thing, she felt, well,
making one complete day.

To Understand

1. Summarize what the woman has done. Is it a large accomplishment? How do you decide if it is large or small?

2. Consider the number *four,* mentioned three times in this short poem. Is there significance to this number?

3. Review the poem's last two lines. How does the poet want us to feel about the woman in the poem and what she has accomplished?

To Write

1. How do you define success in working? Regardless of the particular job, what are the common factors in a working person's success?

J. *California Cooper*

$100 and Nothing!

*In 1987 J. California Cooper was named Black Play-
wright of the Year. By that time she had established her
reputation writing for the theater. Only after that did she
turn to writing fiction with her first collection of short stories,* A Piece of Mine *(from which this is the first story),
and several more award-winning books including* Homemade Love *(winner of the American Book Award),* Family,
and recently The Future Has a Past. *Her work is known
for its colloquial style and engaging storytelling. In "$100
and Nothing!" Cooper introduces us to characters that
allow us to think about the value of hard work, the roles of
men and women, and the ways in which we define success
and failure in life.*

Before Reading: Think about how one partner in a marriage can either
help or hinder the other person in achieving success and happiness.

Where we live is not a big town like some and not a little town like some, but somewhere in the middle, like a
big little town. Things don't happen here very much like
other places, but on the other hand, I guess they do. Just
ever once in awhile, you really pay tension to what is
going on around you. I seen something here really was
something! Let me tell you!

Was a woman, friend of mind born here and her mama
birthed her and gave her to the orphan house and left
town. Her mama had a sister, but the sister had her own
and didn't have time for no more mouths, she said. So the
orphan home, a white one, had to keep her. They named
her "Mary." Mary. Mary lived there, well, "worked" there

bout fifteen years, then they let her do outside work too and Mary saved her money and bought an acre of land just outside town for $5.00 and took to plantin it and growing things and when they were ready, she bring them into town and sell em. She made right smart a money too, cause soon as she could, she bought a little house over there at the end of the main street, long time ago, so it was cheap, and put up a little stall for her vegetables and added chickens and eggs and all fresh stuff, you know. Wasn't long fore she had a little store and added more things.

Now the mens took to hanging round her and things like that! She was a regular size woman, she had real short hair and little skinny bow legs, things like that, but she was real, real nice and a kind person . . . to everybody.

Anyway, pretty soon, one of them men with a mouth full of sugar and warm hands got to Mary. I always thought he had a mouth full of "gimme" and a hand full of "reach," but when I tried to tell her, she just said, with her sweet soft smile, "maybe you just don't know him, he alright." Anyway, they got married.

Now he worked at Mr. Charlie's bar as a go-for and a clean-up man. After they got married I thought he would be working with Mary, in the field and in the store, you know. But he said he wasn't no field man and that store work was woman's work lessen he stand at the cash register. But you know the business wasn't that fast so wasn't nobody gonna be standing up in one spot all day doing nothing over that cigar box Mary used for a cash register.

Anyway, Mary must have loved him cause she liked to buy him things, things I knew that man never had; nice suits and shirts and shoes, socks and things like that. I was there once when she was so excited with a suit to give him and he just looked at it and flipped its edges and told her to "hang it up and I'll get to it when I can," said, "I wouldn'ta picked that one, but you can't help it if you got no eye for good things!" Can you magine!? That man hadn't had nothing!! I could see he was changing, done spit that sugar out!!

Well, Mary's business picked up more and more and everybody came to get her fresh foods. It was a clean little store and soon she had a cash register and counters and soda water and canned goods and oh, all kinds of stuff you see in the big stores. She fixed that house up, too, and doing alright!! But, she didn't smile so much anymore . . . always looking thoughtful and a little in pain inside her heart. I took to helping her round the store and I began to see why she had changed. HE had changed! Charles, her husband! He was like hell on wheels with a automatic transmission! She couldn't do nothing right! She was dumb! Called her store a hole in the wall! Called her house "junk!" Said wasn't none of that stuff "nothing."

But I notice with the prosperity he quit working for Mr. Charlie and got a car and rode around and walked around and played around! Just doing nothing! And when people go to telling Mary how smart she was and how good she doing and they glad she there, I heard him say at least a hundred times, "I could take $100 and nothing and have more than this in a year!!" Didn't like to see her happy and smiling! I think he was jealous, but he coulda been working right beside her! When he married her it was his business, too! I heard her tell him that and guess what he answered? "I don't need that hole in the wall with stuff sitting there drawing flies, I'll think of something of my own!" Lord, it's so many kinds of fools in the world you just can't keep up with them!!

I went home to lunch with Mary once and he got mad cause we woke him up as we was talking softly and eating. Lord, did he talk about Mary! Talked about her skinny legs and all under her clothes and her kinky hair. She tried to keep it up but she worked and sweat too hard, for him! She just dropped her head deeper down into her plate and I could see she had a hard time swallowing her food.

Then, she try to buy him something nice and he told her to give it to the Salvation Army cause he didn't want it and that he was going to give everything he had to the Salvation Army that she had picked cause it ain't what he liked! Ain't he something! Somebody trying to be good to you and you ain't got sense enough to understand kindness and love.

She cook good food for him, too, and he mess with it and throw it out saying he don't like her cooking, he feel like eating out! Now!

Just let me tell you! She want a baby. He say he don't want no nappy head, skinny, bow-leg baby and laughed at her.

She want to go out somewhere of a evening, he say he ain't going nowhere with the grocery bag woman!

I didn't mean to, but once I heard her ask him why he slept in the other bedroom stead of with her one night— she had three bedrooms—and he said he couldn't help it, sometime he rather sleep with a rock, a big boulder, than her. She came back with tears in her eyes that day, but she never complain, not to me anyway and I was her best friend.

Anyway, Mary took to eatin to get fat on her legs and bout five or six months, she was fat! Bout 200 pounds but her legs was still small and skinny and bowed. He really went to talking about her then, even in the store, front of other people. Called her the Hog! Said everybody else's Hog was a Cadillac but his was his wife! And laugh! He all the time laughing at her. They never laugh together, in front of me, anyway.

So, one day Mary say she going to take care of some business for a few days and she went off alone. He say "Go head, do what she want to do." He don't care bout what she do! "Do whatever!" Just like that! Whatever! Whatever! Didn't finish it like other people do, like "Whatever you want to," just, "Whatever!" I guess he heard it somewhere and thought it was smart to say it like that. Well, when

Mary come back, I coulda fell out cause she brought one of her cousins, who was a real looker; long hair, big busts, and big legs and a heart full of foolishness. Maybelline was her name and she worked in the store all day, I can't lie about that, she sure did help Mary, but where she got the strength, I don't know, cause she worked the men all night! In three or four months she had gone through all the legible men in town, some twice, and then all the married illegible ones, some of them twice too. She was a go-getter, that Maybelline. But she did help Mary and Mary seemed to need more help cause she was doing poorly in her health. She was sighing, tired and achy all the time now.

But she still took care of her business, the paper work and all, you know. Once, I saw Charles come into the store and she needed him to sign a few things, if you please, and he took them papers and bragged to the fellas in the store that "See, I got to sign things around here to keep things goin." He didn't even read them, just waved his hand and signed them and handed them to Mary without even looking at her, like she was a secretary or something, and went on out and drove off with a big grin looking 50¢ worth of importance, to me anyway.

Well, Mary just kep getting worse off. I told her to see a doctor and she said she had in the big city and she had something they couldn't cure but she wish I wouldn't tell nobody, so I didn't. But I felt so bad for her I loved her. I knew whatever was killing her was started by a heavy sad heart, shaking hands, a sore spirit, hot tears, deep, heavy sighs, hurtful swallows and oh, you know, all them kinda things.

Soon she had to stay home in bed. Wasn't no long sickness though, I could see she was going fast. Near the end, one day I saw her out in her back yard picking up rocks and I knew the dear soul must be losing her mind also and I took her back in the house and tried to get her to loose the rocks and throw them away, but she wouldn't let go. She was sick but she was strong in her hands, from all that work, I guess, she just held on to them, so I said, "Shit, you ain't never had too much you wanted to hold on to so hold the rocks if that what you want!" And she did.

Now, she asked Charles to take Maybelline back to the city to get the rest of Maybelline's things to move down there and Charles didn't mind at all cause I had seen him looking that Maybelline upways, downways, and both sideways and I could tell he like what he saw and so could Maybelline cause she was always posing or prancing. Anyway, they went for a day, one night and back the next day. Before they went, I saw Charles sit on the side of Mary's bed and, first time I ever saw him do it, take her hand and hold it, then bend down and kiss her on the forehead. Musta been thinking bout what he was going to do to Maybelline while they was gone, but anyway, I'm glad he did do it. It brought tears to Mary's eyes. Then, they were gone and before they got back, Mary was gone.

I have to stop a minute cause everytime I think of that sweet woman. . . .

She had told me what to do, the funeral and all, so I had taken care of some of those things and Mary was already gone to the funeral home and the funeral was the next day.

When they come home or back, whatever!, all they had to do was get ready to go to the parlor. I don't know when or nothing like that, but when Charles went to the closet to get something to wear, the closet was bare, except for a note: "Dear Charles," it say, "They gone to the Salvation Army just like you always say you want. Yours truly, Mary."

Now that man run all over trying to find some way to get them back but they was nice things and somebody had done bought them or either kept them, you know what I mean? Then, he rush over to the bank to get some money and found out his name wasn't on the account no more! The manager gave him a letter say: "Dear Charles,

You told me so many times you don't need me or nothing that is mine. Not going to force you to do nothing you don't want to do! Always, Mary."

His named was replaced with Maybelline's so naturally he went to see her at the store. She say sure, and give him $50 and he say, "Come go with me and help me pick it out," and she say she ain't got time. So he told her take time. She say, "I got to take care this business and close the store for the funeral." He say, "I'll close the store, this ain't your business to worry about." She say, "This my store." He say, "Are your crazy?" She say, "I ain't crazy. I'm the boss!" He say, "I'm Mary's husband, what's hers is mine!" She say, "That's true, but this store ain't hers, it's mine! I bought it from her!" He say, "With what? You can't afford to buy no store as nice as this!" She say, "Mary lent me the money; it's all legal; lawyer and everything!" He say, "How you gon' pay her back? You got to pay me, bitch!" She say, "No . . . no . . . when Mary died, all debt clear." He say, "I'll see about that!" She say, "Here, here the lawyer's name and number." He snatched it and left. He musta found out she was right and it was legal cause I never heard no more about it.

Now everybody bringing food and all, the house was full, but I was among the last to go and when Charles got ready to go to bed he say he wasn't going to sleep in the room Mary died in and he went into the third bedroom. I heard him holler and went in there and the covers was pulled back and the bed was full of rocks . . . and a note say: "Dear Charles, Tried to get what you wanted, couldn't carry no boulder, honest. Yours, Mary." Me, I just left.

Next morning he opens the food cupboard and it was almost empty, but for a note and note say: "Dear Charles, here is 30 days supply of food. Waste that too. Yours, Mary." I'm telling you, his life was going upside down. He and Maybelline stayed in that house alone together and that old Charles musta had something going on that was alright cause pretty soon they were married. I knew he thought he was marrying that store again, but let me tell you, Maybelline was pretty and fleshy but she couldn't count and didn't like to pay bills or the workers on that little piece of land of Mary's and pretty soon she was broke and the store was closed cause nothing wasn't in there but some old brown dead lettuce and turned up carrots and empty soda bottles and tired squashy tomatoes didn't nobody want. Charles didn't have nothing but an almost empty house. They cussed and fought and she finally left saying she wasn't really his wife cause she didn't have no divorce from her last husbands! So there!

Now, that ought to be all but let me finish telling you this cause I got to go now and see bout my own life.

Exactly a year passed from the day Mary had passed and a white lady and a black lady came to Mary's house with some papers and I heard a lot of hollering and shouting after a bit and Charles was putting them out. They waved those papers and said they would be back . . . and they did, a week later, with the Sheriff. Seems like Mary had give Charles one year to live there in the house and then it was to go, all legally, to be a orphan home for black children.

Welllll, when everything was over, I saw him sitting outside in his car, kinda raggedy now, just sitting there looking at the house. I took a deep breath and went to my dresser and got the envelope Mary had give me to give him one year from her death, at this time. I looked at it awhile thinking bout all that had happened and feeling kind of sorry for Charles till I remembered we hoe our own rows and what we plants there, we picks. So I went on out and handed him the envelope through the car window. He rolled me red eyes and a dirty look and opened the envelope and saw a one hundred dollar bill and . . . a note. He read it with a sad, sad look on his face. "Dear Charles, here is $100. Take all the nothing you want and in a year you'll have everything. Yours truly, your dead wife, Mary." Well, he just sat there a minute, staring at the money and the note, then started his car up and slowly drove away without so much as "good-by." Going somewhere to spend that money I guess, or just stop and stare off into space . . . Whatever!

To Understand

1. How does the narrator characterize both Mary and Charles at the beginning of the story? Why does Mary agree to marry Charles?

2. List the ways in which Charles mistreats Mary. What kind of person is Charles?

3. How does Mary get her revenge against Charles, and how are readers supposed to feel about this?

4. Is there a moral to this story? If so, what is it?

To Write

1. Do you know anyone who is like Charles or like Mary? Compare this person to the character in the story.

2. Do most people you know help or hinder their spouses in achieving success? Write a response to this question by giving specific examples of men or women who make life easier or harder for the other person in that relationship.

☙❧

Scott Russell Sanders

The Men We Carry in Our Minds

Scott Russell Sanders' many books include Staying Put, Hunting for Hope, The Country of Language, *and* The Force of Spirit. *Among his honors he has received a Lannan Literary Award for his collected work in nonfiction. Sanders is Distinguished Professor of English at Indiana University and is also contributing editor at* Audubon. *In this essay Sanders writes about the men he observed when he was young, the kinds of hard work they did, and the effect this had on his perception of men and women's lives.*

Before Reading: Recall the kinds of jobs you saw men engaged in when you were a child. Were these jobs in factories, in office buildings, in fields? Were many men unemployed?

The first men, besides my father, I remember seeing were black convicts and white guards, in the cottonfield across the road from our farm on the outskirts of Memphis. I must have been three or four. The prisoners wore dingy gray-and-black zebra suits, heavy as canvas, sodden with sweat. Hatless, stooped, they chopped weeds in the fierce heat, row after row, breathing the acrid dust of boll-weevil poison. The overseers wore dazzling white shirts and broad shadowy hats. The oiled barrels of their shotguns flashed in the sunlight. Their faces in memory are utterly blank. Of course those men, white and black, have become for me an emblem of racial hatred. But they have also come to stand for the twin poles of my early vision of manhood—the brute toiling animal and the boss.

When I was a boy, the men I knew labored with their bodies. They were marginal farmers, just scraping by, or welders, steelworkers, carpenters; they swept floors, dug ditches, mined coal, or drove trucks, their forearms ropy with muscle; they trained horses, stoked furnaces, built tires, stood on assembly lines wrestling parts onto cars and refrigerators. They got up before light, worked all day long whatever the weather, and when they came home at night they looked as though somebody had been whipping them. In the evening and on weekends they worked on their own places, tilling gardens that were lumpy with clay, fixing broken-down cars, hammering on houses that were always too drafty, too leaky, too small.

The bodies of the men I knew were twisted and maimed in ways visible and invisible. The nails of their hands were black and split, the hands tattooed with scars. Some had lost fingers. Heavy lifting had given many of them finicky backs and guts weak from hernias. Racing against conveyer belts had given them ulcers. Their ankles and knees ached from years of standing on concrete. Anyone who had worked for long around machines was hard of hearing. They squinted, and the skin of their faces was creased like the leather of old work gloves. There were times, studying them, when I dreaded growing up. Most of them coughed, from dust or cigarettes, and most of them drank cheap wine or whiskey, so their eyes looked bloodshot and bruised. The fathers of my friends always seemed older than the mothers. Men wore out sooner. Only women lived into old age.

As a boy I also knew another sort of men, who did not sweat and break down like mules. They were soldiers, and so far as I could tell they scarcely worked at all. During my early school years we lived on a military base, an arsenal in Ohio, and every day I saw GIs in the guardshacks, on the stoops of barracks, at the wheels of olive drab Chevrolets. The chief fact of their lives was boredom. Long after I left the Arsenal I came to recognize the sour smell the soldiers gave off as that of souls in limbo. They were all waiting—for wars, for transfers, for leaves, for promotions, for the end of their hitch—like so many braves waiting for the hunt to begin. Unlike the warriors of older tribes, however, they would have no say about when the battle would start or how it would be waged. Their waiting was broken only when they practiced for war. They fired guns at targets, drove tanks across the churned-up fields of the military reservation, set off bombs in the wrecks of old fighter planes. I knew this was all play. But I also felt certain that when the hour for killing arrived, they would kill. When the real shooting started, many of them would die. This was what soldiers were *for*, just as a hammer was for driving nails.

Warriors and toilers: those seemed, in my boyhood vision, to be the chief destinies for men. They weren't the only destinies, as I learned from having a few male teachers, from reading books, and from watching television. But the men on television—the politicians, the astronauts, the generals, the savvy lawyers, the philosophical doctors, the bosses who gave orders to both soldiers and laborers—seemed as removed and unreal to me as the figures in tapestries. I could no more imagine growing up to become one of these cool, potent creatures than I could imagine becoming a prince.

A nearer and more hopeful example was that of my father, who had escaped from a red-dirt farm to a tire factory, and from the assembly line to the front office. Eventually he dressed in a white shirt and tie. He carried himself as if he had been born to work with his mind. But his body, remembering earlier years of slogging work, began to give out on him in his fifties, and it quit on him entirely before he turned sixty-five. Even such a partial escape from man's fate as he had accomplished did not seem possible for most of the boys I knew. They joined the Army, stood in line for jobs in the smoky plants, helped build highways. They were bound to work as their fathers had worked, killing themselves or preparing to kill others.

A scholarship enabled me not only to attend college, a rare enough feat in my circle, but even to study in a university meant for the children of the rich. Here I met for the first time young men who had assumed from birth that they would lead lives of comfort and power. And for the first time I met women who told me that men were guilty of having kept all the joys and privileges of the earth for themselves. I was baffled. What privileges? What joys? I thought about the maimed, dismal lives of the men back home. What had they stolen from their wives and daughters? The right to go five days a week, twelve months a year, for thirty or forty years to a steel mill or a coal mine? The right to drop bombs and die in war? The right to feel every leak in the roof, every gap in the fence, every cough in the engine, as a wound they must mend? The right to feel, when the layoff comes or the plant shuts down, not only afraid but ashamed?

I was slow to understand the deep grievances of women. This was because, as a boy, I had envied them. Before college, the only people I had ever known who were interested in art or music or literature, the only ones who read books, the only ones who who ever seemed to enjoy a sense of ease and grace were the mothers and daughters. Like the menfolk, they fretted about money, they scrimped and made-do. But, when the pay stopped coming in, they were not the ones who had failed. Nor did they have to go to war, and that seemed to me a blessed fact. By comparison with the narrow, ironclad days of fathers, there was an expansiveness, I thought, in the days of mothers. They went to see neighbors, to shop in town, to run errands at school, at the library, at church. No doubt, had I looked harder at their lives, I would have envied them less. It was not my fate to become a woman, so it was easier for me to see the graces. Few of them held jobs outside the home, and those who did filled thankless roles as clerks and waitresses. I didn't see, then, what a prison a house could be, since houses seemed to me brighter, handsomer places than any factory. I did not realize—because such things were never spoken of—how often women suffered from men's bullying. I did learn about the wretchedness of abandoned wives, single mothers, widows; but I also learned about the wretchedness of lone men. Even then I could see how exhausting it was for a mother to cater all day to the needs of young children. But if I had been asked, as a boy, to choose between tending a baby and tending a machine, I think I would have chosen the baby. (Having now tended both, I know I would choose the baby.)

So I was baffled when the women at college accused me and my sex of having cornered the world's pleasures. I think something like my bafflement has been felt by other boys (and by girls as well) who grew up in dirt-poor farm country, in black ghettos, in Hispanic barrios, in the shadows of factories, in Third World nations—any place where the fate of men is as grim and bleak as the fate of women. Toilers and warriors. I realize now how ancient these identities are, how deep the tug they exert on men, the undertow of a thousand generations. The miseries I saw, as a boy, in the lives of nearly all men I continue to see in the lives of many—the body-breaking toil, the tedium, the call to be tough, the humiliating powerlessness, the battle for a living and for territory.

When the women I met at college thought about the joys and privileges of men, they did not carry in their minds the sort of men I had known in my childhood. They thought of their fathers, who were bankers, physicians, architects, stockbrokers, the big wheels of the big cities. These fathers rode the train to work or drove cars that cost more than any of my childhood houses. They were attended from morning to night by female helpers, wives and nurses and secretaries. They were never laid off, never short of cash at month's end, never lined up for welfare. These fathers made decisions that mattered. They ran the world.

The daughters of such men wanted to share in this power, this glory. So did I. They yearned for a say over their future, for jobs worthy of their abilities, for the right to live at peace, unmolested, whole. Yes, I thought, yes yes. The difference between me and these daughters was that they saw me, because of my sex, as destined from birth to become like their fathers, and therefore as an enemy to their desires. But I knew better. I wasn't an enemy, in fact or in feeling. I was an ally. If I had known, then, how to tell them so, would they have believed me? Would they now?

To Understand

1. What jobs did the men that Sanders knew as a boy have? How did their occupations affect their lives?

2. Sanders says, "Warriors and toilers: those seemed, in my boyhood vision, to be the chief destinies for men." Explain this statement with examples of what he is referring to.

3. Why was Sanders "slow to understand the deep grievances of women"?

4. How did Sanders view the lives of women—as compared to men—as he was growing up?

To Write

1. Think back to the men you observed when you were a child. Were they like the "warriors and toilers" Sanders describes? Describe the men you observed and how they were like or unlike the men Sanders observed.

2. At the end of the essay, Sanders questions if women now would believe that he is their ally in the quest for equality. After reading this essay, do you believe most women would see him as an ally? To support your response, refer to particular parts of the essay.

Robert Wrigley

To Work

Robert Wrigley has two other poems—"A Photo of Immigrants, 1903" (p. 17) and "Winter Love" (p. 167)—in this book. A brief biography of Wrigley can be found on page 17. In "To Work" Wrigley captures, from a child's perspective, one mother's never-ending job of doing laundry.

Before Reading: Consider the various tasks under the heading housework. How do most people view these jobs? How do you view them?

The three-bladed, dunce-capped agitator pulsed,
and steam billowed into the basement rafters.
Monday mornings, in a broth of soap and clothes,
my mother wielded her stick, bleached dun
and blunted with probing, then fed the works
through wringers to a galvanized tub.
Those summers the neighborhood blossomed
with laundry. Sheets snapped and dresses swayed,
a shirt dragged its cuffs through the dandelions.
By early afternoon, by the basket load
lugged in, the laundry stiff with sun was spread
across the kitchen table for sprinkling.
I remember my mother's easy motions,
her thumb mostly over the bottle's hole
and the clothes rolled tight and stacked
like cordwood in the cooler.

And when the light leaned into dusk—
when my father in the gap between two jobs arrived,
dinner done, dishes washed, my father gone again,
the tiny, round-eyed television squinting

over us—my mother hauled from the hallway closet
the rickety wooden ironing board
and began her final Monday chore.
I sprawled across the rug
and picked at the pills of the hand-me-down sofa,
the whole house filling with the smell of heat
and watery steel, the ironing board's creak,
the iron's dull thunk and glide.
Last thing she pressed was sheets,
one set for each bed in the house,
each bed remade in my sleep
before she lifted me off the floor
and eased me away for the night.

Then the night itself unwrinkling,
new sheets warming into sleep.
That last summer in the old house
many times I woke up late,
my father finally come home and collapsed
in bed alone, while I wandered the halls
to the kitchen, my mother at the table
in a bright wedge of light. I looked up
past the bulb on her sewing machine
at a thicket of pins between her lips.
And in my sleepiness it was one gesture—
her palm across her mouth, a shaken head—
and I was asleep on my feet,
hand in my mother's hand
as she walked me back to bed.
I don't remember ever arriving there,
nor the straightening of the covers,
nor the kiss she might have given me.
I don't remember the house we walked through,
nor the colors of the walls, nor the colors of the clothes
she labored over each night,
the clothes she made for herself,
in which, come September, she would look for work.

To Understand

1. How does the speaker feel about his mother's work? Point to specific lines in the poem as evidence.

2. What role does the father have in this poem? Explain.

3. How do the central images of laundry—being washed, hanging on the line, being ironed and folded—make a reader feel? Explain.

4. How are we readers supposed to interpret and respond to the last line?

To Write

1. Write about the kinds of work your mother did—at home or at her job—when you were a child. What impressions did these tasks have on you?

Work and Dreams: Ideas for Writing

1. Think of a person whose work ethic you admire. Write a paper about this person, mentioning the main qualities of his or her work ethic and giving examples of how it is admirable.

2. How good of a worker are you? Write a paper in which you evaluate yourself as a worker. Think of the places and situations that require work of you: your job, school, home. Are you a better worker in some places than in others? How do you rate overall?

3. Write a paper about one occupation you may want to pursue. What is it about this occupation that makes it appealing? Start by brainstorming reasons for going into this field; then focus your discussion around the three or four strongest reasons.

4. Using the guidelines in assignment 3, write about an occupation that you definitely *do not* want to pursue.

5. Write a paper about the work of one of your parents—whether at home, in a factory, or in an office. Identify the job, describe it in detail, and offer an opinion about it. Then support your opinion by offering detailed examples.

6. Write a paper about how work fits into your overall dreams for the future. How important will your job be in your life? What other parts of your life will compete with your job for your time and energy? Explain in detail how you think you will weigh these competing interests, and offer examples of people who, in your opinion, model the lifestyle you want.

7. People work for a variety of reasons: to provide for themselves and their families, to be with people who have similar interests, to help other people, to provide meaning for their lives, or, simply, to keep busy. Write a paper in which you examine these or other reasons people work. What, in your opinion, are the best and worst reasons? Offer examples of people who clearly fit into each category you write about.

7

Issues/Positions

Issues/Positions

In nearly every forum of our daily lives, we encounter controversial issues. We struggle with these issues to take the right positions, although no absolutely correct position may exist. In our own families, we may face the issue of how to punish children or whether we should put Grandma in a nursing home. In school, your instructors discuss and debate which instructional methods are best for their classes while you may grapple with the question of which course of study will be best for your future. There are controversial issues at your workplace, in your community, in your state, and in our country. It's fair to say that we encounter these issues every day. Struggling with them is a part of what makes us human.

Perhaps that is why writers so frequently imbed controversial issues within their work. They know that controversy is part of the human experience and that it causes people anxiety. If this anxiety or tension is present in a poem or story, it causes readers to take notice and to become involved in the issue at hand.

This chapter includes

- a story about a man and his wife who argue about interracial marriage;
- an essay by a writer who recalls his inner struggle about whether or not to heed his draft notice for the Vietnam War;
- a poem in which the speaker decides whether or not to try saving an unborn fawn;
- an essay in which the author struggles with the issue of how important her appearance is—to herself and to others.

You'll find controversial issues in many of the other chapters of this book as well. As a reader, try to understand the issue in a piece and how the characters are responding to it. Do they appear reasonable or unreasonable? Ask yourself how the author wants you to stand on the issue. Of course, use the *To Understand* and *To Write* questions to help you with your reading, and think about issues in your life that are worthy of writing about.

Tobias Wolff

Say Yes

Tobias Wolff's short story "Powder" as well as a brief biography of the author appear on page 22. In "Say Yes," from Back in the World, *a man and his wife argue over the issue of interracial marriage and come to know each other in a different way in the process.*

Before Reading: Ask yourself what you think about interracial marriages. Are they significantly different from other marriages?

They were doing the dishes, his wife washing while he dried. He'd washed the night before. Unlike most men he knew, he really pitched in on the housework. A few months earlier he'd overheard a friend of his wife's congratulate her on having such a considerate husband, and he thought, *I try.* Helping out with the dishes was a way he had of showing how considerate he was.

They talked about different things and somehow got on the subject of whether white people should marry black people. He said that all things considered, he thought it was a bad idea.

"Why?" she asked.

Sometimes his wife got this look where she pinched her brows together and bit her lower lip and stared down at something. When he saw her like this he knew he should keep his mouth shut, but he never did. Actually it made him talk more. She had that look now.

"Why?" she asked again, and stood there with her hand inside a bowl, not washing it but just holding it above the water.

"Listen," he said, "I went to school with blacks, and I've worked with blacks and lived on the same street with blacks, and we've always gotten along just fine. I don't need you coming along now and implying that I'm a racist."

"I didn't imply anything," she said, and began washing the bowl again, turning it around in her hand as though she were shaping it. "I just don't see what's wrong with a white person marrying a black person, that's all."

"They don't come from the same culture as we do. Listen to them sometime—they even have their own language. That's okay with me, I *like* hearing them talk"—he did; for some reason it always made him feel happy—"but it's different. A person from their culture and a person from our culture could never really *know* each other."

"Like you know me?" his wife asked.

"Yes, like I know you."

"But if they love each other," she said. She was washing faster now, not looking at him.

Oh boy, he thought. He said, "Don't take my word for it. Look at the statistics. Most of those marriages break up."

"Statistics." She was piling dishes on the drainboard at a terrific rate, just swiping at them with the cloth. Many of them were greasy, and there were flecks of food between the tines of the forks. "All right," she said, "what about foreigners? I suppose you think the same thing about two foreigners getting married."

"Yes," he said, "as a matter of fact I do. How can you understand someone who comes from a completely different background?"

"Different," said his wife. "Not the same, like us."

"Yes, different," he snapped, angry with her for resorting to this trick of repeating his words so that they sounded crass, or hypocritical. "These are dirty," he said, and dumped all the silverware back into the sink.

The water had gone flat and gray. She stared down at it, her lips pressed tight together, then plunged her hands under the surface. "Oh!" she cried, and jumped back. She took her right hand by the wrist and held it up. Her thumb was bleeding.

"Ann, don't move," he said. "Stay right there." He ran upstairs to the bathroom and rummaged in the medicine chest for alcohol, cotton, and a Band-Aid. When he came back down she was leaning against the refrigerator with her eyes closed, still holding her hand. He took the hand and dabbed at her thumb with the cotton. The bleeding had stopped. He squeezed it to see how deep the wound was and a single drop of blood welled up, trembling and bright, and fell to the floor. Over the thumb she stared at him accusingly. "It's shallow," he said. "Tomorrow you won't even know it's there." He hoped that she appreciated how quickly he had come to her aid. He'd acted out of concern for her, with no thought of getting anything in return, but now the thought occurred to him that it would be a nice gesture on her part not to start up that conversation again, as he was tired of it. "I'll finish up here," he said. "You go and relax."

"That's okay," she said. "I'll dry."

He began to wash the silverware again, giving a lot of attention to the forks.

"So," she said, "you wouldn't have married me if I'd been black."

"For Christ's sake, Ann!"

"Well that's what you said, didn't you?"

"No, I did not. The whole question is ridiculous. If you had been black, we probably wouldn't even have met. You would have had your friends and I would have had mine. The only black girl I ever really knew was my partner in the debating club, and I was already going out with you by then."

"But if we had met, and I'd been black?"

"Then you probably would have been going out with a black guy." He picked up the rinsing nozzle and sprayed the silverware. The water was so hot that the metal darkened to a pale blue, then turned silver again.

"Let's say I wasn't," she said. "Let's say I am black and unattached and we meet and fall in love."

He glanced over at her. She was watching him and her eyes were bright. "Look," he said, taking a reasonable tone, "this is stupid. If you were black you wouldn't be you." As he said this he realized it was absolutely true. There was no possible way of arguing with the fact that she would not be herself if she were black. So he said it again: "If you were black you wouldn't be you."

"I know," she said, "but let's just say."

He took a deep breath. He had won the argument but he still felt cornered. "Say what?" he asked.

"That I'm black, but still me, and we fall in love. Will you marry me?"

He thought about it.

"Well?" she said, and stepped close to him. Her eyes were even brighter. "Will you marry me?"

"I'm thinking," he said.

"You won't, I can tell. You're going to say no."

"Let's not move too fast on this," he said. "There are lots of things to consider. We don't want to do something we would regret for the rest of our lives."

"No more considering. Yes or no."

"Since you put it that way—"

"Yes or no."

"Jesus, Ann. All right. No."

She said, "Thank you," and walked from the kitchen into the living room. A moment later he heard her turning the pages of a magazine. He knew that she was too angry to be actually reading it, but she didn't snap through the pages the way he would have done. She turned them slowly, as if she were studying every word. She was demonstrating her indifference to him, and it had the effect he knew she wanted it to have. It hurt him.

He had no choice but to demonstrate his indifference to her. Quietly, thoroughly, he washed the rest of the dishes. Then he dried them and put them away. He wiped the counters and the stove and scoured the linoleum where the drop of blood had fallen. While he was at it, he decided, he might as well mop the whole floor. When he was done the kitchen looked new, the way it looked when they were first shown the house, before they had ever lived here.

He picked up the garbage pail and went outside. The night was clear and he could see a few stars to the west, where the light of the town didn't blur them out. On El Camino the traffic was steady and light, peaceful as a river. He felt ashamed that he had let his wife get him into a fight. In another thirty years or so they would both be dead. What would all that stuff matter then? He thought of the years they had spent together, and how close they were, and how well they knew each other, and his throat tightened so that he could hardly breathe. His face and neck began to tingle. Warmth flooded his chest. He stood there for a while, enjoying these sensations, then picked up the pail and went out the back gate.

The two mutts from down the street had pulled over the garbage can again. One of them was rolling around on his back and the other had something in her mouth. Growling, she tossed it into the air, leaped up and caught it, growled again and whipped her head from side to side. When they saw him coming they trotted away with short, mincing steps. Normally he would heave rocks at them, but this time he let them go.

The house was dark when he came back inside. She was in the bathroom. He stood outside the door and called her name. He heard bottles clinking, but she didn't answer him. "Ann, I'm really sorry," he said. "I'll make it up to you, I promise."

"How?" she asked.

He wasn't expecting this. But from a sound in her voice, a level and definite note that was strange to him, he knew that he had come up with the right answer. He leaned against the door. "I'll marry you," he whispered.

"We'll see," she said. "Go on to bed. I'll be out in a minute."

He undressed and got under the covers. Finally he heard the bathroom door open and close.

"Turn off the light," she said from the hallway.

"What?"

"Turn off the light."

He reached over and pulled the chain on the bedside lamp. The room went dark. "All right," he said. He lay there but nothing happened. "All right," he said again. Then he heard a movement across the room. He sat up, but he couldn't see a thing. The room was silent. His heart pounded the way it had on their first night together, the way it still did when he woke at a noise in the darkness and waited to hear it again—the sound of someone moving through the house, a stranger.

To Understand

1. Why does the man in this story have a negative opinion about interracial marriage? Are his reasons valid?

2. Explain why the wife objects to her husband's position. Who seems most reasonable? Refer to particular sentences to support your answer.

3. Review the section in which the husband helps his wife with her bleeding thumb. How are we readers supposed to respond to this part?

4. In the last paragraph, the husband imagines his wife as "a stranger." Explain how, if they have been married for a number of years, she could be a stranger to him.

To Write

1. Where do you stand on the issue of interracial marriage? Support your stance with concrete reasons. If you know someone in an interracial marriage, you might include information about this person as an example.

Tim O'Brien

Beginning

The author of six novels including Northern Lights,
Going After Cacciato, Nuclear Age, In the Lake of the
Woods, Tomcat in Love, *and most recently* July, July, *Tim
O'Brien has intrigued readers with his characters who
have experienced the Vietnam War. His book of Vietnam
stories,* The Things They Carried, *a memoir* If I Die in a
Combat Zone, Box Me Up and Ship Me Home, *and his
novels constitute for many the best writing available
about the war, a controversial period in American history.
In the following essay, O'Brien recalls the difficult decision of heeding his draft notice while some young men
were fleeing to Canada to escape the draft.*

Before Reading: Think about what you know of the Vietnam War.
What was controversial about it? Why were many young men reluc-
tant to fight for their country?

The summer of 1968, the summer I turned into a soldier, was a good time for talking about war and peace.
Eugene McCarthy was bringing quiet thought to the subject. He was winning votes in the primaries. College students were listening to him, and some of us tried to help
out. Lyndon Johnson was almost forgotten, no longer forbidding or feared; Robert Kennedy was dead but not
quite forgotten; Richard Nixon looked like a loser. With
all the tragedy and change that summer, it was fine
weather for discussion.

And, with all of this, there was an induction notice
tucked into the corner of my billfold.

So with friends and acquaintances and townspeople, I
spent the summer in Fred's antiseptic cafe, drinking coffee

and mapping out arguments on Fred's napkins. Or I sat in Chic's tavern, drinking beer with kids from the farms. I played some golf and tore up the pool table down at the bowling alley, keeping an eye open for likely looking high school girls.

Late at night, the town deserted, two or three of us would drive a car around and around the town's lake, talking about the war, very seriously, moving with care from one argument to the next, trying to make it a dialogue and not a debate. We covered all the big questions: justice, tyranny, self-determination, conscience and the state, God and war and love.

College friends came to visit: "Too bad, I hear you're drafted. What will you do?"

I said I didn't know, that I'd let time decide. Maybe something would change, maybe the war would end. Then we'd turn to discuss the matter, talking long, trying out the questions, sleeping late in the mornings.

The summer conversations, spiked with plenty of references to the philosophers and academicians of war, were thoughtful and long and complex and careful. But, in the end, careful and precise argumentation hurt me. It was painful to tread deliberately over all the axioms and assumptions and corollaries when the people on the town's draft board were calling me to duty, smiling so nicely.

"It won't be bad at all," they said. "Stop in and see us when it's over."

So to bring the conversations to a focus and also to try out in real words my secret fears, I argued for running away.

I was persuaded then, and I remain persuaded now, that the war was wrong. And since it was wrong and since people were dying as a result of it, it was evil. Doubts, of course, hedged all this: I had neither the expertise nor the wisdom to synthesize answers; the facts were clouded; there was no certainty as to the kind of government that would follow a North Vietnamese victory or, for that matter, an American victory, and the specifics of the conflict were hidden away—partly in men's minds, partly in the archives of government, and partly in buried irretrievable history. The war, I thought, was wrongly conceived and poorly justified. But perhaps I was mistaken, and who really knew, anyway?

Piled on top of this was the town, my family, my teachers, a whole history of the prairie. Like magnets, these things pulled in one direction or the other, almost physical forces weighting the problem, so that, in the end, it was less reason and more gravity that was the final influence.

My family was careful that summer. The decision was mine and it was not talked about. The town lay there, spread out in the corn and watching me, the mouths of old women and Country Club men poised in readiness to find fault. It was not a town, not a Minneapolis or New York, where the son of a father can sometimes escape scrutiny. More, I owed the prairie something. For twenty-one years I'd lived under its laws, accepted its education, eaten its food, wasted and guzzled its water, slept well at night, driven across its highways, dirtied and breathed its air, wallowed in its luxuries. I'd played on its Little League teams. I remember Plato's *Crito,* when Socrates, facing certain death—execution, not war—had the chance to escape. But he reminded himself that he had seventy years in which he could have left the country, if he were not satisfied or felt the agreements he'd made with it were unfair. He had not chosen Sparta or Crete. And, I reminded myself, I hadn't thought much about Canada until that summer.

The summer passed this way. Golden afternoons on the golf course, an illusive hopefulness that the war would grant me a last-minute reprieve, nights in the pool hall or drug store, talking with townsfolk, turning the questions over and over, being a philosopher.

Near the end of that summer the time came to go to the war. The family indulged in a cautious sort of Last Supper together, and afterward my father, who is brave, said it was time to report at the bus depot. I moped down to my bedroom and looked the place over, feeling quite stupid, thinking that my mother would come in there in a day or two and probably cry a little. I trudged back up to the kitchen and put my satchel down. Everyone gathered around, saying so long and good health and write and let us know if you want anything. My father took up the induction papers, checking on times and dates and all the last-minute things, and when I pecked at my mother's face and grabbed the satchel for comfort, he told me to put it down, that I wasn't supposed to report until tomorrow. I'd misread the induction date.

After laughing about the mistake, after a flush of red color and a flood of ribbing and a wave of relief had come and gone, I took a long drive around the lake. Sunset Park, with its picnic table and little beach and a brown wood shelter and some families swimming. The Crippled Children's School. Slater Park, more kids. A long string of split-level houses, painted every color.

The war and my person seemed like twins as I went around the town's lake. Twins grafted together and forever together, as if a separation would kill them both.

The thought made me angry.

In the basement of my house I found some scraps of cardboard. I printed obscene words on them. I declared my intention to have no part of Vietnam. With delightful viciousness, a secret will, I declared the war evil, the draft board evil, the town evil in its lethargic acceptance of it all. For many minutes, making up the signs, making up my mind, I was outside the town. I was outside the law. I imagined myself strutting up and down the sidewalks outside the depot, the bus waiting and the driver blaring his horn, the *Daily Globe* photographer trying to push me into line with the other draftees, the frantic telephone calls, my head buzzing at the deed.

On the cardboard, my strokes of bright red were big and ferocious looking. The language was clear and certain and burned with a hard, defiant, criminal, blasphemous sound. I tried reading it aloud. I was scared. I was sad.

Later in the evening I tore the signs into pieces and put the shreds in the garbage can outside. I went back into the basement. I slipped the crayons into their box, the same stubs of color I'd used a long time before to chalk in reds and greens on Roy Rogers cowboy boots.

I'd never been a demonstrator, except in the loose sense. I'd taken a stand in the school newspaper on the war, trying to show why it seemed wrong. But, mostly, I'd just listened.

"No war is worth losing your life for," a college acquaintance used to argue. "The issue isn't a moral one. It's a matter of efficiency: What's the most efficient way to stay alive when your nation is at war? That's the issue."

But others argued that no war is worth losing your country for, and when asked about the case when a country fights a wrong war, those people just shrugged.

Most of my college friends found easy paths away from the problem, all to their credit. Deferments for this and that. Letters from doctors or chaplains. It was hard to find people who had to think much about the problem. Counsel came from two main quarters, pacifists and veterans of foreign wars, but neither camp had much to offer. It wasn't a matter of peace, as the pacifists argued, but rather a matter of when and when not to join others in making war. And it wasn't a matter of listening to an ex-lieutenant colonel talk about serving in a right war, when the question was whether to serve in what seemed a wrong one.

On August 13, I went to the bus depot. A Worthington *Daily Globe* photographer took my picture standing by a rail fence with four other draftees.

Then the bus took us through corn fields, to the little towns along the way—Rushmore and Adrian—where other recruits came aboard. With the tough guys drinking beer and howling in the back seats, brandishing their empty cans and calling one another "scum" and "trainee" and "GI Joe," with all this noise and hearty farewelling, we went to Sioux Falls. We spent the night in a YMCA. I went out alone for a beer, drank it in a corner booth, then I bought a book and read it in my room.

At noon the next day our hands were in the air, even the tough guys. We recited the oath—some of us loudly and daringly, others in bewilderment. It was a brightly lighted room, wood paneled. A flag gave the place the right colors. There was smoke in the air. We said the words and we were soldiers.

I'd never been much of a fighter. I was afraid of bullies: frustrated anger. Still, I deferred to no one. Positively lorded myself over inferiors. And on top of that was the matter of conscience and conviction, uncertain and surface-deep but pure nonetheless. I was a confirmed liberal. Not a pacifist, but I would have cast my ballot to end the Vietnam war, I would have voted for Eugene McCarthy, hoping he would make peace. I was not soldier material, that was certain.

But I submitted. All the soul searching and midnight conversations and books and beliefs were voided by abstention, extinguished by forfeiture, for lack of oxygen, by a sort of sleepwalking default. It was no decision, no chain of ideas or reasons, that steered me into the war.

It was an intellectual and physical standoff, and I did not have the energy to see it to an end. I did not want to be a soldier, not even an observer to war. But neither did I want to upset a peculiar balance between the order I knew, the people I knew, and my own private world. It was not just that I valued that order. I also feared its opposite—inevitable chaos, censure, embarrassment, the end of everything that had happened in my life, the end of it all.

And that standoff is still there. I would wish this book could take the form of a plea for everlasting peace, a plea from one who knows, from one who's been there and come back, an old soldier looking back at a dying war.

That would be good. It would be fine to integrate it all to persuade my younger brother and perhaps some others to say no to wrong wars.

Or would it be fine to confirm the old beliefs about war: It's horrible, but it's a crucible of men and events and, in the end, it makes more of a man out of you.

But, still, none of this seems right.

Now, war ended, all I am left with are simple, unprofound scraps of truth. Men die. Fear hurts and humiliates. It is hard to be brave. It is hard to know what bravery *is*. Dead human beings are heavy and awkward to carry, things smell different in Vietnam, soldiers are dreamers, drill sergeants are boors, some men thought the war was proper and others didn't and most didn't care. Is that the stuff for a morality lesson, even for a theme?

Do dreams offer lessons? Do nightmares have themes, do we awaken and analyze them and live our lives and advise others as a result? Can the foot soldier teach anything important about war, merely for having been there? I think not. He can tell war stories.

To Understand

1. What kind of town did O'Brien live in? Describe it.
2. What objection did O'Brien have to the war? What made his decision so difficult?
3. Why did O'Brien paint obscene words on cardboard?
4. What impressions of the war does O'Brien leave readers with at the end of the essay? Does he have a message?

To Write

1. Imagine that you have been drafted into military service. Write about your reaction. In what ways would your reaction be similar to O'Brien's, in what ways different?

~~~~~~

Grace Suh

The Eye of the Beholder

Grace Suh first published this essay in A Magazine. *In this piece, she looks at the issue of how important appearance is to her and, in turn, to all of us. She is frank in revealing her self-image as it pertains to her facial features and how others perceive her.*

Before Reading: Think about how important physical appearance is to you. Compared to other people, are you very concerned about it?

Several summers ago, on one of those endless August evenings when the sun hangs suspended just above the horizon, I made up my mind to become beautiful.

It happened as I walked by one of those mirrored glass-clad office towers, and caught a glimpse of my reflection out of the corner of my eye. The glass on this particular building was green, which might have accounted for the sickly tone of my complexion, but there was no explaining away the limp, ragged hair, the dark circles under my eyes, the facial blemishes, the shapeless, wrinkled clothes. The overall effect—the whole being greater than the sum of its parts—was one of stark ugliness.

I'd come home from college having renounced bourgeois suburban values, like hygiene and grooming. Now, home for the summer, I washed my hair and changed clothes only when I felt like it, and spent most of my time sitting on the lawn eating mini rice cakes and Snickers and reading dogeared back issues of *National Geographic.*

But that painfully epiphanous day, standing there on the hot sidewalk, I suddenly understood what my mother had been gently hinting these past months: I was no longer just plain, no longer merely unattractive. No, I had broken the Unsightliness Barrier. I was now UGLY, and aggressively so.

And so, in an unusual exertion of will, I resolved to fight back against the forces of entropy. I envisioned it as reclamation work, like scything down a lawn that has grown into meadow, or restoring a damaged fresco. For the first time in ages, I felt elated and hopeful. I nearly sprinted into the nearby Neiman Marcus. As I entered the cool, hushed, dimly lit first floor and saw the gleaming counters lined with vials of magical balm, the priestesses of beauty in their sacred smocks, and the glassy photographic icons of the goddesses themselves—Paulina, Linda, Cindy, Vendella—in a wild, reckless burst of inspiration I thought to myself, Heck, why just okay? Why not BEAUTIFUL?

At the Estée Lauder counter, I spied a polished, middle-aged woman whom I hoped might be less imperious than the aloof amazons at the Chanel counter.

"Could I help you?" the woman (I thought of her as Estée) asked.

"Yes," I blurted. "I look terrible. I need a complete makeover—skin, face, everything."

After a wordless scrutiny of my face, she motioned me to sit down and began. She cleansed my skin with a bright blue mud masque and clear, tingling astringent and then applied a film of moisturizer, working extra amounts into the rough patches. Under the soft pressure of her fingers, I began to relax. From my perch, I happily took in the dizzying, colorful swirl of beautiful women and products all around me. I breathed in the billows of perfume that wafted through the air. I whispered the names of products under my breath like a healing mantra: cooling eye gel, gentle exfoliant, night time neck area reenergizer, moisture recharging intensifier, ultra-hydrating complex, emulsifying immunage. I felt immersed in femininity, intoxicated by beauty.

I was flooded with gratitude at the patience and determination with which Estée toiled away at my face, painting on swaths of lip gloss, blush, and foundation. She was not working in vain, I vowed, as I sucked in my cheeks on her command. I would buy all these products. I would use them every day. I studied her gleaming, polished features—her lacquered nails, the glittering mosaic of her eyeshadow, the complex red shimmer of her mouth, her flawless, dewy skin—and tried to imagine myself as impeccably groomed as she.

Estée's voice interrupted my reverie, telling me to blot my lips. I stuck the tissue into my mouth and clamped down, watching myself in the mirror. My skin was a blankly even shade of pale, my cheeks and lips glaring bright in contrast. My face had a strange plastic sheen, like a mannequin's. I grimaced as Estée applied the second lipstick coat: Was this right? Didn't I look kind of—fake? But she smiled back at me, clearly pleased with her work. I was ashamed of myself: Well, what did I expect? It wasn't like she had anything great to start with.

"Now," she announced, "Time for the biggie—Eyes."

"Oh. Well, actually, I want to look good and everything, but, I mean, I'm sure you could tell, I'm not really into a complicated beauty routine. . ." My voice faded into a faint giggle.

"So?" Estée snapped.

"Sooo. . ." I tried again, "I've never really used eye makeup, except, you know, for a little mascara sometimes, and I don't really feel comfortable—"

Estée was firm. "Well, the fact is that the eyes are the windows of the face. They're the focal point. An eye routine doesn't have to be complicated, but it's important to emphasize the eyes with some color, or they'll look washed out."

I certainly didn't want that. I leaned back again in my chair and closed my eyes.

Estée explained as she went: "I'm covering your lids with this champagne color. It's a real versatile base, 'cause it goes with almost any other color you put on top of it." I felt the velvety pad of the applicator seep over my lids in a soothing rhythm.

"Now, being an Oriental, you don't have a lid fold, so I'm going to draw one with this charcoal shadow. Then, I fill in below the line with a lighter charcoal color with a bit of blue in it—frosted midnight—and then above it, on the outsides of your lids, I'm going to apply this plum color. There. Hold on a minute. . . Okay. Open up."

I stared at the face in the mirror, at my eyes. The drawn-on fold and dark, heavy shadows distorted and re-proportioned my whole face. Not one of the features in the mirror was recognizable, not the waxy white skin or the redrawn crimson lips or the sharp, deep cheekbones, and especially, not the eyes. I felt negated; I had been blotted out and another face drawn in my place. I looked up at Estée, and in that moment I hated her. "I look terrible," I said.

Her back stiffened. "What do you mean?" she demanded.

"Hideous. I don't even look human. Look at my eyes. You can't even see me!" My voice was hoarse.

She looked. After a moment, she straightened up again, "Well, I'll admit, the eyeshadow doesn't look great." She began to put away the pencils and brushes. "But at least now you have an eyelid."

I told myself that she was a pathetic, middle-aged woman with a boring job and a meaningless life. I had my whole life before me. All she had was the newest Richard Chamberlain miniseries.

But it didn't matter. The fact of the matter was that she was pretty, and I was not. Her blue eyes were re-cessed in an intricate pattern of folds and hollows. Mine bulged out.

I bought the skincare system and the foundation and the blush and the lip liner pencil and the lipstick and the primer and the eyeliner and the eyeshadows—all four colors. The stuff filled a bag the size of a shoebox. It cost a lot. Estée handed me my receipt with a flourish, and I told her, "Thank you."

In the mezzanine level washroom, I set my bag down on the counter and scrubbed my face with water and slimy pink soap from the dispenser. I splashed my face with cold water until it felt tight, and dried my raw skin with brown paper towels that scratched.

As the sun sank into the Chicago skyline, I boarded the Burlington Northern Commuter for home and found a seat in the corner. I set the shopping bag down beside me, and heaped its gilt boxes and frosted glass bottles into my lap. Looking out the window, I saw that night had fallen. Instead of trees and backyard fences I saw my profile—the same reflection, I realized, that I'd seen hours ago in the side of the green glass office building. I did have eyelids, of course. Just not a fold. I wasn't pretty. But I was familiar and comforting. I was myself.

The next stop was mine. I arranged the things carefully back in the rectangular bag, large bottles of toner and moisturizer first, then the short cylinders of masque and scrub and powder, small bottles of foundation and primer, the little logs of pencils and lipstick, then the flat boxed compacts of blush and eyeshadow. The packages fit around each other cleverly, like pieces in a puzzle. The conductor called out, "Fairview Avenue," and I stood up. Hurrying down the aisle, I looked back once at the neatly packed bag on the seat behind me, and jumped out just as the doors were closing shut.

To Understand

1. Why does Suh decide to get a makeover? Describe her attitude early in the essay.

2. Describe the way in which Estée treats Suh. What are we readers to conclude about Estée?

3. Why does Suh wash her face after her makeover?

4. Why does Suh first buy all of the beauty products (at considerable expense) and then leave them on the bus when she gets off?

To Write

1. Critics of our contemporary culture argue that we are obsessed with our appearance. They claim that we spend too much time and money on beauty products, exercise equipment, and fad diets. Write about whether you would agree with this assessment.

Pat Mora

Immigrants

The author of many children's books as well as poetry collections for adults, Pat Mora has received acclaim for writing about the people and places of the Southwest and for drawing connections between cultures and communities. She has won awards from the National Endowment for the Arts and was granted the Kellogg National Leadership Fellowship. In this poem, Mora writes about the hopes and dreams immigrant parents have for their children.

Before Reading: Ask yourself what parents immigrating to America want for their children. Are there similarities from family to family, culture to culture? Also, note that this is the kind of poem in which the title leads right into the first line.

wrap their babies in the American flag,
feed them mashed hot dogs and apple pie,
name them Bill and Daisy,
buy them blonde dolls that blink blue
eyes or a football and tiny cleats
before the baby can even walk,
speak to them in thick English,
hallo, babee, hallo,
whisper in Spanish or Polish
when the babies sleep, whisper
in a dark parent bed, that dark
parent fear, "Will they like
our boy, our girl, our fine american
boy, our fine american girl?"

To Understand

1. List the images of American life that Mora mentions in the first half of the poem. Do the images accurately represent what immigrant parents want for their children?

2. Explain the parents' fears. What are they concerned about?

3. What is the speaker's attitude toward the immigrant parents in this poem? Are we readers to admire the immigrants for their hopes and fears?

To Write

1. In your opinion, is it more important for immigrant children to maintain the identity of their old culture or to develop a new American identity? Write about this as it pertains to families you know, and also think about the immigrants in your family—even if they came to the United States a long time ago.

Amy Tan

Mother Tongue

In 1989, Amy Tan received immediate acclaim for her novel, The Joy Luck Club, *which delves into the relationships between Chinese women and their Chinese-American daughters. This book, winner of the Bay Area Book Reviewers Award and the Commonwealth Club Gold Award, was later made into a major motion picture. Since then, Tan has published three more novels and two children's books. "Mother Tongue" was first published in* The Threepenny Review *and was included in the 1991 Best American Essays. In this essay, she explores the various kinds of English she has used as a child and as an educated adult.*

Before Reading: Think about the different ways you speak: in school, with your family, with friends, on the job, or in other situations.

I am not a scholar of English or literature. I cannot give you much more than personal opinion on the English language and its variations in this country or others.

I am a writer. And by that definition, I am someone who has always loved language. I am fascinated by language in daily life. I spend a great deal of my time thinking about the power of language—the way it can evoke an emotion, a visual image, a complex idea, or a simple truth. Language is the tool of my trade. And I use them all—all the Englishes I grew up with.

Recently, I was made keenly aware of the different Englishes I do use. I was giving a talk to a large group of people, the same talk I had already given to half a dozen other groups. The nature of the talk was about my writing, my life, and my book, *The Joy Luck Club*. The talk was going along well enough, until I remembered one major difference that made the whole talk sound wrong. My mother was in the room. And it was perhaps the first time she had heard me give a lengthy speech, using the kind of English I have never used with her. I was saying things like, "The intersection of memory upon imagination" and "There is an aspect of my fiction that relates to thus-and-thus"—a speech filled with carefully wrought grammatical phrases, burdened, it suddenly seemed to me, with nominalized forms, past perfect tenses, conditional phrases, all the forms of standard English that I had learned in school and through books, the forms of English I did not use at home with my mother.

Just last week, I was walking down the street with my mother, and I again found myself conscious of the English I was using, and the English I do use with her. We were talking about the price of new and used furniture and I heard myself saying this: "Not waste money that way." My husband was with us as well, and he didn't notice any switch in my English. And then I realized why. It's because over the twenty years we've been together I've often used that same kind of English with him, and sometimes he even uses it with me. It has become our language of intimacy, a different sort of English that relates to family talk, the language I grew up with.

So you'll have some idea of what this family talk I heard sounds like, I'll quote what my mother said during a recent conversation which I videotaped and then transcribed. During this conversation, my mother was talking about a political gangster in Shanghai who had the same last name as her family's, Du, and how the gangster in his early years wanted to be adopted by her family, which was rich by comparison. Later, the gangster became more powerful, far richer than my mother's family, and one day showed up at my mother's wedding to pay his respects. Here's what she said in part:

"Du Yusong having business like fruit stand. Like off the street kind. He is Du like Du Zong—but not Tsung-ming

Island people. The local people call putong, the river east side, he belong to that side local people. That man want to ask Du Zong father take him in like become own family. Du Zong father wasn't look down on him, but didn't take seriously, until that man big like become a mafia. Now important person very hard to inviting him. Chinese way, came only to show respect, don't stay for dinner. Respect for making big celebration, he shows up. Mean gives lots of respect. Chinese custom. Chinese social life that way. If too important won't have to stay too long. He come to my wedding. I didn't see, I heard it. I gone to boy's side, they have YMCA dinner. Chinese age I was nineteen."

You should know that my mother's expressive command of English belies how much she actually understands. She reads the *Forbes* report, listens to *Wall Street Week,* converses daily with her stockbroker, reads all of Shirley MacLaine's books with ease—all kinds of things I can't begin to understand. Yet some of my friends tell me they understand 50 percent of what my mother says. Some say they understand 80 to 90 percent. Some say they understand none of it, as if she were speaking pure Chinese. But to me, my mother's English is perfectly clear, perfectly natural. It's my mother tongue. Her language, as I hear it, is vivid, direct, full of observation and imagery. That was the language that helped shape the way I saw things, expressed things, made sense of the world.

Lately, I've been giving more thought to the kind of English my mother speaks. Like others, I have described it to people as "broken" or "fractured" English. But I wince when I say that. It has always bothered me that I can think of no way to describe it other than "broken," as if it were damaged and needed to be fixed, as if it lacked a certain wholeness and soundness. I've heard other terms used, "limited English," for example. But they seem just as bad, as if everything is limited, including people's perceptions of the limited English speaker.

I know this for a fact, because when I was growing up, my mother's "limited" English limited *my* perception of her. I was ashamed of her English. I believed that her English reflected the quality of what she had to say. That is, because she expressed them imperfectly her thoughts were imperfect. And I had plenty of empirical evidence to support me: the fact that people in department stores, at banks, and at restaurants did not take her seriously, did not give her good service, pretended not to understand her, or even acted as if they did not hear her.

My mother has long realized the limitations of her English as well. When I was fifteen, she used to have me call people on the phone to pretend I was she. In this guise, I was forced to ask for information or even to complain and yell at people who had been rude to her. One time it was a call to her stockbroker in New York. She had crashed out her small portfolio and it just so happened we were going to New York the next week, our very first trip outside California. I had to get on the phone and say in an adolescent voice that was not very convincing, "This is Mrs. Tan."

And my mother was standing in the back whispering loudly, "Why he don't send me check, already two weeks late. So mad he lie to me, losing me money."

And then I said in perfect English, "Yes, I'm getting rather concerned. You had agreed to send the check two weeks ago, but it hasn't arrived."

Then she began to talk more loudly. "What he want, I come to New York tell him front of his boss, you cheating me?" And I was trying to calm her down, make her be quiet, while telling the stockbroker, "I can't tolerate any more excuses. If I don't receive the check immediately, I am going to have to speak to your manager when I'm in New York next week." And sure enough, the following week there we were in front of this astonished stockbroker, and I was sitting there red-faced and quiet, and my mother, the real Mrs. Tan, was shouting at his boss in her impeccable broken English.

We used a similar routine just five days ago, for a situation that was far less humorous. My mother had gone to the hospital for an appointment, to find out about a benign brain tumor a CAT scan had revealed a month ago. She said she had spoken very good English, her best English, no mistakes. Still, she said, the hospital did not apologize when they said they had lost the CAT scan and she had come for nothing. She said they did not seem to have any sympathy when she told them she was anxious to know the exact diagnosis, since her husband and son had both died of brain tumors. She said they would not give her any more information until the next time and she would have to make another appointment for that. So she said she would not leave until the doctor called her daughter, me, who spoke in perfect English—lo and behold—we had assurances the CAT scan would be found, promises that a conference call on Monday would be held, and apologies for any suffering my mother had gone through for a most regrettable mistake.

I think my mother's English almost had an effect on limiting my possibilities in life as well. Sociologists and linguists probably will tell you that a person's developing language skills are more influenced by peers. But I do think that the language spoken in the family, especially in immigrant families which are more insular, plays a large role in shaping the language of the child. And I believe it affected my results on achievement tests, IQ tests, and the SAT. While my English skills were never judged as poor, compared to math, English could not be considered my strong suit. In grade school I did moderately well, getting perhaps B's, sometimes B-pluses, in English and scoring perhaps in the sixtieth or seventieth percentile on achievement tests. But those scores were not good enough to override the opinion that my true abilities lay in math and science, because in those areas I achieved A's and scored in the ninetieth percentile or higher.

This was understandable. Math is precise; there is only one correct answer. Whereas, for me at least, the answers on English tests were always a judgment call, a matter of opinion and personal experience. Those tests were constructed around items like fill-in-the-blank sentence completion, such as, "Even though Tom was _____, Mary thought he was _____." And the correct answer always seemed to be the most bland combinations of thoughts, for example, "Even though Tom was shy, Mary thought he was charming," with the grammatical structure "even though" limiting the correct answer to some sort of semantic opposites, so you wouldn't get answers like, "Even though Tom was foolish, Mary thought he was ridiculous." Well, according to my mother, there were very few limitations as to what Tom could have been and what Mary might have thought of him. So I never did well on tests like that.

The same was true with word analogies, pairs of words in which you were supposed to find some sort of logical, semantic relationship—for example, "*Sunset* is to *nightfall* as _____ is to _____." And here you would be presented with a list of four possible pairs, one of which showed the same kind of relationship: *red* is to *stoplight, bus* is to *arrival, chills* is to *fever, yawn* is to *boring*. Well, I could never think that way. I knew what the tests were asking, but I could not block out of my mind the images already created by the first pair, "*sunset* is to *nightfall*"—and I would see a burst of colors against a darkening sky, the moon rising, the lowering of a curtain of stars. And all the other pairs of words—red, bus, stoplight, boring—just threw up a mass of confusing images, making it impossible for me to sort out something as logical as saying: "A sunset precedes nightfall" is the same as "a chill precedes a fever." The only way I could have gotten that answer right would have been to imagine an associative situation, for example, my being disobedient and staying out past sunset, catching a chill at night, which turns into feverish pneumonia as punishment, which indeed did happen to me.

I have been thinking about all this lately, about my mother's English, about achievement tests. Because lately I've been asked, as a writer, why there are not more Asian Americans represented in American literature. Why are there few Asian Americans enrolled in creative writing programs? Why do so many Chinese students go into engineering? Well, these are broad sociological questions I can't begin to answer. But I have noticed in surveys—in fact, just last week—that Asian students, as a whole, always do significantly better on math achievement tests than in English. And this makes me think that there are other Asian American students whose English spoken in the home might also be described as "broken" or "limited." And perhaps they also have teachers who are steering them away from writing and into math and science, which is what happened to me.

Fortunately, I happen to be rebellious in nature and enjoy the challenge of disproving assumptions made about me. I became an English major my first year in college, after being enrolled as a pre-med. I started writing nonfiction as a freelancer the week after I was told by my former boss that writing was my worst skill and I should hone my talents toward account management.

But it wasn't until 1985 that I finally began to write fiction. And at first I wrote using what I thought to be wittily crafted sentences, sentences that would finally prove that I had mastery over the English language. Here's an example from the first draft of a story that later made its way into *The Joy Luck Club*, but without this line: "That was my mental quandary in its nascent state." A terrible line, which I can barely pronounce.

Fortunately, for reasons I won't get into today, I later decided I should envision a reader for the stories I would write. And the reader I decided upon was my mother, because these were stories about mothers. So with this reader in mind—and in fact she did read my early drafts—I began to write stories using all the Englishes I grew up with: the English I spoke to my mother, which for lack of a better term might be described as "simple"; the English she used with me, which for lack of a better term might be described as "broken"; my translation of her Chinese, which could certainly be described as "watered down"; and what I imagined to be her translation of her Chinese if she could speak in perfect English, her internal language, and for that I sought to preserve the essence, but neither an English nor a Chinese structure. I wanted to capture what language ability tests can never reveal: her intent, her passion, her imagery, the rhythms of her speech and the nature of her thoughts.

Apart from what any critic had to say about my writing, I knew I had succeeded where it counted when my mother finished reading my book and gave me her verdict: "So easy to read."

To Understand

1. What occasion made Tan particularly aware of the different kinds of English she speaks?
2. Describe Tan's attitude about her mother's "broken" or "limited" English. Has it changed over the years? What parts of the essay inform you about her attitude?
3. Explain why Tan had difficulty on English achievement tests.
4. Tan explains that in her first attempts at fiction writing she used "wittily crafted sentences." Why didn't this work for her? How did her writing change in response to her early drafts?

To Write

1. Write about the different kinds of English you use. How does your English change according to the people you are with?

2. Tan says that she was encouraged to pursue math and science because that is where her "true abilities lay" and to avoid careers that involved writing. Write about how your math skills and language skills are influencing your choice of career. Are there other important factors in addition to these two?

⚜

Don DeLillo

Videotape

Don DeLillo was born in New York City and grew up in the Bronx. Considered a master of dark humor and a keen observer of contemporary American culture, he has written eleven novels including Americana, Mao II, White Noise, *and* Underworld. *His work has earned him a National Book Award and a Pen / Faulkner Award. In the following story, he involves his readers in a murder videotaped by a child.*

Before Reading: Ask yourself how powerful home video is when you see it on television. Is there anything special about this medium compared to films produced in a professional studio?

It shows a man driving a car. It is the simplest sort of family video. You see the man at the wheel of a medium Dodge.

It is just a kid aiming her camera through the rear window of the family car at the windshield of the car behind her.

You know about families and their video cameras. You know how kids get involved, how the camera shows them that every subject is potentially charged, a million things they never see with the unaided eye. They investigate the meaning of inert objects and dumb pets and they poke at family privacy. They learn to see things twice.

It is the kid's own privacy that is being protected here. She is twelve years old and her name is being withheld even though she is neither the victim nor the perpetrator of the crime but only the means of recording it. It shows the man in a sport shirt at the wheel of his car. There is nothing else to see. The car approaches briefly, then falls back.

You know how children with cameras learn to work the exposed moments that define the family cluster. They break every trust, spy out the undefended space, catch Mom coming out of the bathroom in her cumbrous robe and turbaned towel, looking bloodless and plucked. It is not a joke. They will shoot you sitting on the pot if they can manage a suitable vantage.

The tape has the jostled sort of noneventness that marks the family product. Of course the man in this case is not a member of the family but a stranger in a car, a random figure, someone who has happened along in the slow lane.

It shows a man in his forties wearing a pale shirt open at the throat, the image washed by reflections and sunglint, with many jostled moments.

It is not just another video homicide. It is a homicide recorded by a child who thought she was doing something simple and maybe halfway clever, shooting some tape of a man in a car.

He sees the girl and waves briefly, wagging a hand without taking it off the wheel—an underplayed reaction that makes you like him.

It is unrelenting footage that rolls on and on. It has an aimless determination, a persistence that lives outside the subject matter. You are looking into the mind of a home video. It is innocent, it is aimless, it is determined, it is real.

He is bald up the middle of his head, a nice guy in his forties whose whole life seems open to the hand-held camera.

But there is also an element of suspense. You keep on looking not because you know something is going to happen—of course you do know something is going to happen and you do look for that reason but you might also keep on looking if you came across this footage for the first time without knowing the outcome. There is a crude power operating here. You keep on looking because things combine to hold you fast—a sense of the random, the amateurish, the accidental, the impending. You don't think of the tape as boring or interesting. It is crude, it is blunt, it is relentless. It is the jostled part of your mind, the film that runs through your hotel brain under all the thoughts you know you're thinking.

The world is lurking in the camera, already framed for the boy or girl who will come along and take up the device, learn the instrument, shooting old Granddad at breakfast, all stroked out so his nostrils gape, the cereal spoon baby-gripped in his pale fist.

It shows a man alone in a medium Dodge. It seems to go on forever.

There's something about the nature of the tape, the grain of the image, the sputtering black-and-white tones, the starkness—you think this is more real, truer-to-life than anything around you. The things around you have a rehearsed and layered and cosmetic look. The tape is superreal, or maybe underreal is the way you want to put it. It is what lies at the scraped bottom of all the layers you have added. And this is another reason why you keep on looking. The tape has a searing realness.

It shows him giving an abbreviated wave, stiff-palmed, like a signal flag at a siding.

You know how families make up games. This is just another game in which the child invents the rules as she goes along. She likes the idea of videotaping a man in his car. She has probably never done it before and she sees no reason to vary the format or terminate early or pan to another car. This is her game and she is learning it and playing it at the same time. She feels halfway clever and inventive and maybe slightly intrusive as well, a little bit of brazenness that spices any game.

And you keep on looking. You look because this is the nature of the footage, to make a channeled path through time, to give things a shape and a destiny.

Of course if she had panned to another car, the right car at the precise time, she would have caught the gunman as he fired.

The chance quality of the encounter. The victim, the killer, and the child with a camera. Random energies that approach a common point. There's something here that speaks to you directly, saying terrible things about forces beyond your control, lines of intersection that cut through history and logic and every reasonable layer of human expectation.

She wandered into it. The girl got lost and wandered clear-eyed into horror. This is a children's story about straying too far from home. But it isn't the family car that serves as the instrument of the child's curiosity, her inclination to explore. It is the camera that puts her in the tale.

You know about holidays and family celebrations and how somebody shows up with a camcorder and the relatives stand around and barely react because they're numbingly accustomed to the process of being taped and decked and shown on the VCR with the coffee and cake.

He is hit soon after. If you've seen the tape many times you know from the hand-wave exactly when he will be hit. It is something, naturally, that you wait for. You say to your wife, if you're at home and she is there, Now here is where he gets it. You say, Janet, hurry up, this is where it happens.

Now here is where he gets it. You see him jolted, sort of wire-shocked—then he seizes up and falls toward the door or maybe leans or slides into the door is the proper way to put it. It is awful and unremarkable at the same time. The car stays in the slow lane. It approaches briefly, then falls back.

You don't usually call your wife over to the TV set. She has her programs, you have yours. But there's a certain urgency here. You want her to see how it looks. The tape has been running forever and now the thing is finally going to happen and you want her to be here when he's shot.

Here it comes, all right. He is shot, head-shot, and the camera reacts, the child reacts—there is a jolting movement but she keeps on taping, there is a sympathetic response, a nerve response, her heart is beating faster but she keeps the camera trained on the subject as he slides into the door and even as you see him die you're thinking of the girl. At some level the girl has to be present here, watching what you're watching, unprepared—the girl is seeing this cold and you have to marvel at the fact that she keeps the tape rolling.

It shows something awful and unaccompanied. You want your wife to see it because it is real this time, not fancy movie violence—the realness beneath the layers of cosmetic perception. Hurry up, Janet, here it comes. He dies so fast. There is no accompaniment of any kind. It is very stripped. You want to tell her it is realer than real but then she will ask what that means.

The way the camera reacts to the gunshot—a startle reaction that brings pity and terror into the frame, the girl's own shock, the girl's identification with the victim.

You don't see the blood, which is probably trickling behind his ear and down the back of his neck. The way his head is twisted away from the door, the twist of the head gives you only a partial profile and it's the wrong side, it's not the side where he was hit.

And maybe you're being a little aggressive here, practically forcing your wife to watch. Why? What are you telling her? Are you making a little statement? Like I'm going to ruin your day out of ordinary spite. Or a big statement? Like this is the risk of existing. Either way you're rubbing her face in this tape and you don't know why.

It shows the car drifting toward a guardrail and then there's a jostling sense of two other lanes and part of another car, a split-second blur, and the tape ends here, either because the girl stopped shooting or because some central authority, the police or the district attorney or the TV station, decided there was nothing else you had to see.

This is either the tenth or eleventh homicide committed by the Texas Highway Killer. The number is uncertain because the police believe that one of the killings may have been a copycat crime.

And there is something about videotape, isn't there, and this particular kind of serial crime? This is a crime designed for random taping and immediate playing. You sit there and wonder if this kind of crime became more possible when the means of taping and playing an event—playing it immediately after the taping—became part of the culture. The principal doesn't necessarily commit the sequence of crimes in order to see them taped and played. He commits the crimes as if they were a form of taped-and-played event. The crimes are inseparable from the idea of taping and playing. You sit there thinking that this is a crime that has found its medium, or vice versa—cheap mass production, the sequence of repeated images and victims, stark and glary and more or less unremarkable.

It shows very little in the end. It is a famous murder because it is on tape and because the murderer has done it many times and because the crime was recorded by a child. So the child is involved, the Video Kid as she is sometimes called because they have to call her something. The tape is famous and so is she. She is famous in the modern manner of people whose names are strategically withheld. They are famous without names or faces, spirits living apart from their bodies, the victims and witnesses, the underage criminals, out there somewhere at the edges of perception.

Seeing someone at the moment he dies, dying unexpectedly. This is reason alone to stay fixed to the screen. It is instructional, watching a man shot dead as he drives along on a sunny day. It demonstrates an elemental truth, that every breath you take has two possible endings. And that's another thing. There's a joke locked away here, a note of cruel slapstick that you are completely willing to appreciate. Maybe the victim's a chump, a dope, classically unlucky. He had it coming, in a way, like an innocent fool in a silent movie.

You don't want Janet to give you any crap about it's on all the time, they show it a thousand times a day. They show it because it exists, because they have to show it, because this is why they're out there. The horror freezes your soul but this doesn't mean that you want them to stop.

To Understand

1. Summarize what actually happens in this story. Are there surprises in the course of events?

2. Why does DeLillo use the second-person pronoun "you" throughout the story? What is the effect of this point of view?

3. Several times throughout the story, the narrator tells us, "You keep on looking." What point about human nature is the author making?

4. The final four paragraphs of the story suggest reasons to be captivated by such videotape. Review these paragraphs and summarize the reasons.

To Write

1. If you were to see the videotape in this story on television, how would you react? Write about whether you would be drawn to it in the way DeLillo's story suggests and whether DeLillo has accurately captured human nature here.

Thomas Lux

The Swimming Pool

Thomas Lux's poem "You Go to School To Learn" and a brief biography appear on page 100 in this book. In the following poem, Lux describes a scene of children at a swimming pool to characterize a particularly negative aspect of human nature.

Before Reading: Ask yourself why people, under any circumstances, are cruel to other people. Are there any general reasons you can think of?

All around the apt. swimming pool
the boys stare at the girls
and the girls look everywhere but the opposite
or down or up. It is
as it was a thousand years ago: the fat
boy has it hardest, he
takes the sneers,
prefers the winter so he can wear
his heavy pants and sweater.
Today, he's here with the others.
Better they are cruel to him in his presence
than out. Of the five here now (three boys,
two girls) one is fat, three cruel,
and one, a girl, wavers to the side,
all the world tearing at her.
As yet she has no breasts
(her friend does) and were it not
for the forlorn fat boy who she joins
in taunting, she could not bear her terror,
which is the terror
of being him. Does it make her happy

that she has no need, right now, of ingratiation,
of acting fool to salve
her loneliness? She doesn't seem
so happy. She is like
the lower-middle class, that fatal group
handed crumbs so they can drop a few
down lower, to the poor, so they won't kill
the rich. All around
the apt. swimming pool
there is what's everywhere: forsakenness
and fear, a disdain for those beneath us
rather than a rage
against the ones above: the exploiters,
the oblivious and unabashedly cruel.

To Understand

1. In your own words, describe the plight of the fat boy. What difficulties does he face?

2. Why does the girl who "wavers to the side" join in mocking the "forlorn fat boy"? What does Lux want us to understand about this girl?

3. The speaker says that the girl, who joins the others in treating the fat boy cruelly, "is like the lower middle class. . . ." Explain this.

4. Review the poem's final seven lines. What is the speaker saying about "what's everywhere"?

To Write

1. The poem's speaker says we have "a disdain for those beneath us / rather than a rage / against the ones above. . . ." Do you believe this is true for most people? Use examples of people you have observed to support or refute this statement.

Edwin Arlington Robinson

Richard Cory

In 1869, Edwin Arlington Robinson was born in Head Tide, Maine, and early on he devoted his life to poetry. Recognized for his control of traditional forms, Robinson's career was given a great opportunity when President Theodore Roosevelt arranged for him a job at a New York customs house at which he was required to do little but write poetry. However, it wasn't until later, when an anonymous donor gave him a monthly income to write, that Robinson did his best work, winning three Pulitzer Prizes—for Collected Poems, The Man Who Died Twice, *and* Tristram. *In the following poem, Robinson offers readers a message about a character who seems to have everything.*

Before Reading: Think of people you know who seem to have everything other people want. How well do you know these people?

Whenever Richard Cory went down town,
We people on the pavement looked at him:
He was a gentleman from sole to crown,
Clean favored and imperially slim.

And he was always quietly arrayed,
And he was always human when he talked;
But still he fluttered pulses when he said,
"Good morning," and he glittered when he walked.
And he was rich—yes, richer than a king—
And admirably schooled in every grace:
In fine, we thought that he was everything
To make us wish that we were in his place.

So on we worked, and waited for the light,
And went without the meat and cursed the bread;
And Richard Cory, one calm summer night,
Went home and put a bullet through his head.

To Understand

1. Reread the poem and list what Richard Cory has going for him—those things that others admired.

2. In what position are the people who observe Richard Cory? What hints do we have about their lives?

3. What does Robinson want us readers to conclude about Richard Cory? How should we respond to the surprise ending?

To Write

1. Speculate about the reasons Richard Cory (or any other person who seems to have everything) would commit suicide.

∗∞⚙⚘∞∗

Linda Pastan

Ethics

Linda Pastan's poem, "Marks," and a brief biography can be found on page 144. In ethics, Pastan writes about a class of children presented with a difficult ethical question by their teacher.

Before Reading: Think about Pastan's one-word title. What kinds of issues does this word bring to mind for you?

In ethics class so many years ago
our teacher asked this question every fall:
if there were a fire in a museum
which would you save, a Rembrandt painting
or an old woman who hadn't many
years left anyhow? Restless on hard chairs
caring little for pictures or old age
we'd opt one year for life, the next for art
and always half-heartedly. Sometimes
the woman borrowed my grandmother's face
leaving her usual kitchen to wander
some drafty, half imagined museum.
One year, feeling clever, I replied
why not let the woman decide herself?
Linda, the teacher would report, eschews
the burdens of responsibility.
This fall in a real museum I stand
before a real Rembrandt, old woman,
or nearly so, myself. The colors
within this frame are darker than autumn,
darker even than winter—the browns of earth,
though earth's most radiant elements burn

through the canvas. I know now that woman
and painting and season are almost one
and all beyond saving by children.

To Understand

1. Describe the speaker and her classmates. How does Pastan's brief image of them influence your understanding of the poem?

2. How does Pastan describe the Rembrandt painting, and how is her description significant?

3. Read the poem again and explain the final sentence.

To Write

1. Write your own response to the poem's initial question. Give specific reasons for your answer.

William Stafford

Traveling through the Dark

The author of more than sixty-five books of poetry and prose, William Stafford achieved notoriety for a writing style that was deceptively simple. Among his honors, he won a Western States Lifetime Achievement Award in Poetry, a Shelley Memorial Award, and a Guggenheim Fellowship. Stafford taught for over thirty years at Lewis and Clark College in Oregon before his death in 1993. The following piece is the title poem from Stafford's first major collection, which won the National Book Award. In it the speaker faces a dilemma when he encounters a dead deer beside a rural road.

Before Reading: Consider the word "dark" in the title, and pay attention to the effect of the nighttime images in this poem.

Traveling through the dark I found a deer
dead on the edge of Wilson River road.
It is usually best to roll them into the canyon:
that road is narrow; to swerve might make more dead.

By glow of the tail-light I stumbled back of the car
and stood by the heap, a doe, a recent killing;
she had stiffened already, almost cold.
I dragged her off; she was large in the belly.

My fingers touching the side brought me the reason—
her side was warm; her fawn lay there waiting,
alive, still, never to be born.
Beside that mountain road I hesitated.

The car aimed ahead its lowered parking lights;
under the hood purred the steady engine.
I stood in the glare of the warm exhaust turning red;
around our group I could hear the wilderness listen.

I thought hard for all of us—my only swerving—
then pushed her over the edge into the river.

To Understand

1. After the speaker discovers the fawn, he says, "Beside that mountain road I hesitated." Why does he hesitate? Explain the dilemma.

2. Review the images in the fourth stanza. What impression or message should a reader receive from these images?

3. Why does the speaker decide to push the doe "over the edge into the river"?

To Write

1. What would you have done if you had been in the speaker's position? Give and explain reasons for your answer.

Raymond Carver

Popular Mechanics

A writer of both poetry and short stories, Raymond Carver was one of the most influential American fiction writers of the 1970's and 1980's. His books including What We Talk About When We Talk About Love *(from which this story is taken),* Cathedral, *and* Will You Please Be Quiet, Please? *are notable for their portrayal of working-class people and for their spare style. Before his death in 1988, Carver won a Mildred and Harold Strauss Living Award, which payed him $35,000 a year for five years and required that he give up all employment except for writing. In the following story, Carver presents a domestic struggle that turns, in a matter of minutes, very dangerous.*

Before Reading: Think about how and why domestic strife between men and women can turn violent. Are there any common factors to such events?

Early that day the weather turned and the snow was melting into dirty water. Streaks of it ran down from the little shoulder-high window that faced the backyard. Cars slushed by on the street outside, where it was getting dark. But it was getting dark on the inside too.

He was in the bedroom pushing clothes into a suitcase when she came to the door.

I'm glad you're leaving! I'm glad you're leaving! she said. Do you hear?

He kept on putting his things into the suitcase.

Son of a bitch! I'm so glad you're leaving! She began to cry. You can't even look me in the face, can you?

Then she noticed the baby's picture on the bed and picked it up.

He looked at her and she wiped her eyes and stared at him before turning and going back to the living room.

Bring that back, he said.

Just get your things and get out, she said.

He did not answer. He fastened the suitcase, put on his coat, looked around the bedroom before turning off the light. Then he went out to the living room.

She stood in the doorway of the little kitchen, holding the baby.

I want the baby, he said.

Are you crazy?

No, but I want the baby. I'll get someone to come by for his things.

You're not touching this baby, she said.

The baby had begun to cry and she uncovered the blanket from around his head.

Oh, oh, she said, looking at the baby.

He moved toward her.

For God's sake! she said. She took a step back into the kitchen.

I want the baby.

Get out of here!

She turned and tried to hold the baby over in a corner behind the stove.

But he came up. He reached across the stove and tightened his hands on the baby.

Let go of him, he said.

Get away, get away! she cried.

The baby was red-faced and screaming. In the scuffle they knocked down a flower pot that hung behind the stove.

He crowded her into the wall then, trying to break her grip. He held on to the baby and pushed with all his weight.

Let go of him, he said.

Don't, she said. You're hurting the baby, she said.

I'm not hurting the baby, he said.

The kitchen window gave no light. In the near-dark he worked on her fisted fingers with one hand and with the other hand he gripped the screaming baby up under an arm near the shoulder.

She felt her fingers being forced open. She felt the baby going from her.

No! she screamed just as her hands came loose.

She would have it, this baby. She grabbed for the baby's other arm. She caught the baby around the wrist and leaned back.

But he would not let go. He felt the baby slipping out of his hands and he pulled back very hard.

In this manner, the issue was decided.

To Understand

1. Reread the opening paragraph. How do the images there contribute to your understanding of the story?

2. How would you characterize the man's behavior? The woman's? Point to specific sentences to support your answers.

3. The final sentence reads, "In this manner, the issue was decided." How exactly has the issue been decided? Use your imagination. What happens next for the characters in this story?

To Write

1. What is wrong in the way this couple is trying to resolve their differences? In your opinion, what should they be doing differently?

Issues/Positions: Ideas for Writing

Note that for any of the writing ideas below, you should make certain the scope of your issue is appropriate for the length of paper you will write. Don't write about too large an issue in a very brief paper. Before beginning, consult with your instructor to make sure you have a topic that will give you a chance of writing a good paper.

1. Go back to one of the readings in this chapter and write a paper in which you take a position on an issue in that piece. Identify exactly what the issue is, make a clear and emphatic statement of your position, and organize your paper around three to five of your strongest reasons to support it.

2. What are some issues that are controversial in your community? You might read a local newspaper to familiarize yourself with them. Choose one issue, clearly define it for your readers, and write a paper in which you take a position on it.

3. Choose a controversial issue that concerns one particular age group—young children, teenagers, or the elderly, for example. Write a paper that takes a position on this issue.

4. Write a paper on an issue pertaining to education or, in particular, to your school. What is the controversy, and where do you stand on the issue?

5. Think about an issue within your own household. Perhaps you think a problem needs solving, but others in the house don't. Write a paper in which you define the problem and argue for a particular solution.

6. Choose a controversial issue related to the world of
   - entertainment or sports;
   - the environment or an environmental policy;
   - health care;
   - law enforcement or a particular law;
   - other.

   Write a paper in which you clearly explain what the issue is, and argue your position on that issue.

Glossary

The following words are found in the literary selections in this text. The particular poem, story, or essay is indicated in parentheses following the definition. These definitions do not denote the many possible meanings you will find in a good dictionary. Rather, they define the word according to its context in the piece of literature. Likewise, words are identified by their usage in the work. For instance, although astringent *can be a noun or an adjective, it is identified as a noun here because that is the way it is used in Grace Suh's essay.*

aberrant: adj. deviating from the ordinary ("Death of the Right Fielder")

abstention: n. refraining from doing something ("Beginning")

academicians: n. people who promote science, art, or literature; those who follow a tradition of ideas ("Beginning")

acquaintanceship: n. a relationship in which people know each other but are not necessarily close ("Paper Pills")

acrid: adj. bitter or unpleasant in taste or odor ("The Men We Carry in Our Minds")

affluent: adj. having many material possessions ("Daddy Tucked the Blanket")

agitator: n. a device for stirring or shaking ("To Work")

alienate: v. to cause something or someone to be separate from you ("My Oedipus Complex" and "The Case Against Chores")

amiable: adj. friendly, sociable ("My Oedipus Complex")

analogies: (analogy): n. correspondence between a pair of words that can be compared to another pair of words ("Mother Tongue")

antiseptic: adj. very clean; resisting contamination ("Beginning")

arbitrary: adj. selected at random ("Birthday Poem")

archives: n. public documents or records; a collection of works ("Beginning")

arrayed: v. dressed in fine clothes ("Richard Cory")

arsenal: n. storage or collection of weapons ("The Men We Carry in Our Minds")

associative: adj. relating to the act of forming a mental connection between ideas, memories, or sensations ("Mother Tongue")

astringent: n. a substance that draws together skin or tissue ("The Eye of the Beholder")

aurora borealis: n. a spectacle in the night sky notable for arcing and waving light—seen most commonly in the Arctic and northern regions ("Work")

axioms: n. ideas or propositions widely held as truths ("Beginning")

baffled: adj. confused or frustrated ("The Men We Carry in Our Minds")

bantams: n. small or miniature foul such as chickens ("Catfish in the Bathtub")

biographers: n. people who tell or write the story of another person's life (Nikki-Rosa)

blasphemous: adj. showing a lack of respect for God or something sacred ("Beginning")

bourgeois: adj. relating to the middle class ("The Eye of the Beholder")

braceros: n. Mexican laborers working in the U.S., especially in agriculture ("The Circuit")

brindled: adj. coloring of dark streaks on a gray or light brown background ("The Witness")

buoyant: adj. capable of floating ("Winter Love")

burnished: adj. made shiny by rubbing ("Two on Two")

cajoled: v. deceived by flattery ("My Oedipus Complex")

calamity: n. an event that causes great loss, pain, and suffering ("My Oedipus Complex")

ceaselessly: adv. constant; never stopping ("Paper Pills")

censure: n. a condemning judgment or official reprimand ("Beginning")

cloaca: n. a cavity into which a bird's waste and eggs discharge before leaving its body ("Winter Love")

cocksure: adj. overconfident ("Two on Two")

codded: v. tricked; joked ("My Oedipus Complex")

coercion: n. the act of being made or forcefully persuaded to do something ("Powder")

compelled: v. driven to do something ("The Chase")

confound: v. to cause confusion; to put to shame ("Paper Pills")

conspicuous: adj. attracting attention ("Father")

conscience: n. the part of one's personality that feels an obligation to do what is right or good; moral sense ("Beginning")

corollaries: (corollary): n. something that naturally follows another thing; a result ("Beginning")

corridos: n. (Spanish) songs; popular ballads ("The Circuit")

crass: adj. insensitive; stupid ("Say Yes")

credulous: adj. unduly ready to believe ("The Witness")

crenellated: adj. furnished with battlements; open spaces on a wall used for defense ("The Chase")

crucible: n. a container used for melting something with high heat ("Beginning")

cumbrous: adj. cumbersome; heavy ("Videotape")

curios: n. items considered rare, unusual, or precious ("My Oedipus Complex")

demonstrative: adj. displaying much feeling ("My Oedipus Complex")

depot: n. a station for bus or train travelers ("The Woman Who Makes Swell Doughnuts")

deteriorating: (deteriorate): v. to fall apart; to worsen in quality ("Daddy Tucked the Blanket")

disdain: n. a feeling of scorn over one in a lesser position ("It's Over" and "The Swimming Pool")

dispose: v. to get rid of ("The Witness")

disposed: v. arranged ("The Witness")

dissonance: n. discord; an inconsistency between one's beliefs and one's actions ("The Woman Who Makes Swell Doughnuts")

dissuade: v. to advise against doing something; to persuade a person not to act in a certain way ("The Struggle to Be an All-American Girl")

dotty: adj. crazy; mentally unbalanced ("My Oedipus Complex")

dromedaries: n. camels ("Catfish in the Bathtub")

drone: n. sustained, deep buzzing or humming sound ("The Circuit")

duster: n. a housecoat to protect ones clothes from dust ("Paper Pills")

elemental: adj. fundamental; an essential part of something ("Videotape")

embossed: adj. decorated with a raised surface ("Books")

emigrated: v. having left one place or country to live else-where ("Not Skin Deep—Heart Deep")

empirical: adj. relying on observation or experience ("Mother Tongue")

emulsifying: (emulsify): v. converting into an emulsion, a mixture of two liquids in which one is suspended in small droplets (as in oil and water) ("The Eye of the Beholder")

epiphanous: adj. relating to a sudden realization of reality ("The Eye of the Beholder")

epitaph: n. an inscription at a grave; a brief statement to honor a dead person ("Death of the Right Fielder")

eradicate: v. to get rid of or do away with; to exterminate ("Death of the Right Fielder")

ethics: n. moral standards or values ("Ethics")

eulogy: n. a praising statement, most often after a person's death ("Father")

exfoliant: n. a substance that removes rough or scaly skin ("The Eye of the Beholder")

forbidding: adj. disagreeable; unapproachable ("Beginning")

forfeiture: n. a loss of something (usually money or property) due to a breech in legal agreement ("Beginning")

forlorn: adj. miserable, sad, lonely ("The Swimming Pool")

forsakenness: n. something renounced or quit ("The Swimming Pool")

fresco: n. a painting done on fresh lime plaster ("The Eye of the Beholder")

furrow: n. a groove in soil made by a plow ("My Father's Song")

futility: n. a useless act ("Daddy Tucked the Blanket")

galvanized: adj. iron or steel coated with zinc ("The Circuit" and "To Work")

gleaned: v. gathered ("The Case Against Chores")

hackneyed: adj. lacking originality; trite ("Pricing")

hairpins: n. abrupt turns in a road ("Powder")

humaneness: n. showing compassion for other human beings ("The Case Against Chores")

hypocritical: adj. acting in a way that contradicts one's true beliefs ("Say Yes")

ideograph: n. a picture or symbol used in writing ("The Struggle to Be an All-American Girl")

illumine: v. to give off light ("My Oedipus Complex")

illusive: adj. deceptive ("Beginning")

immunage: n. a kind of beauty product ("The Eye of the Beholder")

impelled: v. driven forward by a moral sense ("The Chase")

impending: adj. about to occur ("Videotape")

imperially: adj. royally; regally ("Richard Cory")

implacable: adj. not capable of being changed or appeased ("It's Over")

implication: n. the act of drawing a connection; incriminating ("The Two-Twenty Low Hurdle Race")

imploring (implore): v. begging; calling for earnestly ("It's Over")

imply: v. to express an idea indirectly, without direct statement ("Father")

inclination: n. a disposition to do something ("Videotape")

incomprehensible: adj. impossible to understand ("The Witness")

inconsolably: adv. incapable of being consoled; intense grief ("It's Over")

incredulously: adv. skeptically ("My Oedipus Complex")

indifferent: adj. unbiased; no special liking or disliking of something ("Powder" and "Say Yes")

indignantly: adj. reacting as if something is unworthy or unjust ("The Witness")

indignation: n. angry reaction to something unjust ("The Two-Twenty Low Hurdle Race")

indignity: n. an act that humiliates; loss of honor ("My Oedipus Complex")

indispensable: adj. absolutely necessary ("The Case Against Chores")

induction: n. initiation ("Beginning")

instantaneous: adj. done without delay; immediate ("Death of the Right Fielder")

intercession: n. prayer or petition ("My Oedipus Complex")

invoices: n. lists of goods or services; bills ("Work")

ironclad: adj. unchangeable ("The Men We Carry in Our Minds")

irretrievable: adj. not to be recovered ("Beginning")

jaded: adj. exhausted; cynical ("Paper Pills")

jalopy: n. an old dilapidated automobile ("The Circuit")

jockeying (jockey): v. to maneuver or change position ("Rite of Passage")

kowtow: n. to kneel and touch the forehead to the ground in respect or worship ("The Struggle to Be an All-American Girl")

labyrinths: n. maze in hedges or walls; passageways ("The Chase")

lethargic: adj. sluggish or indifferent ("Beginning")

liberate: v. to set free ("The Two-Twenty Low Hurdle Race")

limbo: n. a place or state of transition; in between ("The Men We Carry in Our Minds")

loping (lope): v. the easy striding of a horse or other animal ("Driving Lessons")

lorded: v. to act superior ("Beginning")

luminous: adj. giving off light; glowing ("Picture Bride" and "You Go To School To Learn")

maestra: n. Spanish, master or teacher ("Office Hour")

magnanimous: adj. showing courage and/or generosity ("My Oedipus Complex")

malevolent: adj. showing ill will; hatred ("Winter Love")

maniacal: adj. unusual enthusiasm; characterized by madness ("The Struggle to Be an All-American Girl")

meticulously: adv. careful; with extreme care for details ("Two on Two")

mijito: n. Spanish, a slang term of endearment, often used by parent or grandparent toward a child ("Office Hour")

mincing: adj. delicate ("The Witness")

monochrome: adj. in a single hue or color ("Cannery Town in August")

moorage: n. the act of securing a boat—to a dock, for instance ("A Photo of Immigrants, 1903")

morphine: n. an addictive narcotic ("The Witness")

mortified: adj. caused great shame ("My Oedipus Complex")

nascent: adj. starting to develop ("Mother Tongue")

negate: v. to say no; to deny ("It's Over" and "The Eye of the Beholder")

nominalized: adj. a word changed to function as a noun ("Mother Tongue")

nondescript: adj. not distinguishable from others ("The Sanctuary of School")

oblivious: adj. unaware or forgetful ("The Swimming Pool")

odyssey: n. a long voyage; an intellectual or spiritual journey ("It's Over")

ominous: adj. foreboding; frightful ("My Oedipus Complex")

pacifists: n. those opposed to war and violence ("Beginning")

perfunctorily: adv. routinely; mechanically ("The Chase")

perpetrator: n. one who commits a crime ("Videotape")

perished: adj. weakened (by cold or hunger) ("My Oedipus Complex")

petrified: adj. frozen; like stone ("My Oedipus Complex")

plausible: adj. seemingly convincing; worthy of belief ("Death of the Right Fielder")

plowshare: n. the part of a plow that cuts a furrow ("My Father's Song")

porcelain: adj. a nonporous ceramic ware fired in high heat ("Henry Manley, Living Alone, Keeps Time")

prose: n. writing that is distinguished from poetry, usually presented in paragraphs ("A Photo of Immigrants, 1903")

quandary: n. a state of doubt; being uncertain ("Mother Tongue")

quicksilver: adj. mercury; moving like mercury ("Two on Two")

quince: n. (Spanish) fifteen ("The Circuit")

quinceañeras: n. (Spanish) celebrations (often including Mass and party) of girl's fifteenth birthday ("Office Hour")

rationale: n. an explanation or reason ("The Case Against Chores")

reclamation: n. the act of reclaiming; recovering ("The Eye of the Beholder")

rendezvous: n. a planned (romantic) meeting ("It's Over")

reprieve: n. relief; a delay of punishment ("Beginning")

resolve: n. of a firm mind; determination ("It's Over")

retrospect: n. to think about something again; to go back; considering the past ("Daddy Tucked the Blanket")

salve: v. to assist in healing; to soothe or assuage ("The Swimming Pool")

scribe: v. to write ("Death of the Right Fielder")

scything (scythe): v. to cut, as if with a scythe ("The Eye of the Beholder")

self-determination: n. free choice over one's own actions; people determining their own fate ("Beginning")

semantic: adj. related to the *meaning* of language ("Mother Tongue")

sentimentalist: n. one who has exceedingly romantic or nostalgic feelings ("Paper Pills")

sharecropper: n. a person who raises a crop on another person's farm and is paid an agreed upon share of the profits ("The Circuit")

sinister: adj. evil; leading to disaster ("My Oedipus Complex")

slipstream: n. an area of reduced air pressure and increased suction behind a speeding car ("Powder")

spar: n. a stout pole or rounded piece of wood ("Winter Love")

spherical: adj. shaped like a ball or globe ("The Chase")

spindle: n. a rod or pin that holds yarn or thread ("Not Skin Deep—Heart Deep")

squalls: n. violent winds, often with rain or snow ("Powder")

stoically: adv. not responding to passion; indifferent to distress or change ("The Struggle to Be an All-American Girl")

switchbacks: n. zigzagging parts of a road in the mountains or on a hillside ("Powder")

synthesize: v. to combine ideas or concepts to draw a conclusion ("Beginning")

tack: n. parts of a harness; saddle and bridle ("The Case Against Chores")

"Tienen que tener cuidado": (Spanish) "Watch out" or "Be careful" ("The Circuit")

toady: v. to flatter in hopes of getting something in return ("The Two-Twenty Low Hurdle Race")

turret: n. a gunner's enclosure on an airplane or a warship ("Rite of Passage")

tyranny: n. oppressive power ("Beginning")

unabashedly: adv. not disguised; straightforward ("The Swimming Pool")

unadorned: adj. plain; without decoration ("Not Skin Deep—Heart Deep")

unrelenting: adj. stern; not letting up; not relenting ("The Case Against Chores")

unwieldy: adj. not easy to handle; cumbersome ("Winter Love")

vamanos: (Spanish) let's go; hurry ("Powder" and "The Circuit")

vexed: adj. irritated ("My Oedipus Complex")

vistas: n. distant views ("Powder")

wretchedness: n. in a very bad state; miserable ("The Men We Carry in Our Minds")

Acknowledgements

Robert Wrigley, "A Photograph of Immigrants, 1903" from *Moon in A Mason Jar*; and, *What My Father Believed: Two Volumes of Poetry*. Copyright 1986, 1991, 1998 by Robert Wrigley. Used with permission of the poet and the University of Illinois Press.

"Picture Bride" from *Picture Bride*. Copyright © 1983. Reprinted by permission of Yale University Press.

"Powder" from *The Night in Question: Stories* by Tobias Wolff, copyright © 1996 by Tobias Wolff. Used by permission of Alfred A. Knopf, a division of Random House, Inc.

Permission granted by author Simon J. Ortiz. "My Father's Song" originally published in *Woven Stone*, University of Arizona Press, 1992.

"Father" from *Living Up the Street* (Dell) © 1985 by Gary Soto. Used by permission of the author.

"Nikki-Rosa" from *Black Feeling, Black Talk, Black Judgement* by Nikki Giovanni. Copyright © 1968, 1970 by Nikki Giovanni. Reprinted by permission of HarperCollins Publishers Inc.

Susan Straight, "Not Skin Deep—Heart Deep" copyright © 1999 by Susan Straight. This essay first appeared in *Mothers Who Think*, a Salon book published by Villard Books. Reprinted by permission of The Richard Parks Agency.

"Driving Lessons" is reprinted by permission of Louisiana State University Press from *Out of the South* by Neal Bowers. Copyright © 2002 by Neal Bowers.

"Catfish in the Bathtub" from *The Woman Warrior* by Maxine Hong Kingston, copyright © 1975, 1976 by Maxine Hong Kingston. Used by permission of Alfred A. Knopf, a division of Random House, Inc.

Thomas Lux. Reprinted by permission of Houghton Mifflin Company. All rights reserved.

"Yuba City School" from *Leaving Yuba City* by Chitra Banerjee Divakaruni, © 1997 by Chitra Banerjee Divakaruni. Used by permission of Doubleday, a division of Random House, Inc.

Dorianne Laux, "Books" from *Smoke*. Copyright © 2000 by Dorianne Laux. Reprinted with the permission of BOA Editions, Ltd.

"The Sanctuary of School" by Lynda Barry. Copyright © 1992 by The New York Times Co. Reprinted with permission.

Carol Lem, "Office Hour" found in *The Geography of Home: California's Poetry of Place*, Heydey Books. Reprinted by permission of the author.

Elizabeth Wong, "The Struggle to Be an All-American Girl," *Los Angeles Times*, September 7, 1980. Reprinted by permission of the author.

"Manners" from *The Complete Poems: 1927–1979* by Elizabeth Bishop. Copyright © 1979, 1983 by Alice Helen Methfessel. Reprinted by permission of Farrar, Straus and Giroux, LLC.

"The Two-Twenty Low Hurdle Race" copyright 1943 and renewed 1971 by William Saroyan, reprinted by permission of Harcourt, Inc.

Ann Darr, "Advice I Wish Someone Had Given Me." From *St. Ann's Gut*. Copyright © 1971 by Ann Darr. Published by William Morrow & Company, Inc. Reprinted by permission of the author.

"The Lesson," copyright © 1972 by Toni Cade Bambara, from *Gorilla, My Love* by Toni Cade Bambara. Used by permission of Random House, Inc.

"Ethics," from *Waiting for My Life* by Linda Pastan. Copyright © 1981 by Linda Pastan. "Marks," from *The Five Stages of Grief* by Linda Pastan. Copyright © 1978 by Linda Pastan. Used by permission of W.W. Norton & Company, Inc.

Lucille Clifton, "Homage to My Hips." Copyright © 1980 by Lucille Clifton. First appeared in *Two-Headed Woman*, published by University of Massachusetts Press. Reprinted by permission of Curtis Brown, Ltd.

"Daddy Tucked the Blanket," copyright © 1975 by The New York Times Co. Reprinted with permission.

"Leslie in California" from *Selected Stories* by Andre Dubus. Reprinted by permission of David R. Godine, Publisher, Inc. Copyright © 1988 by Andre Dubus.

"Oranges" from *New and Selected Poems* by Gary Soto. Copyright © 1995. Used with permission of Chronicle Books LLC. Visit http://www.chroniclebooks.com

"Paper Pills," from *Winesburg, Ohio* by Sherwood Anderson, copyright 1919 by B. W. Huebsch. Copyright 1947 by Eleanor Copenhaver Anderson. Used by permission of Viking Penguin, a division of Penguin Group (USA) Inc.

"To Work" and "Winter Love," from *In the Bank of Beautiful Sins* by Robert Wrigley, copyright © 1995 by Robert Wrigley. Used by permission of Penguin, a division of Penguin Group (USA) Inc.

Gerald W. Haslam, "It's Over" is reprinted from *Condor Dreams and Other Fictions* by Gerald W. Haslam. © 1994 University of Nevada Press. By permission of the publisher.

"Loyal" from *Selected Poems & Translations, 1969–1991* by William Matthews. Copyright © 1992 by William Matthews. Reprinted by permission of Houghton Mifflin Company. All rights reserved.

Brian Doyle, "Two on Two" as published in *Creative Nonfiction* (No. 9), Lee Gutkind, Ed. Copyright © 2003 by Brian Doyle. Reprinted by permission of the author.

"What Work Is" from *What Work Is* by Philip Levine, copyright © 1992 by Philip Levine. Used by permission of Alfred A. Knopf, a division of Random House, Inc.

"Work" is from *Family Reunion: Selected and New Poems*, by Paul Zimmer, © 1983. Reprinted by permission of the University of Pittsburgh Press.

"The Witness" from *The Leaning Tower and Other Stories*, copyright 1935 and renewed 1963 by Katherine Ann Porter, reprinted by permission of Harcourt, Inc.

Jane Smiley, "The Case Against Chores" copyright © 1995 by *Harper's Magazine*. All rights reserved. Reproduced from the June issue by special permission.

Francisco Jiminez, "The Circuit" from *The Circuit: Stories from the Life of a Migrant Child*, 1997, University of New Mexico Press. Reprinted by permission.

"Cannery Town in August" from *Emplumada,* by Lorna Dee Cervantes, © 1981 by Lorna Dee Cervantes. Reprinted by permission of the University of Pittsburgh Press.

"$100 and Nothing" from *A Piece of Mine* by J. California Cooper, copyright © 1984 by J. California Cooper. Used by permission of Doubleday, a division of Random House, Inc.

Scott Russell Sanders, "The Men We Carry in Our Minds." Copyright © 1984 by Scott Russell Sanders; first appeared in Milkweed Chronicle; from *The Paradise of Bombs.* Reprinted by permission of the author and the author's agents, the Virginia Kidd Agency, Inc.

Tobias Wolff, "Say Yes," from *Back in the World.* Reprinted by permission of International Creative Management, Inc. Copyright © 1985 by Tobias Wolff.

"Beginning" from *If I Die in a Combat Zone* by Tim O'Brien, copyright © 1973 by Tim O'Brien. Used by permission of Dell Publishing, a division of Random House, Inc.

Grace Suh, "The Eye of the Beholder" from *aMagazine.* Copyright © 1993 by Grace Suh. Reprinted by permission of the author.

"Immigrants" by Pat Mora is reprinted with permission from the publisher of *Borders* (Houston: Arte Publico Press— University of Houston, 1986).

Amy Tan, "Mother Tongue." Copyright © 1990 by Amy Tan. First appeared in *The Threepenny Review.* Reprinted by permission of the author and the Sandra Dijkstra Literary Agency.

"Videotape" (pp. 155–160), as first published in *Antaeus,* is reprinted with the permission of Scribner, an imprint of Simon & Schuster Adult Publishing Group, from *Underworld* by Don DeLillo. Copyright © 1997 by Don DeLillo.

"Traveling through the Dark" copyright 1962, 1998 by the Estate of William Stafford. Reprinted from *The Way It Is: New & Selected Poems* with the permission of Graywolf Press, Saint Paul, Minnesota.

"Popular Mechanics" from *What We Talk About When We Talk About Love* by Raymond Carver, copyright © 1981 by Raymond Carver. Used by permission of Alfred A. Knopf, a division of Random House, Inc.

Author and Title Index